18·99

Making People Behave

Making People Behave
Anti-social behaviour, politics and policy

Elizabeth Burney

WILLAN
PUBLISHING

Published by

Willan Publishing
Culmcott House
Mill Street, Uffculme
Cullompton, Devon
EX15 3AT, UK
Tel: +44(0)1884 840337
Fax: +44(0)1884 840251
e-mail: info@willanpublishing.co.uk
website: www.willanpublishing.co.uk

Published simultaneously in the USA and Canada by

Willan Publishing
c/o ISBS, 920 NE 58th Ave, Suite 300,
Portland, Oregon 97213-3786, USA
Tel: +001(0)503 287 3093
Fax: +001(0)503 280 8832
e-mail: info@isbs.com
website: www.isbs.com

First published 2005

ISBN 1-84392-138-3 (cased)
ISBN 1-84392-137-5 (paper)

British Library Cataloguing-in-Publication Data

A catalogue record for this book is available from the British Library

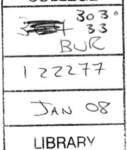

Project managed by Deer Park Productions, Tavistock, Devon
Typeset by GCS, Leighton Buzzard, Bedfordshire, LU7 1AR
Printed and bound by T.J. International Ltd, Padstow, Cornwall

Contents

Foreword

This book is about a right idea that went wrong from the start. The right idea that the Labour Party developed in the 1990s, and acted upon in office, was that there were some neighbourhoods where people were living daily with abuse, intimidation and disorder that seriously undermined their quality of life and that of their locality. Recognising that these situations were not being effectively dealt with, a new policy was formed. Unfortunately the chosen instrument, and others that have followed, rely on often disproportionately intrusive and punitive restraints on individuals held responsible for disrupting their communities, while doing nothing to deal with the possible causes of bad behaviour, either those arising from individual circumstances or, less directly, from the marginalised and impoverished nature of the communities worst afflicted. The weakness of the communities was recognised, but it was conceived as a moral weakness, induced by the presence of a selfish and uncivil minority.

The use of legal enforcement as the sole response arose out of an earlier legal anomaly, which had appropriated housing law, wielded by social landlords, as the main instrument for dealing with bad behaviour. A small gap in the law limited the power to deal with minors, although children were very often the source of complaints. Plugging that gap was deemed necessary, and it was from that almost technical difficulty that the now familiar anti-social behaviour order, or ASBO, was born.

The following chapters are critical of the manner in which the

Labour government has created and developed the concept of anti-social behaviour. This criticism is not meant to deny the serious reality for those worst affected, about which I have written elsewhere. But we are talking about a pyramid of different kinds and degrees of incivility, where only the tip is the painfully sharp experience, compared with a wide base of mere distaste or annoyance. These distinctions are lost in an all-embracing approach that extends control and regulation into ever-increasing categories of behaviour.

A note on semantics: anti-social behaviour has no clear legal definition. But the term has been in longstanding use by behavioural psychologists and developmental criminologists. I have deliberately avoided referring to their work except briefly in passing. In my view, although some very damaged individuals are often involved, the concept of anti-social behaviour in the way it is used politically is a social construct which, although echoing, does not require scientific validation.

Some thanks are due. The British Academy supplied a grant which took me to the Netherlands and Sweden to compare their way of dealing with incivilities. All those I interviewed for that comparison, and for the comparison of crime and disorder practices in Milton Keynes and Nottingham, must be thanked warmly for their interest, frankness and patience. Special thanks also to Jennifer Davis, Martin Davis, David Downes, Felipe Estrada, Barrie Irving, Nicola Padfield, Kevin Stenson and Rene van Swaaningen who took the trouble to comment constructively on my draft. Any mistakes left are mine alone.

As ever I am grateful for the facilities provided by the Cambridge Institute of Criminology: in particular, as my bibliography testifies, to the Radzinowicz Library.

Elizabeth Burney

Chapter 1

Why 'anti-social behaviour'?

It is sometimes claimed, currently in the context of terrorism, that governments rely upon scaring people in order to prove that they are in control and doing something about a particular threat. In 1997 the newly elected Labour government introduced a cherished piece of legislation, Clause 1 of the Crime and Disorder Bill, which created the Anti-Social Behaviour Order (ASBO). 'Anti-social behaviour is a menace on our streets; it is threat to our communities',[1] declared Lord Williams to the House of Lords. Just what was the nature of this menace, which has become the springboard for so much government action, providing an ever-increasing range of penalties and enforcement agents? And why has the notion of anti-social behaviour been embraced so keenly by the British public, who formerly might barely have been familiar with the term?

I hope to show why this has happened, what form the sanctions take and what influences lie behind them, and to address also the question: has offensive behaviour really become more widespread and/or intense and if so why? Is this significantly more than a recycling of permanent concerns about the behaviour of neighbours, and youths, and defilers/ disturbers of public space? Is it a category distinct from crime, or – as is increasingly apparent – simply a way of relabelling criminal acts in a manner that permits short-cut punishment? The book will therefore look at the political process involved in the promotion of the idea of anti-social behaviour; the nature and application of the expanding body of legislation introduced in its name; the elements contributing to the perception that bad behaviour in the public domain has got worse; the way that some local authorities are addressing the issue; and, finally, whether there are signs that Britain is not alone in western Europe in increased anxiety relating to anti-social behaviour, or, to use a less emotive term, 'incivilities'.

The difference in terminology is not without significance. In recent years different names have been attached to a clutch of common phenomena associated usually, though not exclusively, with impoverished, run-down neighbourhoods. When American academics turned their attention to the plight of rustbelt cities in the 1970s and 1980s they used terms such as 'incivilities' and 'disorder' to describe a cocktail of social unpleasantness and environmental mess found in decaying neighbourhoods. Similar studies followed in Britain, with parallel concerns about the fate of urban areas blighted by the loss of jobs. But in the mid-1990s Britain (not America) began to become familiar with another name: 'anti-social behaviour'. Over the years this name has been applied to most of the things itemised in American studies as 'incivilities' or 'disorder'.[2] But it has always had a distinct, personal, implication. 'Disorder' is a term applied collectively to communities; 'anti-social behaviour' is something done by individuals who are thereby singled out and blamed for the harm they inflict upon communities. One is about outcomes; the other about inputs. 'Disorder' focuses on a standard list of recognisable elements; 'anti-social behaviour' on the other hand has no clear identity, but results in the targeting of individuals or groups through predetermined instruments of restraint. It has politicised an almost limitless range of behaviour drawn into the net of new controls. It signals exclusion and rejection, trumpeted as a means of rescuing social order and strengthening communities.

It is indisputable that in the 1990s many poor neighbourhoods were indeed plagued and intimidated by persistent bad behaviour on the lower edge of criminality. New Labour recognised a serious need and linked it directly to a philosophy that set communities and their miscreant members at odds, expressed in a new law of rejection and banishment. Yet scapegoating individual perpetrators of neighbourhood disturbance and destruction enables the authorities to evade acknowledging the social and economic decline of those neighbourhoods, of which the objectionable behaviour might be seen as a symptom or a response. As Jock Young (1999) has argued, exclusion is the inevitable consequence of the condition in which late modernity leaves those deprived of status and opportunity in a market-driven society. Whole neighbourhoods are 'socially excluded' and their condition worsened by the harm inflicted by some of their inhabitants. The welfare interventions that might once have prevented some of the deviant behaviour are few and far between. Informal social control has weakened, to be replaced by formal instruments of a punitive nature. These instruments increasingly assume what Pratt (2000) calls 'emotive and ostentatious' forms, recalling past eras of branding, stocks and pillory. He cites a sex offender in the United States obliged to display a notice saying 'Dangerous Sexual Offender – No Children Allowed'. There have been demands in Britain for similar public identification of sex offenders, so far resisted. But the deliberate identification of people – even children – on anti-social behaviour orders, including photographs and addresses, has been supported by the courts and is now commonplace.

This book examines how the concept of anti-social behaviour has come to dominate Britain's law and order discourse, and what have been the consequences in terms of the way what Americans would still term 'incivilities' have been dealt with – often by methods directly copied from America. The introduction of the label 'anti-social behaviour' into the realm of public order enforcement was the direct responsibility of the first New Labour government of 1997. Until then it was a term used either in a clinical context by psychologists and criminologists to describe a certain type of personality or propensity, or alternatively in popular use simply as a loosely pejorative expression applied to behaviour offensive to tastes or norms. But since its introduction into the law and order discourse it has acquired a burgeoning life of its own in the public arena, assisted by an increased volume of legislation. *The Times* used the words 'anti-social' or 'antisocial' 74 times in 1993 but by 2003 this had risen to 292. The acronym 'ASBO' has passed into the nation's vocabulary and regularly provides a source of shocking or entertaining news stories (at the time of writing, headlines concerned a Norfolk farmer dealt an ASBO for failing to contain a herd of pigs).

'Anti-social behaviour' has been described as 'a vague term, with a broad definition, which in the last few years has become a rallying call for some onerous and intrusive measures against individuals' (Ashworth, 2004: 263). The Parliamentary Joint Committee on Human Rights said: '[W]e do not think that people would be able to establish what it means by any predictable ojective standard'.[3] As one American observer has remarked: '[B]y making antisocial behaviour into a major social policy problem, and by giving it sustained high-visibility attention, Labour has made a small problem larger, thereby making people more aware of it and less satisfied with their lives and their government' (Tonry, 2004: 57).

It is a 'small problem' in the sense that for a vast majority of the population anti-social behaviour is a very small or non-existent concern

(Millie et al., 2005). A minority are affected in varying degrees, with a very small number devastated by it. It would be a great mistake to be dismissive about nasty forms of rampant and persistent bad behaviour which have afflicted certain neighbourhoods or vulnerable people. Racial abuse, threats and intimidation, serious damage to property, intrusive loud noise and the environment created by drug dealing cannot be ignored. Yet most of these things are plainly criminal and all can be targeted by existing legal instruments without recourse to anti-social behaviour orders. As we shall see, it was the perceived inefficiency of the criminal justice system that led to demands for something that would give the authorities a freer hand. It was this, rather than a more general concern about minor nuisances, that was the initial focus of the anti-social behaviour agenda. Yet, once the label 'anti-social behaviour' became current, it was very easy to adopt it as a description of any local irritation or the presence of any persons attracting disapproval in the public domain. It reflects back a perception that society is falling apart and that this process is driven by people who have no sense of civilised norms.

Doom-sayers like Frank Field, the MP for Birkenhead, take this to extremes. He has naturally been sincerely outraged by the sufferings inflicted on 'respectable working-class' constituents by a few grossly anarchic neighbours, usually children. In his book *Neighbours From Hell* (2003: 10) he describes how this first came to his notice by a visit from a group of pensioners.

> Nothing had prepared me for the description of what they were enduring and the hell which had engulfed them. Young lads who ran across their bungalow roofs, peed through their letterboxes, jumped out of the shadows as they returned home at night, and, when they were watching television, tried to break their sitting room windows, presumably with the hope of showering the pensioners with shattered glass.

Birkenhead is indeed a vulnerable place, ravaged by years of unemployment and heroin addiction (Pearson, 1987). The worst cases of anti-social behaviour are likely to occur in such areas.[4] But Field goes on to extrapolate from similar examples of persistent horrible behaviour, garnered from his constituents and elsewhere, arguing that the whole country is suffering from an onslaught against old-fashioned values led by feckless families who have no interest in instilling behavioural standards in their children. Not only are these families seen by Mr Field as a local menace: he believes that they actually infect society as a whole, driving down behaviour towards their own level. Society becomes dominated by selfish, yobbish behaviour because we have lost the certainties and mutual responsibilities of religion and the welfare state. His main remedy consists of harsh measures, including the removal of benefits, to force parents to act responsibly.

The problem with this presentation is that it has no shades of grey. The bad cases are indeed very bad but they are the tip of a pyramid of lesser incivilities, sometimes upsetting but not devastating. People who are annoyed to see schoolchildren dropping litter at the bus stop when there is a bin right beside them may readily buy into Field's worst-case scenario.

Disorder and fear

The government's anti-social behaviour policy has succeeded in its own terms not only because it resonates with people at the sharp end, but also because it builds upon pre-existing causes of social unease. There is long-standing evidence that people (or some people in some places) are psychologically more affected by disorderly behaviour and messy environments than they are by more serious crime. The association of these perceptions with fear of crime – as a phenomenon distinct from measurable crime rates – has been the subject of academic study and debate, mainly in America, for over thirty years. It is therefore appropriate at this point to summarise this debate, which has affected policing methods both sides of the Atlantic and can be shown to have fed into the political process which is a main focus of this book.

> We have found that the attitudes of citizens regarding crime are less affected by their past victimisation than by their ideas about what is going on in their community – fears about a weakening of social controls on which they feel their safety and the broader fabric of social life is ultimately dependent. (p. 160)

So wrote the authors of a report to the US federal government in 1967 (Biderman et al.). Since then there have been numerous studies, only a few of which will be referred to here, developing this theme and exploring the processes involved. Many involve questioning people about their perceptions of disorder (or 'incivilities') in the neighbourhood – social disorder, such as rowdy youths on street corners, public drinking and drug dealing, and environmental disorder such as litter, vandalism and abandoned or ill-kept buildings. Some researchers travel the streets themselves to assess visible disorders. People are also questioned about their experience of crime and their fear of the same – or avoidance behaviour, such as not going out at night. It was soon shown that neighbourhoods, and even subsections of neighburhoods, differed significantly in both levels of fear and perceptions of disorder, and that the two were somehow related.

For instance, when Lewis and Maxfield (1980) investigated Chicago neighbourhoods they found striking differences from place to place. The fear of crime was more associated with perceptions of incivilities than with crime rates, even where people had a realistic awareness of the crimes being committed in their area. They concluded (p. 185) that crime rates did matter, but that 'levels of perceived risk are greatest when where there is a combination of high concern about crime and incivility'. High crime rates produced far less concern in tidy neighbourhoods. The theme was picked up in a highly influential magazine article (Wilson and Kelling, 1982), which argued that unless early signs of disorder were dealt with promptly, deterioration and fear would set in, leading eventually to an increase in predatory crime. (The history of this 'broken windows' thesis will be described in a later chapter.)

The idea of risk was taken up by Lagrange et al. (1992), arguing that incivilities were mainly seen by people as indicating a risk of crime, and that fear was an outcome of this perception. The most fearful people, it was often pointed out, were those with a low actuarial risk of victimisation (e.g. Hough, 1995). Ditton et al. (1999) argued that 'fear of crime' was a misleading shorthand for a mix of emotions, such as anger, experienced differentially. Some recent studies have focused on the way that disadvantaged neighbourhoods may feel threatened because of a sense of powerlessness, amplified by signs of disorder and the erosion of trust (Ross et al., 2001), a view which ties in with the 'social disorganisation' theory discussed in a later chapter. Again, not all high crime neighbourhoods suffer in this way (Walklate and Evans, 1999; Evans et al., 1996). Innes and Fielding (2002), like Lagrange et al., prefer to talk of risk rather than fear. They argue that certain common types of disorder in public space, both social and environmental, are 'signal crimes', sending a message that the neighbourhood is unsafe. If there are signs that these things are being taken in hand, the public are reassured (hence the term 'reassurance policing'). This interpretation has a strong bearing on recent government policy.

Jackson (2004) has analysed expressions of 'fear' as relating to a variety of mental processes – knowledge or perceptions of the characteristics of the neighbourhood on the one hand and broader socio-cultural concerns which shape what he calls 'expressive fear' on the other. People might be concerned about their own vulnerability, interpreting local disorders as 'representational of a community that lacked trust, moral consensus, and informal social control' (p. 960). But this unease was linked to more general attitudes about social decline:

> Wider social attitudes shaped the social meaning of disorder and its links to community aspects. Respondents who held more authoritarian views about law and order, and who were concerned about a long-term deterioration of community, were more likely to perceive disorder in their environment. They were also more likely to link these physical cues to problems of social cohesion and consensus, of declining quality of social bonds and informal social control. (p. 960)

These observations fit with the findings of Bottoms and Wilson (2004) concerning contrasting attitudes found in two deprived, high-crime areas of Sheffield, discussed in another chapter, where punitiveness was far higher in the area most concerned about disorder. They also find an echo in the psychological survey conducted by Maruna and King (2004) where punitiveness is strongly linked to socio-economic insecurity.

How far people's sense of insecurity therefore feeds into their concern about disorder, or more generally anti-social behaviour, is therefore a subject of much interest. There is no shortage of theories around the effects of late (or 'post-') modern society on people's lives and relationships to each other, describing the unravelling of traditional bonds and the rising dominance of risk as the key paradigm (e.g. Giddens, 1990; Beck, 1992; Taylor, 1999; Boutellier, 2004), leading to more punitive desires. Against this background, it is no surprise that government in Britain has tapped into some very broad areas of unease, in which the large but imprecise threat of anti-social behaviour finds much resonance.

What is anti-social behaviour?

It is clear from the previous discussion that there are a number of problem types of behaviour in the public domain which can upset people, and sometimes affect them very badly indeed. But there is no satisfactory way of encompassing them all under one label. The elastic nature of the idea of anti-social behaviour (ASB) finds no limits in the official definition given in Section 1 of the Crime and Disorder Act – behaviour that 'has caused or is likely to cause harassment, alarm or distress' to persons beyond the perpetrator's immediate household. This reflects the context of social housing which gave rise to the legislation originally (see Chapter 2). Local authorities, social landlords and others have produced many definitions of their own, either focusing on the effect rather than the substance of ASB, or simply giving examples of the kind of behaviour that qualifies for the label. The Chartered Institute of Housing offered:

> Behaviour that unreasonably interferes with other people's rights to use and enjoyment of their home and community

but there are of course no legally constituted rights that fit this broad approach. The homeless charity Shelter focused more directly on possible adverse effects:

> Anti-social behaviour occurs where behaviour by one household or individuals in an area threatens the physical or mental health, safety or security of other households or individuals

a definition which could just as well apply to criminal activity. The dividing line between ASB and crime is a shifting one: most behaviour which has given rise to ASBOs could in law have been prosecuted as an offence (Chapter 5).

Frequency, intensity and seriousness of the effect on people's lives are necessary considerations which, again, have no legal recognition. Practitioners have to devise their own guidelines when deciding on appropriate action. Cherwell District Council has a definition of ASB which covers several key aspects (cited in Whitehead et al., 2003: 3):

> behaviour causing disturbance, distress, harm or fear which has a significant effect on people's life-styles and routines. Persistence, intensity and numbers involved are relevant factors. The behaviour need not be a breach of the criminal law.

All these definitions are formed around the around the effects that certain types of behaviour have on other people, in line with a new consciousness of the claims of victims for recognition. They do nothing to specify exactly what the trouble is. In 1996 a Parliamentary Scottish Affairs Committee examined the concept of anti-social behaviour in the context of housing and warned against using it to justify the adoption of new legal powers to deal with quite disparate types of crime and nuisance which already had numerous remedies. (Despite this, a version of the ASBO was introduced into Scottish law.)

In introducing legislation purporting to address a recognisable phenomenon, the government grasped one very important theme, although it was not introduced into the statutory definition of anti-social behaviour: that to suffer repeated offensive behaviour can be as bad, or worse, than being a victim of a one-off more serious crime. This resonated with many people's experience – racial harassment, for example, often takes this form. But there was a fundamental weakness in the political presentation, which was based mainly upon a few outstandingly bad examples of individuals or families whose behaviour (often plainly criminal) had come to the attention of politicians. From this was extrapolated a picture of generalised thuggery and harassment affecting the country at large, rebranded as 'anti-social behaviour'.

The details did not even fit the rather sketchy information about the prevalence and intensity of the social and environmental incivilities perceived by respondents to the British Crime Survey (BCS), in a series collected since 1992. Vandalism and rubbish consistently headed this list as big or very big problems prior to the introduction of legislation in 1997/8, features which can certainly make places very unpleasant but are hardly on the same note psychologically as repeated threats, harassment and foul insults. Only subsequently (a matter of a few percentage points) were the environmental concerns briefly matched by concern over 'teenagers hanging around', which peaked in 2002/3 when one-third of people said that this was the worst problem in their neighbourhood. No qualitative research was undertaken to find out just what it was that made these youths so disturbing, but the figures encouraged the focus of enforcement to be directed against young people. Not until 2004 was closer analysis of the experience and intensity of different BCS categories of ASB published, as described in Chapter 4 (Wood, 2004).

The British Crime Survey has always shown that these concerns were much more prevalent in deprived areas, suggesting that the sharp distinction shown in violent and property crime victimisation statistics between a relatively small number of neighbourhoods and the rest – those in the tenth decile towering over the rest (Hope, 1996 and 2001) – also holds good for offensive behaviour outside or lower down the scale of criminality. Perceptions of ASB more or less track trends in fear of crime and both are more likely to be associated with economic insecurity. In other words, poor people do suffer more from crime and disorder but they also have more things to worry about and are more likely to feel things are out of control.

Therefore, while the BCS measures specific environmental and social phenomena now labelled as anti-social such as litter, graffiti and loitering youths, perceptions about such things cannot be disconnected from fear and risk of crime victimisation, which in turn connect to more general sources of affront and anxiety. Citing Smith (1986: 117) Richard Sparks (1992: 84) pointed out that:

9

Whereas fear and risk do tend to coincide, they do not coincide uniformly; the sense of living in a dangerous place also has to do with awareness of economic and political marginality and decline. These perceptions may crystallise in imputations of dangerousness across group (especially racial, but also age) boundaries ... In a similar way ... that fear may result from 'incivilities', where the behavioural improprieties of some groups which may not be specifically criminal, are viewed by others as indices of social disorganisation and of threat.

The readiness with which the public has embraced Labour's take on anti-social behaviour suggests that this analysis is close to the mark. Having recognised that communities needed more protection, the Labour government chose to take a punitive line in rhetoric and legislation – a line which was undoubtedly popular in the vulnerable neighbourhoods. An alternative reading of the known facts might have suggested the need to look more closely at what was happening on the ground, followed by an intensive effort to improve facilities, opportunities and family support in the worst afflicted areas, coupled with early intervention and firm enforcement against the worst behaviour. This was more or less what was suggested by the government's Social Exclusion Unit (2000). But by then the dominant enforcement message was entrenched and rhetoric continued to feed the impression that the whole country was seriously afflicted by the ravages of anti-social behaviour. As a result, concern about anti-social behaviour pervades public discourse much as fear of the dangerous classes did for the Victorians – and is applied to much the same sort of people. Yet (unlike its counterparts in America) it does not begin with specific targets in mind, such as squeegee men or panhandlers. Rather, it begins with generalised disapproval which then settles here and there on objects of local concern.

With the help of the media discourses take on a life of their own. The closely related field of crime and criminal justice is an obvious case in point. Despite a steady drop in most types of recorded crime there is little or no let-up in reporting and highlighting of the subject in Britain, added to which fictional or semi-fictional representations fill television screens daily. Reports of anti-social behaviour have now joined forces with this disquiet. My local paper, the *Cambridge Evening News*, regularly carried anti-social behaviour stories throughout 2003 and 2004, often in tandem with actions against street drinking and other nuisances being taken as part of a concerted drive in a special Home Office funded area initiative. Half a mile from my house, in another area covered by the same initiative, neighbourhood meetings about 'Anti-Social Behaviour' were held – usually ending up with demands for more resources to fill young people's leisure time.

Nationally identified targets of disorder therefore stimulate police and local authorities to gear up their response, making headlines in the local press. Public consciousness is then aroused to identify other disorder problems, which in turn increases sensitivity to anything that might be seen in that category. Growing concern about bad behaviour can be seen in terms described by Stanley Cohen as a 'moral panic', which he describes as follows:

> A condition, episode, person or group of persons emerges to become a threat to societal values; its nature is presented in a stylised and stereotypical fashion by the mass media; the moral barricades are manned by editors, bishops, politicians and other right-thinking people; socially accredited experts pronounce their diagnoses and solutions, ways of coping are evolved or (more often) resorted to; the condition then disappears, submerges or deteriorates and becomes more visible … Sometimes the panic passes over and is forgotten … ; at other times it has a more serious and long-lasting repercussions and might produce such changes as in legal or social policy or even in the way society conceives itself'. (1972: 9)

Risk consciousness besets modern society and anti-social behaviour is only one among many of the issues which seize public attention. Pollution, paedophiles, food scares, medical errors and many more threaten our peace of mind as ever-present dangers which from time to time throw up peaks of alarm triggered by fresh events or 'expert' reports. For all we know the peak of interest in anti-social behaviour may soon be reached, and the discourse may die down to a simmer as some other social concern takes hold. The results from the 2003/4 British Crime Survey (Dodd et al., 2004) indeed show significantly reduced concern in all the chosen indices of anti-social behaviour. Overall, the proportion of people perceiving disorder at a high level in their neighbourhoods fell from 21 per cent to 16 per cent in the course of a year. The pay-off from council programmes to remove abandoned or burnt-out cars was seen in the finding that the proportion of people who thought they were a very big or fairly big problem fell from 25 per cent to 15 per cent. The 'very big problem' for the survey, however, is the qualitative difference concealed in the 'basket' of incivilities making up the index of anti-social behaviour. For example, how does the suffering of 9 per cent of people badly affected by noisy neighbours or loud parties weigh against 29 per cent who see litter and rubbish as a serious problem, and how far might these problems be interrelated?

Wherever it ends up, the anti-social behaviour discourse currently creates a penumbra of disapproval and disquiet, within which an eclectic and ever-shifting range of objects become the focus. The public is encouraged to join in at every opportunity, addressing whatever kind of behaviour they happen to dislike at any particular time. In the words of one local official interviewed who was responsible for recording complaints from the public:

> More and more people are aware of anti-social behaviour because it's so much talked about. So they say 'why should the children be playing ball in the street?'

Because 'anti-social behaviour' resonates in the public mind it increasingly provides a lever which can be used to activate local politicians, council officials and police resources. As anti-social behaviour strategies, action teams and designated officers become the norm, so do many normal functions of local government – street cleaning, tenancy management, truancy prevention – become validated through the stamp of anti-social behaviour reduction.

Several years ago Colin Sumner (1990) described a new 'sociology of censure'. He said:

> The concept of social censure registers several key features of modern social regulation: their political character, their reliance on value judgements, and their formal, bureaucratic character.

Nothing could better describe the nature of the censure conveyed through the label 'anti-social behaviour' and the mechanisms to which it has given rise. The management of strategies to combat anti-social behaviour, however defined, run along the same pre-ordained bureaucratic paths as the 'management' of offenders and crime prevention. And in the attempts to pass responsibility for crime control to 'communities', the message is: as a community you are not performing as you should if you cannot stop people behaving badly.

The latest phase of government policy, in line with the 'responsibilisation strategy' described by David Garland (2001), is an attempt to kick-start a *gemeinschaft* bonding within troubled communities focused around control of bad behaviour. The attempt to induce 'collective efficacy' is unlikely to succeed if it tries to reproduce a nostalgic notion of neighbourliness. We live in a world where the rise of individualism and the fragmentation of social structures means that we are neither connected to each other vertically, by social institutions and hierarchies, nor horizontally by local ties. As Durkheim observed, crime can provide a template against which people affirm collective norms. So, from time to time, neighbours may still come together to confront some local blight, criminal or otherwise, but in the absence of any such challenge there is little incentive to co-operate. Some frightened and demoralised people will never summon the will to do so, even where the need is greatest.

Structuring the scene

Because the developments outlined above are so dependent upon political choices, the next chapter (Chapter 2) tells the story of New Labour's invention of anti-social behaviour: its origins in the complaints of constituents in Labour heartlands, and the British government's borrowings from American sources to define and deal with it. The chapter describes how policy has evolved in the years since 1997 – moving to embrace environmental as much as social nuisances as a means of reducing public fear and gaining credit for the drop in crime. The concept of 'collective efficacy' – the ability of communities to act together to defend norms of behaviour – has been adopted and community policing reinvented under the name of 'reassurance policing', underlining the purpose not only to reduce crime but to make people feel safer.

As a reminder that, under various guises, bad behaviour has always attracted social control, Chapter 3 provides a brief historical survey, ranging from medieval to Victorian times. The urban scene may be more disorderly now than it was fifty years ago, but go back a bit further and we are living in a remarkably clean and quiet way by comparison with the noise, smells and filth of mid-Victorian towns. Chapter 4 proceeds to the rather important question of whether it is possible to say that offensive behaviour in Britain has seriously worsened in recent years. Are we dealing with new phenomena or just new versions of old animosities and threats? Just how widespread are the worst experiences? What are the features of modern life that might explain both the possible increases and the changes in perceptions of what is or is not acceptable behaviour? Are people nowadays more sensitive to incivilities and more easily threatened by assertive/intrusive encounters? Do we simply lack the moral fibre to deal with people who transgress norms? The chapter seeks some explanations in three related phenomena: the social polarisation evident in neighbourhood characteristics; the behaviour, experience and demonised image of young people today; and the local impact of illicit drugs and problem drinking.

The development of the legal instruments devised to control bad behaviour and how they are applied are the focus of Chapter 5, which leaves no doubt that the marginalised poor have been the main objects of control and the consequences often disproportionate to the actions that triggered the intervention. How this agenda is played out in different local authorities (with a focus on two study areas) is the subject of Chapter 6, showing that local history, experiences and cultures, even in cities not 70 miles apart, determine different approaches to anti-social behaviour.

Chapter 7 opens out the perspective to show that Britain is not alone in western Europe in developing hard policies against nuisance and disorder in the name of calming public feelings of insecurity. The bulk of the chapter makes comparisons with policy and practice in Holland and Sweden, based on interviews with public servants in those countries as well as documentary sources. The Dutch political climate is now such that controls that would have been unthinkable a few years ago are now proliferating and Britain is envied for its anti-social behaviour orders.

The pairing of 'rights' with 'responsibilities', which now shapes social policy in a number of different fields, has been adopted in the cause of behaviour control, although more often as a rhetorical device than a practical mechanism. No British legislation, as yet, goes quite as far as Frank Field would like, but instruments such as parenting orders, fixed penalty notices for parents of truants and misbehaving children, and for extreme cases whole 'problem family' retraining in social services accommodation, are in the same mould. Parents are a relatively new addition to the groups targeted by anti-social reduction measures, replacing the welfarist approach as social service departments cut back on support roles.

Other targeted groups are (primarily) youths and in specific places prostitutes, drunks and beggars – all three being traditional recipients of street policing. Today's methods may be more sophisticated, but they employ traditional practices: surveillance, 'moving on' and exclusion. These themes will recur throughout this study, as different versions of these practices are examined in relation to these groups and other disfavoured people, illustrating Stanley Cohen's (1985) classic analysis of the effects of imposed social control described as 'net widening' and 'mesh thinning' – in other words catching more and more low-level deviants and applying harsher controls to them. There can be no doubt that these effects are pervasive in our streets today, and driven by the political desire to be seen to be making people behave.

Notes

1 Hansard HL, 3 February 1998, col. 603.
2 The British Crime Survey first categorised its range of perceived local disorders as 'anti-social behaviour' in 2002.
3 Thirteenth Report of 2002–3: HL Paper 120, HC 766 (commenting on the Antisocial Behaviour Bill 2003).
4 Five members of a violent Birkenhead family who had allegedly terrorised their community for four years received one of the strictest ASBOs ever issued, banning them from the entire Wirral peninsula (*Guardian*, 25 and 26 March 2005).

Chapter 2

New Labour, new ideas

The belief that crime and criminal justice must be packaged very differently by New Labour compared with the party's previous emphasis on social causes and social work-type solutions was one of the strongest elements in the preparations leading up to the 1997 election victory. Part and parcel with this package was the proposed 'community safety order' which later evolved into the anti-social behaviour order (S.1, Crime and Disorder Act 1998). It was the adoption of this phrase which launched 'anti-social behaviour' as an increasingly popular focus of public consciousness and the rationale for a series of further policies, structures and legislation.

Anti-social behaviour was the hydra-headed monster that represented a spectrum of bad behaviour, from serious to merely irritating, afflicting neighbourhoods. But how did this particular set of concerns, which were by definition not the high-level index crimes which were the subject of the main political contest, come to play such an important part in Labour Party thinking and rhetoric? And how was it that solutions were developed that elevated administrative and civil law above the procedures of the criminal courts?

Particular policies develop a momentum for a number of reasons. There may be pressure to deal with *identified problems*; there may be *interested parties* who see to it that their ideas appeal to the government, especially a new government anxious to position itself differently from its opponents; there may be *leading politicians* whose own mindsets are predisposed to take policy and legislation in a certain direction; and there are *global influences, especially American* ones offering what seem to be new answers and providing new rhetoric. These things all impinge upon the *political culture* of the time, which during the 1990s was developing in a much more punitive direction.

All these elements were present in the adoption of anti-social behaviour issues as a New Labour trade mark. Problems were identified in poor areas represented by Labour MPs, where concerns about crime became focused on the fear and disruption attributed to a small number of families and individuals in hard-to-manage neighbourhoods of social housing. Interested parties pressing for new powers were the local authorities in their role as landlords. Leading politicians sharing concerns about community breakdown and legal constraints included Tony Blair, as Shadow Home Secretary, and his successor in that role Jack Straw, MP for Blackburn. Both these politicians had visited the United States and been impressed by the way the Democrats under Bill Clinton had adopted a tough law and order stance, and how in New York city and elsewhere tough policing of incivilities appeared to pay off (Rutherford, 2000).

The shift in political culture which so affects styles of crime control has been an international one, most clearly expressed in the United States and Britain. David Garland's analysis (2001) has become the classic description: the social insecurity of late modernity finds its expression in increased risk-consciousness and fear of crime, resulting in more punitive attitudes of the public in general and politicians in particular, and where political advantage is seen to stem from the provision of ever-tougher law and order policies. In Garland's thesis governments are nevertheless aware that crime control is beyond their capability, and they therefore attempt to delegate responsibility to other institutions and to private citizens, thereby creating new systems of social control. This gloomy picture has been criticised as over-generalised, ignoring large exceptions and local or national particularities (Zedner, 2002). Although it fits fairly well with the stance adopted by New Labour and the policies which have emerged from at least eight years of the Blair government, in centralised Britain the government intervenes more directly and relies upon a corporatist approach to engage relevant parties in the enterprise of crime control.

New Labour's realignment was evident when in Opposition in 1993 it did not contest the Criminal Justice and Public Order Bill which introduced harsher treatment of young offenders and powers of 'aggravated trespass' designed to restrain ravers, squatters and hunt saboteurs, who at the time were seen as significant threats to social order.

Tony Blair's famous dictum 'Tough on crime, tough on the causes of crime' was first uttered in a radio interview in January 1993. This phrase neatly summed up the New Labour Party stance and also hinted at Blair's personal perspective. His biographer John Rentoul (1995) describes how as an undergraduate Blair became attracted to the writings of the philosopher John Macmurray (1961), who believed that individuals exist not as isolated entities but in relation to others. Communities are therefore all important. Society and the individual have mutual obligations – society has responsibilities towards the individual, who in turn must give back to society. This fitted with Blair's new-found Christian faith in the brand of Christian Socialism.

Visiting the United States in 1993 Tony Blair became aware of the communitarian ideas which through the writings of Etzioni (1993) had become fashionable, and he realised that these ideas were close to his own – indeed Macmurray's thinking had also been influential in the US (Rentoul, 1995: 287). In a speech in Wellingborough in February 1993 he said:

> The importance of the notion of community is that it defines the relationship not only between us as individuals but between people and the society in which they live, one that is based upon responsibility as well as rights, on obligations as well as entitlements. Self-respect is in part derived from respect for others. (cit. Rentoul, 1995: 291)

The importance of the family was another strong thread. In June 1993 Blair made another speech :

> It is largely from family discipline that social discipline and a sense of responsibility is learnt. A modern notion of society – where rights and responsibilities go together – requires responsibility to be nurtured. Out of a family grows the sense of community. (cit. Rentoul, 1995: 292)

The February speech warned: 'If the value of what is right and wrong is not learnt then taught then the result is simply moral chaos' (cit. Rutherford, 2000: 36). Following the overwhelming effect nationally of the murder of the toddler Jamie Bulger by two 10-year-old boys, Blair wrote in *The Sun* newspaper: 'It's a bargain – we give opportunity, we demand responsibility. There is no excuse for crime' (cit. Rutherford, 2000: 36).

In the heightened atmosphere engendered by the Bulger case, we therefore find Tony Blair translating his belief in mutual responsibilities into a 'no excuses for crime' narrative, phraseology that was later adopted after Labour's election victory in a White Paper on youth justice (*No More Excuses*, 1997). His communitarian beliefs might have taken a different turn: the importance of the family and of communities could have been the focus for social support and regeneration (elements of which did make their way later into neighbourhood renewal programmes).[1] But instead the culture of censure and blame took over: parents were to be punished for the misdeeds of their children and for their own failure to impart proper values, and these aims were later, as we shall see, expressed in legislation.

Tony Blair was not the only Labour politician to espouse the theme of remoralisation. As cited in Chapter 1, Frank Field, MP for Birkenhead, holds this position particularly firmly. Another key player was Jack Straw, who as Shadow Home Secretary created the detailed policies on anti-social behaviour that were incorporated wholesale in the Crime and Disorder Act 1998.

Jack Straw's own experiences chimed with the pleas of social landlords to 'do something' about nasty neighbours. When his parents divorced he and his mother moved onto a council estate where, as a grammar school boy, he stood out. His mother was plagued by a difficult next-door neighbour, and when mutual accusations came to court the teenage Straw had to give evidence on behalf of his mother, who was cleared of assault, while the neighbour was bound over to keep the peace (*The Times*, 23 September 1998, cit. Rutherford, 2000: 39).

The Labour Party paper on dealing with nasty neighbours, entitled *A Quiet Life, Tough Action on Criminal Neighbours* (1995) sounded a rallying cry. It began:

Every citizen, every family, has the right to a quiet life – a right to go about their lawful business without harassment, interference or criminal behaviour by their neighbours. But across Britain there are thousands of people whose lives are made miserable by the people next door, down the street or on the floor above or below. Their behaviour may not be just unneighbourly, but intolerable and outrageous.

The paper was, as the title states, directed against *criminal* acts. The separate notion of 'anti-social behaviour' had not yet emerged. The crimes that Jack Straw was worried about were *repeated* acts of nuisance or aggression, each one in itself not enough to attract significant punishment. The paper argued that many people's lives were being made a misery in this way and that the criminal courts were not able to help them, especially when victims were too intimidated to bear witness. It was for this reason that a new remedy was proposed – a civil order similar to an injunction, with civil standards of proof, but with a criminal offence for breach (thus enabling a much longer maximum than the two years for contempt of court available for breach of an injunction). The implications of this are examined in a later chapter.

Two separate issues were thus highlighted: insufficient punishment for repeat low-level crimes and witness intimidation, both said to plague many poor neighbourhoods. The paper cited two particular examples which were to be recycled in later Home Office documents. The first was 'Family X' from Jack Straw's own constituency of Blackburn, who continued to terrorise their neighbours despite numerous court appearances for attempted robbery, burglary, damage and public disorder. After several evictions they were now living in private rented accommodation and were therefore even beyond the reach of civil action by social landlords.

The second example came from Coventry, and it was no coincidence that Coventry City Council was among the most active in pressing for extra powers to deal with people apparently beyond the reach of both criminal and housing sanctions. The case highlighted, *Coventry City Council* v. *Finnie*[2] was critical in the development of remedies outside the criminal law in dealing with acute neighbourhood problems.

The two Finnie brothers were said to have committed many burglaries and other crimes within the estate where their mother still lived, but at the same time were so menacing that nobody dared bear witness against them. The city council made bold use of powers under S. 222, Local Government Act 1972, giving them the right to bring criminal or civil actions aimed at protecting the interests of citizens. They sought an injunction banning the Finnies from the area affected. The case was contested at successive stages. But in the end it had to be abandoned for a reason that had plagued it from the outset: nobody was willing to appear in person in court to testify against the defendants. The case having been discontinued, the defendants then failed in an application for damages.

The High Court judgment on this final issue, on 18 March 1996,[3] recognised that '[t]he criminal law had proved inadequate to protect the lawful interests of the inhabitants of the particular area of Coventry, so the local authority stepped in to invoke the civil law ... What is clear is that the nature of the plaintiffs' claim had at its very heart law enforcement'.

Coventry City Council's claim, said the judgment, was:

that tenants of their housing stock had over a period of years been subjected to very high levels of crime, including, in particular, burglary, harassment, intimidation and firebombing, causing great distress and fear to the inhabitants. In some instances there were witnesses whom they had interviewed who felt themselves to be in personal danger.

In these circumstances the plaintiffs had concluded that they were prevented from achieving effective use of of their housing stock to discharge their duties and that they had to commit a high and disproportionate extent of staff time to dealing with complaints by tenants about burglary and intimidation, and a number of their houses stood vacant for longer periods than should have been the case.

The defendants are brothers. Both have criminal records and, according to the plaintiffs, were responsible for numerous crimes in the area in question. The purpose of taking these proceedings was to give local inhabitants some respite from the defendants' activities.

The Coventry case broke new ground in openly applying civil law to a crime problem. At the time that it was used by the Labour Party in presenting the argument for a new 'community safety order', it seemed that Coventry had won the day, and it took a while to absorb the message that even civil actions, when used as a form of law enforcement, can fail for lack of willing witnesses. Witness intimidation and related evidential problems have always been at the heart of the legal saga in pursuit of serious anti-social behaviour. This is quite a distinct matter from the perceived failure of the criminal courts to deal adequately with repeated low-level aggravation. The two issues were encapsulated in the examples of 'Family X' and the Finnies, whose stories continued to be used in Home Office publications even after the creation of the anti-social behaviour order in 1998.

Jack Straw was closely in touch with the officers of Coventry City who were in charge of this legal initiative. They in turn performed a leading role within a wider pressure group known as the Social Landlords Crime and Nuisance Group (SLCNG), who first obtained tougher sanctions within housing legislation and then lobbied for enhanced injunctive-type powers that could be used in wider contexts (Burney, 1999). The measures proposed in 1995 were essentially a toughened up and widened version of injunctions available against unruly tenants and their associates available in the Housing Act 1996. Social housing remains the main focus of anti-social behaviour restraint, within a now broadened landscape.

Straw and Blair both represented constituencies suffering from the structural problems of deindustrialisation and the accompanying crime and disorder afflicting poor communities: they and other MPs from similar areas (such as Frank Field) were sympathetic to the idea of tougher legal powers to deal with people seen as beyond the reach of the criminal law. The notion that the decent working class deserves protection from a lawless minority was and remains a very powerful sentiment in the mouths of politicians. Tony Blair has referred to the moral values of his constituents and David Blunkett, when Home Secretary, frequently cited the views of Sheffield voters on law and order, which he felt coincided with his own. Along with this goes the not-unjustified claim that people living in more comfortable circumstances have no idea of the havoc that crime and disorder can wreak upon neighbourhoods.

Thus it was that on the day of the Second Reading in the House of Commons of the Crime and Disorder Bill, Jack Straw wrote in an article in *The Times* (8 April 1998): 'For many years, the concerns of those who lived in areas undermined by crime and disorder were ignored or overlooked by people whose comfortable notions of human behaviour were matched only by their comfortable distance from its worst excesses.' He famously told the House of Commons that 'the Bill represents a triumph of community politics over detached metropolitan elites', and in the same *Times* article he explicitly detached the government from single-issue pressure groups, including those concerned with civil liberties – a very distinct signal that the Labour Party's priorities in the field of law and order had changed.[4]

Had Jack Straw chosen to, he could have cited a growing body of academic evidence for the uneven impact of crime and disorder upon neighbourhoods and individuals. While this literature may have informed his policy advisors, it was not used in political debate. The problem of repeat victimisation, a key aspect of the 'nasty neighbour' syndrome, had been highlighted in research and British Crime Survey (BCS) analysis (Trickett et al., 1995; Farrell 1995) and linked to areas with high proportions of both victims and offenders among their populations. The sharp distinction between areas with the highest crime rates and everywhere else was exposed by further BCS analysis (Hope, 1996). This showed that if areas were grouped in ten deciles, from those with the lowest to the highest victimisation rates, the top tenth suffered 76 times more personal crime as the people in the second lowest decile, and 25 times more property crime. Even more strikingly, when compared with the second highest (ninth) decile, victimisation rates were four times higher for personal crime and twice the rate for property crime.

Given that repeat crime was a major plank of the development of anti-social behaviour policy, it is surprising that this concentration was not highlighted.

Well before this statistical exposure, researchers of the criminology school known as 'Left Realism' had shown, mainly through field surveys such as that in Islington (Jones et al., 1986), that the poor indeed suffered most from crime and disorder and had rather different priorities when it came to ideas of crime prevention. This could have fitted well with New Labour thinking but the connection was not made (Rutherford, 2000: 40). In due course, as government policy developed a highly ambiguous approach to social exclusion in conjunction with the containment of anti-social behaviour, the architects of Left Realism became some of New Labour's strongest critics.

Despite the awareness at policy-making level of the inequitable distribution of crime and disorder, and the horror stories coming out of some very troubled areas, there was no input adopted from British academic sources in explaining or devising solutions for local crime and disorder problems. The Crime and Disorder Act (CDA) 1998 created multi-agency structures to address identified local problems, but there were no parameters defining the scope of problems to be included. Not until the Social Exclusion Unit reported in 2000 (see Chapter 4) was there any coherent attempt to define anti-social behaviour and identify its roots.

So where did the Labour government go to find a language to express their concerns at a theoretical level together with practical demonstrations of methods claimed to be effective? The answer is, of course, the United States. However, as Tim Newburn and Richard Sparks have argued (2004), the match in terms of policy transfer is far from perfect. They distinguish between the *content* of specific crime control measures, and 'policy styles, symbols and rhetoric' (130) that may suggest a greater degree of convergence than in fact exists. One can point to the fact that the ASBO was derived, as described above, directly from a basis in housing law and driven by professionals in that field (even though similar injunctive devices were applied in American jurisdictions). Existing public order law also provided a basis for the new remedies against anti-social behaviour. The most obvious American borrowing was the local child curfew (s.14, CDA 1998) which enabled local authorities to introduce area curfews for children under 10. But this was in no way equivalent to the 'teen curfews' imposed in hundreds of American cities and has never been applied. Only in 2003 did similar restraints become available for older children. That said, there are very many Anglo-American parallels, unremarked by Newburn and Sparks, in the use of civil law as crime control, and these have mostly been introduced under New Labour (see below pp. 29–30).

Borrowing American theories

When it came to justifying the theoretical need to crack down on low-level crime and disorder in neighbourhoods, there were convenient American explanations to hand, often of an apparently simple nature which provided political rhetoric and made them easy to 'sell' to the public. As Jones and Newburn point out, New Labour learnt from Bill Clinton's Democrats 'the power and importance of symbolic politics; of using a phrase or action to convey something more powerful and significant' (2004: 133). The term 'zero tolerance' is one such mantra, applied not only in relation to crime and disorder but in many other contexts, such as public service standards. This and other influential American concepts deserve closer scrutiny, especially where they seem to have penetrated policy-making as well as public discourse.

At a neighbourhood meeting in Cambridge in the spring of 2004 an elderly man got up and explained at some length that if litter was not cleared away and fences not mended local youths would inflict more damage and if nothing was done they would assume they had a free hand and eventually turn to burglary and street robbery. This incident encapsulates the extraordinarily tenacious hold that what is known as 'broken windows theory' has on folk wisdom.

Back in 1982, in the midst of rising concern over disorder and crime, an eloquent magazine article was published by a well-known American criminologist, James Q. Wilson, and a senior New York policeman, George Kelling. The title, 'Broken Windows', referred to their central argument:

> [A]t the community level, disorder and crime are usually inextricably linked, in a kind of developmental sequence. Social psychologists and police officers tend to agree that if a window in a building is broken *and is left unrepaired*, [original emphasis], all the rest of the windows will soon be broken. This is as true in nice neighbourhoods as in run-down ones … one unrepaired broken window is a signal that no-one cares. (p. 31)

They argued that 'vandalism can occur anywhere once communal barriers – the sense of mutual regard and the obligations of civility – are lowered by actions that seem to signal that "no-one cares"'. They then went a step further:

We suggest that 'untended' behavior also leads to the breakdown of community controls. A stable neighbourhood of families who care for their homes, mind each other's children, and confidently frown on unwanted intruders can change, in a few years or even a few months, to an inhospitable and frightening jungle. A piece of property is abandoned, weeds grow up, a window is smashed. Adults stop scolding rowdy children; the children, emboldened, become more rowdy. Families move out, unattached adults move in. (pp. 31–2)

And so on. Wilson and Kelling do not think that at this point serious crime becomes inevitable, but they describe how people will come to believe that it is, and will withdraw from the streets and from neighbourly contact. 'Such an area', they say 'is vulnerable to criminal invasion'. They do not see the serious criminals emerging from the original community, but that drunks, prostitutes and robbers preying on them will move in. Fear of strangers and disorderly persons then becomes endemic.

Most of this famous polemic is concerned with styles of policing, in particular new forms of 'community policing'. By bringing back foot patrols and enabling officers to engage more easily with local people the community can be shielded from this doom-laden sequence and helped to maintain informal vigilance. The policeman on foot patrol has direct contact with the vagrants, beggars and street robbers and can keep them in check. 'The essence of the police role in maintaining order is to reinforce the informal control mechanisms of the community itself' (p. 34). The role of community policing in checking social incivilities, thereby reducing fear and increasing public self-confidence, is the core message – one which finds resonance twenty years later in Britain in the method known as 'reassurance policing'.

Incivilities as a sequential *cause* of crime was a further step in the theory and the one which has most political appeal. Wesley Skogan (1990) supported this idea. He interviewed people about their perceptions of environmental disorder (litter, abandoned cars, etc.) and social disorder (including people loitering and drinking in public, insults, gangs) and he compared the results with their reports of crime victimisation, which seemed to correlate. His study used economic variables and residential instability as signifiers of neighbourhood decline. He concluded that there was a causal link from disorder to fear, neighbourhood decay and crime. It seemed for a while that 'broken windows' indeed held the clue to preventing crime and saving civilised living.

The rise of 'zero tolerance policing' as a concept owes its momentum to Will Bratton, police chief in Mayor Giuliani's New York. Bratton's version of this idea involved a strict management style and a centralised approach which, in a denial of 'community policing', scorned the role of beat policemen in reducing crime (Bratton, 1997). Cracking down on offensive behaviour such as aggressive begging, graffiti-writing, public drunkenness and urination, arresting people for minor misdemeanours such as fare-dodging, and conducting intensive car searches were claimed to have led directly to the dramatic falls in homicides, robberies and burglary that took place over four years. This seemed to justify the heavy-handed tactics which produced a sharp increase in complaints of police misconduct and brutality (Greene, 1999).

It did not take long for critics to question this conclusion (see, for instance, Bowling, 1998; Greene, 1999; Harcourt, 2001). It was noted that police numbers had increased to facilitate the street drive, so that their mere presence on the street must have had a deterrent effect. At the same time police efficiency had been transformed by Commissioner Bratton through strict management tools. The main underlying cause of the earlier surge in violence had been drug gang rivalries and changes in the drug market subsequently dampened down the violence. Other factors such as the economic upturn providing more legitimate opportunities were also cited, as well as the fact that crime dropped in other cities which did not apply zero tolerance.

Yet it could not be denied that New York had become a more peaceful place, and pleasanter too as subway cars were routinely cleansed of graffiti, drunks driven from park benches, homeless from doorways and so forth. It needed no crime-reduction justification to gain public support for the visible effects on the streets. It is this sanitising effect that has had the most appeal internationally – Rotterdam's mayor consciously aped Guiliani in his 'street sweeping' policies (Chapter 7). In Britain, the disorders targeted in New York were incorporated into the government's anti-social behaviour canon, and keenly pursued across many British cities. 'Zero tolerance' applied against environmental disorder is more acceptable than its policing equivalent – which with few exceptions is not acceptable to the British authorities or even the police themselves (Jones and Newburn, 2004).

It took a bit longer for any serious challenge to the 'broken windows' claim that social and physical disorder *caused* a subsequent growth of predatory crime. The proposal could only be effectively tested over a long period of time, since what was postulated was a sequence of decline whereby disorder in Year X resulted in a slow process of disintegration ending up with serious criminals in charge by Year Y. It was Ralph Taylor at the University of Baltimore who took up the challenge, with a painstaking longitudinal study (2001). Using a combination of observation and interviews, he surveyed neighbourhoods in Baltimore in 1982 and again in 1994, aiming to measure any independent effect of incivilities on crime and fear of crime.

In 1994 he found marked increases in environmental deterioration in the inner suburbs, in keeping with the economic plight of the city. But people did not report significant increases of either physical or social incivilities. On nearly all counts they were no more fearful than in 1982. And the incivilities counted in 1982, while they did seem linked to some serious crime increases 12 years later, did not display consistent connections. More important was the social structure of neighbourhoods (poverty, private renters replacing owner-occupiers, social status measured by education). Where social and economic disadvantage was more prevalent in 1982, incivilities were also higher and had got worse by 1994, and so had personal crime. In other words, it was structural factors that mattered most rather than the incivilities and crime which stemmed from the same underlying causes.

Taylor concluded that:

> Police planners and leaders should not automatically privilege a program that focuses on the reduction of incivilities. Results here suggest that if those programs achieve reductions in incivilities, there may or may not be an impact on later crime shifts … [T]hey should not presume a priori that incivility reduction will prove more effective than other strategies, nor should they adopt incivility-reduction approaches in lieu of a more contextually sensitive program. (2001: 371–2)

The other major study which has undermined the predictive argument of 'broken windows' is that of Robert Sampson and Stephen Raudenbush (2001) in Chicago. They too found moderate correlations between disorder and predatory crime, but the strongest correlations for both were structural factors and the loss of what they called 'collective efficacy' – the ability of people to relate to others in their neighbourhood in ways that help them to defend common values. Essentially, Sampson and Raudenbush argued that economic decline undermined communities and that disorder and crime were the result, not the cause, of neighbourhood deterioration. They said that reducing signs of disorder may well improve the attractiveness of a neighbourhood for residence and business, but that 'the current fashion in policy circles on cleaning up disorder through law enforcement techniques appears simplistic and largely misplaced, at least in terms of directly fighting crime'. The notion of collective efficacy has taken hold in Britain, and fits nicely with the ideas of Etzioni and Putnam that appeal to one strand of Labour thinking. There is much promotion of the idea that communities need to stick together against behaviour that violates civilised norms. But the related arguments about social and economic infrastructure have not achieved the same prominence.

Bernard Harcourt (2001) used the Sampson and Raudenbush findings to support his reasoned onslaught on the concepts of broken windows and zero tolerance (he did not use the Taylor study). Harcourt was strongly critical of the Skogan studies and reworked the data to show that no valid link had been made between disorder and crime. This does not, of course, invalidate Skogan's other findings, notably the interaction of neighbourhood decay and the housing market. As for zero tolerance, Harcourt looked critically at some of the specific initiatives, such as dispersal of loitering gang members, and found them unconvincing in terms of crime reduction. His put-down of the New York 'quality of life' initiative echoes that of previous critics: it has its uses in terms of improving the environment and helping the police to pick up suspects, but it cannot claim much credit for the drop in violent crime.

Harcourt challenges the psychology of 'broken windows' as an incentive to crime. What evidence have we that the message (or 'social meaning') of disorder, or of the measures taken against it, are processed in the minds of perpetrators in a way that discourages serious crime? There was no qualitative research to support the idea that the message conveyed by disorder was that 'anything goes', and that this message, once absorbed, would encourage people to commit serious criminal acts that they would not otherwise have perpetrated.

What all these analyses show is that, while America has supplied several populist slogans about crime and disorder, it has also provided reasoned and nuanced research that warns against one-idea policies. But politicians tend to turn a deaf ear. Despite the weak foundation for the sequential aspect of broken windows theory, it continued to be echoed in government pronouncements long after the publication of contrary research. David Blunkett's introduction to the 2003 White Paper *Respect and Responsibility – Taking a Stand against Anti-Social Behaviour* stated:

The anti-social behaviour of a few damages the lives of many. We should never underestimate its impact. We have seen the way communities spiral downwards once windows get broken and are not fixed, graffiti spreads and stays there, cars are left abandoned, streets get grimier and dirtier, youths hang around street corners intimidating the elderly. The result: crime increases, fear goes up and people feel trapped.

This was published five years after Ralph Taylor's Baltimore findings became available in summary form, and three years after the publication of his book. Although Home Office researchers must have been aware of this, the political appeal of broken windows continues to be too great to resist. However, there has been a shift in the terms by which disorder is confronted. It is now more common (following the evidence from the British Crime Survey) to see it as an impediment to public awareness of the drop in crime. If disorder, or anti-social behaviour, makes people uneasy and fearful, they will still think there is a high risk of crime (Innes, 2004). So policing must be redirected, more in the direction of the foot patrols advocated twenty years ago by Wilson and Kelling, who wanted policing to be more responsive to local needs. That part of their polemic has come to be viewed more favourably, and is the bit that, for the moment, holds sway.

Civil remedies

It is not just police resources that have been mobilised in American cities to control disorder. In tandem with criminal charges, controls are available through instruments such as injunctions, landlord and tenant law, abatement notices and property forfeiture. The difficulties of applying criminal law to people whose conduct was merely troublesome 'paved the way for increasing reliance on civil remedy actions … the murky in-between concept of "civil remedies" emerged to control potentially troublesome behaviour' (Mazerolle and Roehl, 1998: 11). In this field Britain has adopted many of the same tactics, although in England and Wales home-grown housing law has been the original vehicle for applying quasi-criminal sanctions (see below, Chapter 5). A feature of this type of regulation is that third parties (parents, landlords, liquor stores, etc.) can be made to bear the burden of prevention and can be punished if they fail. Table 2.1 reproduces most of the civil remedies listed in Mazerolle and Roehl's typology (left-hand column). The right-hand column lists the English equivalents. It does not take more than a glance to see how the measures outlined in Blunkett's White Paper *Respect and Responsibility* have been lifted almost wholesale from this menu, although some of the rules, e.g. sale of alcohol to young people, are of longer standing and in Britain come under criminal rather than civil law. Crack house closures, measures against beggars, loitering youths, irresponsible parents and sales of spray paints to youths, plus youth curfews and enforced removal of graffiti and other environmental nuisances have all become part of British law since 2003.

Table 2.1 Typology of U.S. civil remedies

From Mazerolle and Roehl	English equivalents
Suspected offenders	
Gang injunctions	ASBOs
Gang area bans	Dispersal zones
Potential offenders	
Youth curfews	Youth curfews
Evictions	Housing law
Loitering laws	Dispersal, ASBOs
Prohibition of obscene, threatening language	Injunctions, ASBOs
Panhandling laws	Begging bans
Non-offending third parties	
Parental responsibility for delinquent youths	Parenting orders
Public housing lease restrictions	Tenancy rules
Laws against spray paint sales to youths	ASBA 2003
Laws against alcohol sales to youths	Licensing laws
Code enforcement	Environmental health law
Nuisance abatement	Environmental health law
Padlocking	Crack house closures
Mandated graffiti removal	ASBA 2003

The restrictions placed upon American gang members by means of civil injunctions typically restrict association, location in defined geographical areas, even sartorial details. The similarity to the terms of British anti-social behaviour orders is striking. American critics have not been slow to point out that '[p]rohibitions that are too broad or too indefinite may also run afoul of due process requirements that people have fair notice of what conduct is proscribed, and that officials not be permitted to apply the law with completely unfettered discretion' (Cheh, 1998: 62). The same author emphasises the need for effective constitutional challenge to these expanding practices.

Delivering local order

Adoption of many of the ideas outlined above came through the visits of politicians and senior civil servants and policemen to American cities and their filtration into the policy-making sections of the Home Office and the practices of local police forces. America also provided the political rhetoric in which local action against incivilities is presented in terms of 'communities' and a revival of grass-roots social control. The notion of community, a word of emotive but uncertain identity, is in frequent use to validate concepts and policies.[5] 'Community safety' has overtaken the idea of crime prevention so as to encompass an expanding agenda of environmental and nuisance concerns' (Matthews and Pitts, 2001). 'Community' is also the idealised description of people who live together in the same geographical area within which communitarian notions of strong families, supportive neighbours and informal social control are expressed. This vision obscures the fact that 'communities' will continue to rely on public services, and that anything necessary for behaviour control in the present requires effective delivery by the traditional agencies. As Gilling (2001) remarks, '[w]hile community safety may represent a convergence of social and criminal justice policies, it does so on neo-liberal rather than welfare-liberal terms'.

Most of the Labour government's chosen remedies against anti-social behaviour require practical steps to be taken by police and local authorities. The latter are instructed, goaded and offered sweeteners in order to fulfil Home Office priorities. They are also invited to be part of the holistic, Etzionian, moral endeavour. In a 1998 speech (cit. Crawford, 2001: 56), Home Secretary Jack Straw said:

> We are trying to develop the concept of 'the Active Community' in which the commitment of the individual is backed by the duty of all organisations – in the public sector, the private sector and the voluntary sector – to work towards a community of mutual care and a balance of rights and responsibilities.

'Responsibilisation' is the term applied by David Garland (2001) to the process whereby governments, recognising that they have limited power to deliver protection against crime, promote action by other agencies, public and private, to carry out the task at their own level. Actors may be businesses, voluntary agencies or the public at large, as well as the various arms of the local state. This process was given shape in the Crime and Disorder Act 1998, ss. 5 and 6. Multi-agency partnerships (already operating informally in some areas) became compulsory and were given statutory duties. These Crime and Disorder Reduction Partnerships are required to come up with strategies based on local needs in terms of combating crime and disorder, and to work together to achieve them.

This was not an idea that the Labour government had come up with out of the blue. Adam Crawford (1997) describes how from the early 1980s crime prevention began to be recognised as worthy of attention yet beyond the power of the police to deliver on their own. The Morgan report (Home Office, 1991) recommended that crime prevention and community safety should be a local government responsibility – the report was kicked into touch by the Conservative government but provided Labour with an opportunity to enrol local government as responsible partners in their first major piece of Home Office legislation.

By placing these responsibilities in local hands, the new arrangements were intended to show that each CDRP should decide its own priorities and methods of controlling crime and disorder. This ran the risk that central government would not tolerate too much divergence from the way it wanted things to be done, and so it proved. 'Partnership' was clearly not a marriage of equals. In the favourite metaphor of 'steering not rowing', it was (as in many other semi-autonomous service functions) central government pulling the strings – and controlling the purse strings. For all the talk of the 'hollowing out of the state' and the reliance on arm's length government, the hands controlling the rudder strings in the rowing boat can always tweak in a preferred direction. In the field of anti-social behaviour the Home Office has advised, cajoled, bribed and scolded local authorities to do things its own way; when this does not work it issues directives and passes new legislation imposing specific duties and providing different tools. Conferences, training schemes and high-profile publicity show the path to laggard authorities.

Simultaneously the CDRPs must respond to the legitimate expectations that their existence – and their numerous consultation exercises – arouse in local residents. David Blunkett played to this audience when he said (see p. 38) that local officials who did not use ASBOs and other enforcement tools against anti-social behaviour should be sacked.

Implementing the ASBO

The government soon showed its impatience when the initial estimate of 5,000 ASBOs a year was shown to be wildly optimistic. The ASBO became available in April 1999, but by October of that year only five had been made. Home Secretary Jack Straw wrote to all local authorities on 15 October urging full use of this power, pointing out that when they had been consulted on the proposed order 'you (and the police) indicated that they were exactly the sort of weapon you needed to fight the blight of anti-social behaviour in our neighbourhoods'. He assured them that 'despite some of the misconceptions which have gained ground as a result of comments by certain academics and civil libertarians' they should not refrain from making the orders for fear of conflict with the European Court of Human Rights. To which local councils replied that it was supposed to be their job to decide when to use ASBOs.

Even when the human rights issue had died down, few local authorities were keen on ASBOs, partly because of fears about costs and time-consuming processes (Campbell, 2002) but also because, given the statutory need for inter-agency consultation, a range of other interventions were often preferred. Many saw the resort to an ASBO as a failure (Burney, 2002). After the Social Exclusion Unit's report on ASB (2000) had criticised the lack of joined-up government, the Home Office responded with an action plan, promising indicators to measure the scale of anti-social behaviour and targets for reduction.[6] The Local Government Association's (LGA) chair of housing, Paul Jenks, insisted that ASBOs were only one of a range of options available for tackling bad behaviour. Orders began to rise gradually, but for Jack Straw this was not enough. In June 2000 he spoke at the LGA annual conference. Still only 30 orders had been made 'despite them being a powerful tool to make communities safe', although he did acknowledge it was a matter for local discretion.[7] At the same time the Home Office followed its original guidance on ASBOs with a document providing detailed instruction on appropriate protocols (Home Office 2002), picking up on the SEU's recommendation that a named person in each local authority should be designated anti-social behaviour coordinator. Jack Straw's introduction insisted in bold type that there was no need to show that every other remedy had been exhausted before applying for an ASBO.

A year later, with total ASBOs still only in the low hundreds, the new Home Secretary David Blunkett proclaimed his intention to strengthen the orders. 'I hope by ... slimming down the procedures and speeding up the process we shall persuade local authorities and police to take them up ... Far from abandoning them, I want to spread them more widely.' The legislative changes resulting from Mr Blunkett's determination are detailed in Chapter 5. The ASBOs are 'spread more widely' as a result, although they still come nowhere near the volume originally anticipated. Although usage was increasing, little more than 3,000 had been imposed by November 2004. Before then the government had realised that it was time for a new strategy, recasting the whole concept of anti-social behaviour.

The Social Exclusion Unit, based in the Cabinet Office, was the first to take a comprehensive look at the realities of anti-social behaviour and the structures needed to deal with it (2000). It encouraged the Home Office to establish a coordinating body, leading other departments, especially the then Department for Environment, Transport and the Regions, and supplying practical advice to local CDRPs. The stage was set for a much more high-profile approach, fortified by legislative changes.

Gingering-up: the Anti-Social Behaviour Unit and the Anti-Social Behaviour Act 2003

In January 2003 an Anti-Social Behaviour Unit was set up in the Home Office, headed by a rather surprising choice: Louise Casey, previously working for the government on homelessness and before that in the voluntary sector, and long known for a far-left political stance. On 15 March there followed the White Paper *Respect and Responsibility—Taking a Stand Against Anti-Social Behaviour*, and with no formal consultation the associated Anti-Social Behaviour Bill followed two weeks later. These documents signalled a much more diffuse, almost random, selection of misbehaviour to incorporate into the anti-social canon, yet still without providing any satisfactory definition of the meaning of the term.

David Blunkett introduced the Bill to the House of Commons as:

> what I consider to be very important legislation, which will empower people across the country once and for all to get a grip on the scourge that bedevils their communities: the anti-social behaviour that makes other people's lives a misery.[8]

MPs almost without exception agreed (only Liberal Democrats showing some principled objections) and Member after Member rose with tales of anguish from constituents. Tony Banks (West Ham) summed it up when he said:

> The Bill unites all honourable Members, because every one of us can point to examples in our constituencies of people coming to complain to us about anti-social behaviour, and we share our constituents' anger and frustration, and fear for them. Perhaps we should call this a 'letting off steam Bill' as far as Members of Parliament are concerned.[9]

This comment is revealing in the way it highlights the political emotion engendered by contact with victims of very bad cases of harassment. It enabled a Bill which really offered very little that related to such cases to be swept through the House of Commons on a tide of indignation. The Conservatives did not oppose the Bill although Oliver Letwin, Shadow Home Secretary, listed what he described as 'minor disadvantages': the Bill provided only slight changes to existing powers, and amendments to the government's own legislation some of which was not yet implemented, plus it was largely ineffectual, parts unworkable, some of it 'entirely meaningless' and 'part is of questionable good sense'.[10]

The House of Commons stages of the Bill were completed by 22 May, even though, as Nicola Padfield points out (2004a), the Joint Committee on Human Rights was unable to publish its report on the Bill until 17 June. The committee found that:

> the term 'anti-social behaviour' without any definition to limit its meaning is an unacceptably vague term to use when authorising an interference with a Convention Right. We do not think that people would be able to establish what it means by reference to any predictable, objective standards.

The White Paper had indeed acknowledged that the term was a subjective, contextual label, embracing a much wider range of nuisance behaviour than the original target of nasty neighbours:

> Anti-social behaviour means different things to different people – noisy neighbours who ruin the lives of those around them, 'crack houses' run by drug dealers, drunken 'yobs' taking over town centres, people begging by cash points, abandoned cars, litter and graffiti, young people using airguns to threaten or intimidate people or people using fireworks as weapons.

This list incorporates several of the specific measures in the 2003 legislation. The Anti-Social Behaviour Act 2003 (ASBA) ranges from fast-track powers to close down crack houses to restrictions on fireworks and airguns; from extra powers against misbehaving social tenants to a ban on selling spray paints to minors; from stronger enforcement of parental responsibility for misbehaving or truanting schoolchildren to new powers for local authorities to deal with eyesores such as graffiti, abandoned cars and flytips. Most controversially, the police are given powers to disperse groups of two or more people if anti-social behaviour is prevalent in designated areas, and within these areas to impose curfews on under-16s (for more detail see Chapter 5).

The White Paper presented this rag-bag collection in the context of community empowerment and responsibility. The main text opens with the following declaration:

> Every society has to have rules and standards of behaviour. Those rules and standards have to be enforced. People who behave anti-socially should not be allowed to get away with it any longer and we believe it is time for the community to take a stand.

The government role is to be proactive. 'Our job is to take action where none is being taken, to replicate best practice from around the country and to shift the culture away from protecting the rights of the perpetrator towards protecting the rights of decent people' (para. 1.3); thus the dividing line: 'decent people' vs 'perpetrators', the latter being within the community but not of it, and therefore with a lesser claim to legal protection.

Targeting incivilities

The document goes on to reveal another motive for eliminating incivilities. 'Anti-social behaviour gives rise to fear of crime. Since 1997 ... [o]verall crime has dropped by over a quarter ... But the fear of crime has not dropped to the same extent.' The association of visible signs of disorder with fear of crime is well attested, as discussed in Chapter 1, and remains the most valid part of the broken windows thesis. It was obvious that the Labour government would not gain electoral credit for the drop in crime unless people's fear was also reduced.

Findings from the British Crime Survey lay behind the decision to widen the anti-social behaviour campaign to environmental as well as personal nuisances. On most of the main measures – vandalism, graffiti and other deliberate property damage; rubbish and litter; drug use or dealing; teenagers hanging around the streets – the proportions of people seeing these things as a 'very big or fairly big problem' rose from around a quarter in 1996 to about a third in 2001/2. Teenagers were most often seen as 'the biggest problem' – hardly a new perception but one which encouraged the government to supply police with the draconian powers to disperse groups and impose curfews on younger teenagers.

From all this two main themes emerge. One is the targeting of certain types of problem people, some of whom – beggars, youths – become anti-social simply by being in the street. Linked to this is the theme of sanitised public space. Street drinkers and beggars cause offence by their presence and can therefore be banned. Litter, graffiti, rubbish and abandoned cars are deemed 'anti-social' because of their psychological effect which feeds fear of crime. This seems a rather roundabout way of approaching what should be routine municipal duties of keeping public space clean and tidy. It is clear (see Chapter 6) that it is the simple device of allowing fixed penalties for littering, abandoned cars, etc. to be retained by the local authorities that is most effective in getting them to perform their duties keenly. Moreover, cities have good economic reasons for wanting their centres to be clean and free of disorderly people.

No new law was needed to put pressure on beggars: a change in regulations was sufficient to raise the offence of begging (no longer imprisonable) to a recordable offence, which will also enable police to maintain surveillance on persistent beggars. Under the Criminal Justice Act 2003 a third offence qualifies for a community sentence, including a drug treatment and testing order. Begging does not have to be 'aggressive' to become an offence, and it is true some people find that a passive beggar sitting by a cash machine makes them uneasy. The White Paper says that '(w)e need to tackle the nuisance and intimidation caused to those going about their lawful business by people who persistently beg' (p. 47). Yet the policy also clearly relates to the sanitising of public space: beggars, like litter, are an eyesore to be swept away.

Parents are subject to a raft of new controls in ASBA 2003. The White Paper has quite a lot to say about support systems for parents and families, but the legislation is all about enforcement. For instance a new instrument – a parenting contract – is introduced as a way of supplying voluntary improvement in the control exercised over children who have been truanting, excluded from school or referred to a youth offending team (even if no crime has been committed). Contracts carry the proviso that failure to keep to the terms may lead to a compulsory parenting order. Controversially, schools may impose also fixed penalty fines on the parents of truants. David Blunkett pointed out that the new option of a residential requirement in parenting orders can be a way of getting extreme 'problem families' into special accommodation where, on the lines of a scheme pioneered in Dundee, they can be intensively trained into socially acceptable behaviour.

The Act was criticised for replicating many existing powers and introducing 'nanny state' regulation (Padfield, 2004b). But it was trumpeted by the Home Secretary as necessary and 'empowering'. From its title onwards, it was a declaration that the government cared about the fears and annoyances suffered by people on a daily basis and was stepping in to make sure that they were protected.

This was the cue for the crusading efforts of Louise Casey's Anti-Social Behaviour Unit to swing into action. On 14 October 2003 a campaign was launched in flamboyant style to an audience of 700 local delegates, who were treated to a chilling video about people who had suffered gross harassment and had stood up to it. The conference was addressed by both the Prime Minister and the Home Secretary. Each of these emphasised enforcement and the use of the powers now provided, and denigrated the criminal courts for their inability to deal effectively with anti-social behaviour. Tony Blair strongly favoured fixed penalty notices, thus bypassing the courts except for those who choose to contest the evidence. He said:

I want to make one very simple point in this speech. To the police, housing officers, local authorities – we've listened, we've given you the powers, and it's time to use them.

You've got new powers to deal with nuisance neighbours – use them.

You've got new powers to deal with abandoned cars – use them.

You've got new powers to give fixed penalty fines for anti-social behaviour – without going through the court process – use them.

A member of the audience suggested that social exclusion was more important than enforcement and was told by Tony Blair that Connexions, Sure Start and welfare-to-work programmes were dealing with all of that. David Blunkett spoke with characteristic bluntness, saying that local officials and police officers who did not use the available powers should be sacked.

The campaign, entitled 'Together', indicates by its name the focus inspired by social theorists, such as Robert Putnam, who argue that lack of connectedness has weakened communities to the extent that they can no longer function effectively to uphold common standards. In Home Office terms, this means being prepared to bear witness and otherwise stand up against the depredations of the anti-social minority. The inaugural conference was addressed by Mayor O'Malley of Baltimore,[11] who described how the city had reduced its drug-related crime problems with the help of a campaign to persuade people to act as witnesses and mentors, and otherwise get involved.

The campaign was (partly for budgetary reasons) very specifically targeted. Small groups of local authorities were identified to run demonstration projects in the fields selected for attention. Some were environmental nuisances: abandoned cars, graffiti, litter and messy back-alleys. Eye-catching programmes such as the '100-day Clean-up' were launched. Beggars were to be aggressively targeted by five 'trailblazing' councils. In a change of tack, seriously nasty neighbours were acknowledged to be relatively few in number. A Nuisance Neighbour panel would be set up to give expert advice to agencies who had to deal with them; 450 of the worst households were to be 'trailblazed' (a favourite concept) by four local authorities The most problematic families would be taken into specialist residential units, on the model originally created in Dundee – it was not mentioned that Dundee has found it more cost-effective to support such people in their own homes (Dillane et al., 2001).

Impatience with the criminal justice system was reflected in the plan to train specialist prosecutors to deal with anti-social behaviour. Magistrates were to be given new guidelines on dealing with applications for ASBOs and sentencing for breaches. The Home Office strategic plan for 2004–8 promised specialist 'anti-social behaviour courts'.

Over all this the Anti-Social Behaviour Unit presides with training, diffusion of best practice and continual high-profile encouragement on enforcement. A series of roadshows in provincial centres succeeded the 'Together' launch, at which practitioners had it well drilled into them that any type of anti-social problem has an enforcement solution. The campaign has yet to be evaluated but contact with local authority officers suggests that, for the most part, the strong Home Office lead and available advice on particular issues is appreciated and used (especially, of course, where it attracts extra money). There is no doubt that awareness of anti-social behaviour has been raised still higher by the work of the Unit, cheered on by ministers. Tony Blair chose the theme for his first speech on return from summer holiday in 2004, urging all local authorities to copy Manchester's ASBO zeal.

Alcohol – a new focus

Up to this point there had been one curious omission from the 'anti-social' canon – the effects of binge-drinking. For years an obvious source of offensive behaviour, turning many provincial town centres into no-go areas at weekends, it was ignored in political rhetoric and found no place in the 'Together' programme. Several possible reasons can be adduced for this. The proliferation of bars and clubs giving rise to the phenomenon was a deliberate policy by local authorities, encouraged by central government, both as a revenue raiser and in the belief that it would create a 'vibrant' continental-style night-life. Responsibility for policy in this field lay with more than one central government department, with their own perspectives, hampering any serious change of tack. And the binge-drinkers themselves were not the easily identifiable 'youths hanging about' on poor housing estates – although among the latter were often under-age drinkers – but a much larger mass of young people following a culture driven by commercial incentives and imbued with norms adopted by a large proportion of their generation. It would dilute the message about an anti-social minority if it were to be acknowledged that routine mass misbehaviour was an equally serious matter.

Government attitudes towards binge-drinking changed in the course of 2004, spurred by figures showing that violent crime, against the general trend, was on the increase, and that much of it was drink-related. The Prime Minister (whose own son had earlier been picked up by the police dead drunk in Leicester Square) suddenly took an interest, and it was his Strategy Unit within the Cabinet Office which produced a wide-ranging policy document on dealing with alcohol-related harm (2003). The report ranged over the health and economic damage from excessive drinking as well as crime, disorder and environmental nuisance. It supported the controversial liberation of licensing hours contained in the Licensing Act 2003 (intended to reduce disorder through staggered bar closing-times) but by implication condemned the proliferation of licensed premises in town centres, now recognised as a major contributor to night-time disorder and the binge culture. It drew attention to local authorities' responsibility in s. 17 of the Crime and Disorder Act 1998 to consider the effects on crime and disorder of all their functions – which in this context would apply to planning approvals for bars and clubs.

Some detailed remedies (mostly long-term, but including much stricter enforcement) were offered for the three types of drink-related harm associated with nuisance and disorder: under-age drinking, binge-drinking and daytime street drinking by down-and-outs. The first of these was often associated with vandalism, violence and harassment in residential areas as well as town centres.

Spot-fines – another magic bullet?

Control of drink-related nuisance fitted neatly with Tony Blair's long-standing predeliction for on-the-spot fines as a cheap and instant method of punishing bad behaviour. During David Blunkett's reign at the Home Office powers to impose fixed-penalty fines on all kinds of rule-breakers and disorderly people were given to a range of civilian employees as well as the police. The Anti-Social Behaviour Act 2003 strengthened the power of environmental officers to fine polluters and, most controversially, gave teachers the power to fine parents for their children's absenteeism or bad behaviour. The Criminal Justice and Police Act 2001 introduced police-imposed penalty notices for disorder (PNDs) covering a range of street misbehaviour, including being drunk and disorderly, letting off fireworks 'inappropriately' and supplying alcohol to a minor. Tony Blair's original vision of brawling youths being marched off to the cashpoint gave way to something more like a parking ticket, to the tune of £50 or £80, recipients to pay within 21 days or risk prosecution. Amid much scepticism a pilot was run (Halligan-Davis and Spicer, 2004) in which only half the penalties were paid on time – the remainder were converted into fines and eventually an overall payment rate of nearly 70 per cent was achieved.

This heralded wider use of on-the-spot fixed penalty charges. In April 2004 the police were given the power to fine anybody over 16 between £50 and £80 for 21 different offences relating to public order. A drive against binge-drinking disorder took place in the summer of 2004 in which 4,000 PNDs were handed out. Moreover, power had been given in the Anti-Social Behaviour Act 2003 to extend the system to children as young as 10 – an altogether different proposition since parents were to be responsible for payment. January 2005 saw the launch of a pilot of PNDs for under 16s. Probation officers criticised the idea on the grounds that it would create family tension, and police feared it would be no deterrent to children if parents paid. It clearly increases the potential for vicarious punishment of parents, who are already fingered in so many ways for the misbehaviour of their children – and £80 is no small sum for a family on benefit.

The instant justice provided by PNDs has obvious attractions. It saves a great deal of police time compared with an arrest (though fewer than half the PNDs in the pilot went to people who would otherwise have been arrested), and does not involve a criminal record for payers-up. Police say that merely issuing the ticket often has a calming effect. But, even apart from the issue of fines for children, it is not uncontentious. It adds yet another layer to police discretion, and gives powers to civilian support officers who do not have the status or training commensurate with a discretionary decision which could result in a court appearance and a criminal record. It encourages net-widening, especially as more minor offences are added to the list and children become involved. A PND may seem like a parking ticket, but some of the implications are greater.

Housing and bad behaviour

The high-profile Home Office campaigns tend to overshadow the work of the Office of the Deputy Prime Minister, which among other things is responsible for overseeing, and legislating for, the housing issues that are bound up with the problems of anti-social behaviour.[12] The job has become harder as increasing numbers of local authorities have been encouraged to shed their housing management responsibilities and transfer stock to other types of social landlord. These now have most of the same powers as local authority landlords but lack the same political incentive and resources to deal with complaints, and cannot be leant upon so hard by central government.

41

As described later, social landlords mainly use tried and tested methods of warnings and repossessions for controlling anti-social behaviour. The Anti-Social Behaviour Act 2003 widened their power to impose injunctions and deny security of tenure to 'anti-social' tenants. Nevertheless, in June 2004 housing associations were castigated by Louise Casey for a 'culture' alleged to inhibit action against anti-social behaviour, compared with the much keener performance by council landlords. This did not go down well with Tom Manion, chief executive of the large Irwell Valley Housing Association, who declared 'I firmly believe in tough enforcement but also in tough prevention and tough rehabilitation. You can't always lamp these young boys with an ASBO and not consider the possibility of prevention and rehabilitation'.[13]

The fragmentation of council tenancies through the right to buy has resulted in many areas of mixed tenure – where owner occupants are alongside both social and private tenants. The problem of anti-social behaviour in these areas was investigated on behalf of the (then) Department for Environment, Transport, Local Government and the Regions (DETLR) (Nixon et al., 2003) with the conclusion that in these areas the whole range of available preventive powers were needed, applied through close cooperation by all the agencies and services concerned and attention to problem-solving (see Chapter 5). Subsequent legislation (Housing Act 2004) provides for proxy responsibility being imposed on private landlords for tenants' bad behaviour (below p. 168).

Problem families

Scattered throughout mixed tenure areas and in social housing are a small number of individuals and families that undoubtedly fit the 'nasty neighbour' stereotype (see Chapter 4). Such persons provided the original impetus for the anti-social behaviour order and for Frank Field's diatribe against dysfunctional families. Having originally been presented as a very large problem, it took several years for the Home Office to realise that they were a small but very tough problem, requiring intensive supervision and assistance as well as stern treatment. By February 2005 sufficient results had been obtained from the already mentioned pilot scheme with 450 of 'the most challenging nuisance neighbours' for the Home Office Minister Hazel Blears to announce that the treatment would be meted out all over the country in 50 Action Areas, reaching an expected 1,000 families (Home Office press release 030/2005).

Blears said:

It is clear from the work of our expert panels on neighbour nuisance that we must now clamp down further on the problem families who, although small in number, cause disproportionate damage to their communities. That is why we are investing £1.25 million to ensure that those parents who persist in letting their kids run wild, or behave like yobs themselves, will face intensive rehabilitation ... backed by the threat of enforcement.

The programmes, she explained, would provide a package of measures – acceptable behaviour contracts (ABCs), ASBOs, on-the-spot fines, compensation orders for damage done by children under ten. These families were to be the recipients of every kind of behaviour control instrument provided by the government (though at an anticipated £1,250 per family this can hardly be 'intensive').

It was left to others to mention that support measures were also on the agenda as well as enforcement. Thirty per cent of the households, nearly half of all those with children, said they had been helped by increased family support, as well as the 39 per cent who said that warnings, ASBOs, ABCs or threats of eviction had helped them behave better. A spokesman for NCH Children's Homes, a pioneer in this field, said:

> Anti-social behaviour is a very complex problem and if we want to end the distress it creates, addressing its root causes are vital. From our experience working with challenging families, we know that intensive and tailored support for those with a history of anti-social behaviour enables them to reconnect with mainstream society.

The benefit threat

Welfare benefits are sometimes used as a government lever to force people towards a desired end, such as obtaining employment. The recipient is told that benefits will be reduced or removed if he or she does not comply. The Labour government has not hesitated to use this method of getting lone parents and young people into work, and may apply a similar condition to people on incapacity benefit who are deemed fit enough. The principle of conditional benefits has been considered in a report by the Institute of Public Policy Research (Stanley and Asta Lohde, 2004). A foreword by Stuart White sets out three tests for acceptability: a social democratic rationale; evidence that it works; fairness, including effects on the most disadvantaged people and their families.

The proposal to remove housing benefit from badly behaving tenants has not gone away completely. Following a private members bill from Frank Field, the government were minded to include this condition in a Housing Bill. Protests from all sides resulted in a withdrawal, but the government reserved the right to revive the idea. But, as the IPPR report concludes, while civil behaviour is certainly a social democratic attribute, this particular measure would not address root causes, would be difficult to implement justly and would be inequitable as it would only apply to people on housing benefit. That the idea should even be contemplated underlines how, in the pursuit of communitarian aims, Labour is prepared to apply neo-liberal solutions that are manifestly unjust and unfair.

Notes

1 Gordon Hughes (1996) has argued that the exclusionary and authoritarian mindset usually associated with comunitarianism could be replaced with an inclusionary and redistributive version.
2 [1995] QBD 432.
3 [29 HLR 658]
4 Jack Straw took great exception to a reasoned critique of the proposed 'Community Safety Order' by five leading law professors (Ashworth et al. 1998).
5 Lacey and Zedner (1998) note that 'appeals to community are most likely to flourish where structures of community are most fragile'.
6 *Inside Housing*, 7 April 2000.
7 *Inside Housing*, 30 June 2000.
8 Hansard HC, April 2003, col. 136.
9 Ibid., col. 226.
10 Ibid., col. 150.
11 Perhaps not the best choice, as Baltimore has been designated the 'murder capital' of the United States.
12 The ODPM lost out to the Home Office over the sections of the Anti-Social Behaviour Act 2003 that revise housing legislation with regard to anti-social tenants: it was argued that these changes should have awaited the new Housing Bill, then under preparation.
13 *Inside Housing*, 2 July 2004.

Chapter 3

A short history of behaviour control

A concept so fluid and imprecise as 'anti-social behaviour' cannot be measured over time in the way that 'crime' – for all the well-known flaws in official records – does provide some long-term series and comparisons. There is no satisfactory answer to the question 'are people behaving worse?' because there is no baseline apart from the perennial vision of a past, within the lifetime of older members of the community, when things were different and people had more respect for each other. People are often annoyed by rude and inconsiderate behaviour as they go about in public or drive their cars (Phillips and Smith, 2003) but there is no means of comparison with past experiences of incivility.

Without doubt the rapid changes in society indicated in the first chapter have impacted hugely on many people's lives in Britain and elsewhere, in ways that are often for the better but also for the worse. Broad changes in patterns of living and social relations have different consequences for different groups of people and those that are more impoverished and marginalised are most likely to experience, and at the same time be blamed for, some of the more obviously unacceptable behaviour.

History demonstrates that groups of people at the bottom of the social heap have always been subject to condemnation and attempts at control. This may be especially the case at times of rapid social change and economic disruption. And in any society there will always be individuals whose behaviour does not correspond to accepted norms and who may be either tolerated or restrained. But social norms develop over the centuries: what counts as good or bad behaviour varies over time as it does over place. Norbert Elias (1978) has traced 'the civilising process', whereby customs, rules of conduct and standards of acceptability change from one period to another and new constraints on behaviour develop. Some people now maintain that we can no longer rely on common standards of decency and that the civilising process is unravelling – echoing sentiments expressed at regular intervals throughout the Victorian era (Pearson, 1983).

Theorists of 'social control' distinguish between standards of behaviour absorbed through informal social processes, and those imposed, engineered or implied through practices and institutions of governance (Innes, 2004). The mechanisms involved are the subject of continued debate and analysis, which cannot detain us here. But it is abundantly clear that the policies concerning anti-social behaviour described in this book are an overt version of the behaviour control that has been exercised in different forms at different times in the past.

This chapter will look at some examples from the past, illustrating behaviour deemed unacceptable in its time and thus subject to censure or regulation. There are certain recurrent themes from the Middle Ages onwards: changing definitions of bad behaviour, and of which groups, such as vagrants or prostitutes, should be the focus of control; sporadic 'moral panics' and crackdowns; and, from the mid-nineteenth century onwards, the selective exercise of police powers against an increased range of nuisance and disorder, designed to control the urbanised working classes.

Efforts to control and exclude, mainly directed at socially marginalised sub-groups can be found in any historical era. Vagrants and prostitutes are prominent among these. Youths as a focus of complaint and spasmodic outrage are equally present in every age, as Geoff Pearson's classic *Hooligan* (1983) demonstrates. Periodic anxiety about what would now be called anti-social behaviour can be glimpsed anecdotally over the centuries, but the true extent of such behaviour cannot be easily measured through court records that deal with more serious crime. The use of the common law instrument of 'breach of the peace' sometimes reveals situations which nowadays might attract the label 'anti-social' and be dealt with in ways that reflect that perspective, including a convenient lack of imprecision about what kind of conduct would attract the court's censure. Maintaining the 'king's peace' was the job of the justices of the peace, an office which evolved in the unsettled years of the early fourteenth century. It was the community as a whole who were injured when the common peace broke down: individual complainants were not the main focus. The breach occurred through actions likely to evoke an angry response and stir up trouble, and people were often bound over to keep the peace for quite serious matters as well as private annoyances (Cockburn, 1977: 111).

There was (and still is) no legal definition of a breach of the peace. In the Elizabethan period, according to a leading historian:

> One of the hallmarks of the law enforcement system was its flexibility, an attribute which included the correction of a wide variety of conduct which might have defied the precise definition of the statute book ... The power to bind over to keep the peace or to be of good conduct, and the custom of sending petty offenders to the house of correction, gave the authorities almost unlimited discretion in what was, and what was not, illegal or dangerous behaviour. (Sharpe, 1984: 8)

In early modern times 'scolds' were typical of people who disrupted the peace of the community – usually female, but Sharpe (p. 89) quotes the case of Thomas Jackson, of Eccleshall, of whom it was complained in 1599 that 'he useth to call all men yt he falleth out with and women also theeves, rogues, whores and queans and so greatly disquietes the townsmen'. 'Causing dissension' was frowned upon for upsetting community relations: Mary Taylor, of Auckland, was brought before an ecclesiastical court in 1600, where it was said 'that she by her evill and rayling temper misusethe and formethe dissension amonge her neighbours' (Sharpe, 1984: 89). Defamation and discord came before the church courts when the moral character of the plaintiff was impugned. Emmison (1973: 49) remarks that 'not infrequently two women confronted each other with the same term, or such mutual recrimination led to "harlot" being countered by "witch". In such matters the judge usually demanded that they should "reconcile themselves"'. For offences such as keeping a bawdy house punishments could be fining, whipping, public confession in church or excommunication.

Trial records of the time depict individuals who would nowadays rank as 'nasty neighbours'. The following extracts from quarter sessions in seventeenth-century Cheshire, obtained by T. C. Curtis (1977) illustrate this.

> This examinate says upon her oath that she being a door neighbour to the said Mary Mooreton knows ... [that she] is a common drunkard. This examinate says upon her oath that she being a door neighbour to the said Mary Mooreton and hath been within this fortnight drunk twice of one day. And that when she is drunk she

abuses one neighbour or another, calling them whores and thieves. (p. 139).

John Faulkner and his wife are described as 'persons of evil fame and behaviour, causing dissension and variance in the neighbourhood ... they had never heard children use such bad language as the ... children [of John Faulkner] (p. 142).

Alehouse keepers were often in trouble, such as Anne Priestnal, who 'kept a drinking house which may also have housed a brothel. Her activities bitterly offended at least some of her neighbours, who complained of her to the constables, demanding her punishment lest her "naughty carriage" brought " a curse ... upon the town"' (p. 139).

Mental illness could cause anti-social behaviour, then as now. 'Richard Rylands was "a person distracted in his senses, wandering about, and disorderly behaving himself, to the great terror of his majesty's subjects, and has been very abusive in his language and actions"' (p. 137). Similarly 'James Livesey struck and abused a boy in the highway ... it was alleged that ... Livesey used to quarrel with women and children' (p. 137).

The impression given by these seventeenth-century records is of rural communities familiar with, and sometimes greatly offended by, the behaviour of a range of disorderly, eccentric and footloose persons. Parish constables existed to enforce formal rules of behaviour but it was up to private citizens to instigate most of the legal action where behaviour was more than neighbours could tolerate. The examples above concern individuals whose actions were disruptive but not essentially threatening. Social threats derive from ideas rather than individuals, and the imagined threat of witchcraft triggered appalling punishments on people, nearly all women, accused of witchcraft during the moral panic of the late sixteenth and early seventeenth centuries (Rosen, 1991), often singled out simply by reason of rumour or spite.

Strangers became objects of suspicion with the rise in vagabondage in the Elizabethan period, caused by rapid population growth. Sharpe (1984: 100) comments: 'The vagrant emerged as *the* criminal stereotype in the late sixteenth century. His importance in the eyes of those bent on keeping English society orderly was demonstrated by a mass of legislation and a substantial body of popular literature.' Most of these itinerant men and women were looking for employment rather than opportunities to rob or steal, but the demonising and exclusion of 'sturdy beggars' established a lasting image. The Poor Laws were formed to force them back to their place of origin so as to prevent them becoming a burden on the parish. But vagrancy still persisted when impelled by social and economic circumstances. Again by the early nineteenth century urban vagrants were seen as a source of disorder and moral threat. Thus even today the 1823 Vagrancy Act contains the offence of indecent exposure, which at the time Home Secretary Robert Peel claimed 'had been carried to an immense extent in the parks, whereby virtuous females had been shamefully insulted'.[1]

The emphasis on curbing behaviour on grounds of morality had long been apparent, developing new forms after the reformation, in state and church legal control of bad behaviour. Parish records, lay and ecclesiastical, demonstrate the importance placed on disciplining lewdness and drunkenness, as well as enforcing church attendance. By the end of the seventeenth century 'Societies for the Reformation of Manners' had sprung up, in which upright citizens operated surveillance over immorality and bad behaviour, such as rowdy pubs, profanity and poor Sunday observance (Radzinowicz, 1956). But soon such efforts were overwhelmed by rising levels of disorder and crime associated with urbanisation. Drunkenness reached new heights and was a constant source of middle-class concern.

Thus when Peel's new police force was created in 1829 crime prevention and 'public tranquillity' was put above the detection of criminals. Backed up by a wealth of new legislation, the police became active in cleansing the streets of the triple scourges of vagrancy, prostitution and drunkenness, and containing the rowdiness of street leisure. There is some doubt about the extent to which they actually performed the role of 'moral entrepreneurs', imposing middle-class values on the working classes, although this was certainly advocated (Emsley, 1983).

Begging was the main cause of arrests of vagrants. Henry Mayhew (1862/1950) presents an elaborate typology of beggars according to their different methods of attracting sympathy. The presence of beggars was a continual reminder of the underclass known as the 'undeserving poor'. The police often reported that respectable shoppers in the West End were being accosted by beggars (Jones, 1982). Charitable societies sprang up, devoted to the control of mendicants. Their efforts, and waves of police activity, eventually reduced numbers drastically. The problem did not go away, but as ever forceful action made it less visible.

Prostitutes were likewise subject to successive waves of police activity. For most of the century, the numbers of disorderly prostitutes taken into custody in London exceeded those of drunks and vagrants, but the figures show a sequence of peaks and troughs which, though initially attributable to economic conditions, came later to reflect the complaints of ratepayers and anti-vice societies (Jones, 1982: 129, 131). Mayhew provides sympathetic accounts of how unfortunate women came to be prostitutes. Rescuing 'fallen women' was another preoccupation found among the middle-classes even while recourse to brothels was widespread among middle- and upper-class men. A sudden sharp drop in women convicted of soliciting in London in the 1880s was attributed not to any reduction in offending but simply to a change of practice on the part of the police (Emsley, 1996: 28).

Public drunkenness, unlike prostitution, was a crime, and accounted for a third of total arrests in London (Jones, 1982: 129) as well as being rife in other cities. New licensing laws helped to curb public nuisances caused by the enormous number of pubs. Again, police practices varied over time in the way drunks were dealt with, but as provincial cities also acquired police forces so they too focused on reducing drunken behaviour in the streets. The temperance movement gathered pace and played its part in making the manners of the working class more acceptable to their social superiors. Only in the early twenty-first century has public concern about uncontrolled drunkenness again reared its head.

To many propertied people during the Victorian era the social order was felt to be threatened by unruly urban working-class behaviour, especially when the discipline of the factory was not present (Storch, 1977: 139). In terms echoing Frank Field's twenty-first century polemic, some saw the very foundations of society at risk. Storch quotes from W. R. Greg (1831) 'speedily, there are silent but mighty instruments at work … which, ere long, will undermine the system of social union and burst asunder the silken bonds of amity which unite men to their kind'. The rest of the century was devoted in one way and another to making sure that this did not happen, and the means used frequently echo the methods directed against anti-social behaviour today.

Bad behaviour and criminality among children and young people were of particular concern, reflected in the mass of innovation and legislation directed at juvenile delinquency. Boys and girls who behave like disorderly adults are seen as particularly disquieting in their affront to innocence. In 1851 Henry Mayhew recorded that:

The precocity of youth in London is perfectly astounding. The drinking, the smoking, the blasphemy, indecency and immorality that does not ever cause a blush is incredible, and charity schools and the spread of education do not seem to have done much to abate this scourge. (1950. edn: 50)

Complaint about unbridled youthful behaviour is well-recognised as a recurrent theme throughout time and across different societies. Geoffrey Pearson (1983) trawled through historical sources to show how this theme plays louder from time to time, stimulated by moral panics about perceived new forms of juvenile depravity. Pearson traces the way street corner youths were transformed in popular parlance into 'hooligans', perceived as responsible for various outrages against respectable persons. Practices he describes – such as spitting and throwing stones from bridges onto rowers passing beneath (p. 89) – could well attract anti-social behaviour orders today. The division of the working class into 'roughs' and 'respectables' applied equally to the young: it was the latter who were more likely to become involved in the clubs and other activities set up in the 1890s with the conscious purpose of civilising youth (Gillis, 1975). Later, as both Pearson and Gillis point out, the Boy Scout movement created a new milieu, more anarchic and tolerant in character.

By the mid-nineteenth century civilising the adult working classes became the active concern of a wide spectrum of social entrepreneurs. The creation of new institutions by missions and charities, and municipal provision of parks and libraries, were all seen to contribute to underwriting the social order. At the same time the overt police control of disorderly persons – often regarded as the 'undeserving poor' who would not benefit from social improvement – was seen as an essential element in maintaining decencies. The Town Police Clauses Act of 1847 contained detailed powers to control environmental nuisances as well as making innkeepers and others liable for disorderly events on their premises. It has been pointed out that it was one thing for an aggrieved individual to bring a prosecution for, say, assault but

> [I]t was quite a different matter for the ordinary resident to bring a prosecution against the noisy public house, the offensive brothel or the noisy group of drunks who assembled under the window. It was dangerous, unpopular and very difficult to bring and successfully prove a charge concerning such events, so few residents bothered. (Davey, 1983: 45).

Better paving and lighting and removal of nuisances were seen as 'a recipe for physical and moral improvement' (Taylor, 2002: 27) much as the removal of environmental mess has in modern times been seen as a key to improved behaviour.

Replacing overcrowded slum housing was also intended to reduce crime and make people behave better as well as undertaken on health grounds. Later, the municipal housing drive of the 1920s and 1930s aimed to set a standard of decency, in support of which disreputable families were excluded (Burney, 1999).

Research has shown the manner in which police powers were exercised in various provincial towns, backed up by by-laws. Middlesbrough was a particularly unruly industrial town, having sprung up with enormous rapidity. David Taylor (2002: 28) describes how 'behaviour in public places was subject to strict control, in theory at least', including

> anti-social activities such as wilfully ringing doorbells, letting off fireworks or extinguishing street lamps. Above all decency was to be preserved (or instilled) by forbidding indecent exposure of the person or the sale of 'profane, indecent or obscene' material in any form. Abusive and insulting words and behaviour likely to cause a breach of the peace were likewise proscribed.

The watch committee, made up of respectable citizens, expected the police to uphold behavioural standards.

By-laws were increased to maintain/enforce respectability, so that local police had enhanced powers to prevent street nuisances such as swearing, playing pitch and toss, dog and cock fighting, brawling and urinating. 'When Albert Park was opened in 1868 as an alternative and wholesome site of entertainment for working men and their families special by-laws not only forbade alcohol, swearing and brawling in the park but also made provision for the removal of persons 'offensively or indecently clad' (Taylor, 2002: p. 28). By the late nineteenth century the suppression of street gambling replaced drunkeness as a matter of concern. It became a focus of by-laws and statute law, and remained in many places a running sore between police and working-class punters right up to the legalisation of betting shops in 1963.

Taylor (2002: 28) identifies three characteristics of Middlesbrough police activity:

> First, the relatively trivial nature of many of the offences – throwing orange peel on the footpath, obstruction of the footpath by boys playing with tops, the noisy behaviour of both boys and girls at the local ice-cream shop. Second, the underlying continuity of concern, for example with the problem of boys throwing stones or using bad language, throughout the period from the late nineteenth century to the early twentieth century. And third, the sporadic nature of this concern.

The switches of emphasis from, for example, unruly boys in the library to cycling in the park, he believes reflects at least in part pressure from the watch committee and the general public about what they saw as undesirable or reprehensible behaviour at any one time.

Miles Ogbourn (1993) uses his study of Portsmouth police to develop a picture of policing based upon surveillance of public space, which he relates to the increasing power of the state to control the activities of civil society, rather than simply class-based interpretations of the policing function. Reorganisation of the local force produced a greater degree of control over public space, but this was often contested.

> On the streets there were continual confrontations between the police and the 'disorderly' elements who had become increasingly 'visible' as the result of changes in police organisation and legislation … [in committees] there were battles over which places should be protected, which places should be subject to intensive moral regulation, and what forms their policing should take. (p. 518)

Andy Croll's study of Victorian Merthyr Tydfil agrees that 'surveillance played a key role in securing the public spaces of the late Victorian town' (1999: 267). Besides the police, the citizenry were actively involved and were quick to alert the local paper to behaviour that they disapproved of. The press acted as a 'shaming machine' in identifying perpetrators – although this was only effective upon those who could both read and cared about being shamed.

Shaming, surveillance, detailed laws focusing on often petty offences, targeted policing of traditional activities classed as disorderly or on specific groups, rules placing responsibility on third parties such as landlords and publicans plus the belief that environmental improvements improve behaviour and the switching of attention from one source of annoyance to another are all features of modern methods of controlling anti-social behaviour. The difference might be that police in late Victorian times, under the control of local watch committees, were rather more responsive to pressure to attend to matters that annoyed respectable people than perhaps they are today – but this too is changing. The new slogan, 'reassurance policing', indicates that issues that people worry about in communities, criminal or otherwise, should be the focus of police attention. The wheel seems to be coming full circle as 'neighbourhood policing' becomes the favoured practice, and government seeks to engage communities with policing and self-policing. Police are going to have to pay much more attention to the things that people say bother them on their doorstep.

Many things currently labelled anti-social are environmental nuisances, where again during the nineteenth century huge inroads were made to protect public health and the laws relating to nuisance developed to reflect urbanisation and new sources of noise, fumes and other unpleasantness (Burney, 2005 forthcoming). Two principles relevant today in the assessment of 'harassment, alarm or distress' caused by anti-social behaviour were, first, that context matters, and second, that people's sensitivities vary.

In *Sturges* v. *Bridgman*[1] [1878] Lord Justice Thesiger declared that 'What would be a nuisance in Belgrave Square would not necessarily be so in Bermondsey'. (No doubt the judge was more familiar with the former than the latter location.) But in *Brand* v. *Hammersmith Railway Company* [1867][2] Chief Justice Erle stressed the subjective nature of 'nuisance' (even in the minds of judges) and the need for tolerance. He said:

> There is no standard by which to measure degrees of annoyance, or to estimate the effect of circumstances; each neighbour is a source of some annoyance; proximity necessitates mutual forbearance; the degree of forbearance to be required is measured by the sensibility to feelings of delicacy of the tribunal which has to decide the case, and cannot be foreseen until that decision is given.

Other judgments ruled that the natural and reasonable usage of a house might produce some disturbance, for example from piano playing or a children's nursery, but that these were noises reasonably to be expected and in general put up with. Such issues continue to be argued in court under modern environmental health legislation and requests for anti-social behaviour orders.

Historically, the laws of nuisance (tort) and of public order (criminal statute and common law) are the twin pillars of behaviour control as developed in English law (Burney, 2005 forthcoming). From the mid-nineteenth century statutory nuisance controls proliferated with concerns about health and environmental matters. Public order law, developed over time since the Middle Ages, was based on the idea that public conduct must not be so provocative as to arouse an angry reaction. It was not until 1986 that, in recognition that bystanders might be upset or frightened but not provoked to violence, the test of low-level public order offences became that of causing 'harassment, alarm and distress'. How both public order and nuisance laws have been developed in recent legislation to control anti-social behaviour is the subject of another chapter.

Notes

1 *Sturges* v. *Bridgman* [1878] 11 ChD 852; 48 LJ 785.
2 *Brand* v. *Hammersmith Railway Company* [1867] LR 2 QB 246.

Chapter 4

Engines of bad behaviour

When Millie et al. (2005) asked for people's views on the causes of anti-social behaviour, the answers fell into three categories: two of them assumed that the problem was getting worse because of social and moral decline and/or increasing disengagement from mainstream society of a significant minority of youths and families; the third version was simply that youths have always misbehaved but the context is changing and therefore people get more upset. This chapter looks in some detail at factors contributing to these perceptions. The three main themes are communities, youth and substance abuse. The discussion opens with the growth of social and economic polarisation and how this has impacted on certain neighbourhoods and the families living in them. It looks at the 'youth' question from different angles, such as the changes in society that have had particularly adverse effects on the young; the lifestyle and spatial clashes involved in the 'youths hanging about' complaint; and the increase in certain behaviour-related characteristics – such as mental health problems, drinking and drug-taking – as background to a possible growth in anti-social behaviour.

Communities and neighbourhoods

Only by rebuilding cohesive communities and reforming the system to bear down harder on anti-social behaviour can we achieve our vision of a strong and fair society. That is why reforms to restore civic responsibility are not a threat to social justice, but essential for its realisation in a modern society. (Tony Blair, October 2003)

The idea that communities have somehow lost the ability to deal with bad behaviour by informal means drives much government rhetoric in the early twenty-first century, and is at the heart of Labour's communitarian agenda. If this is true, then we need to ask what has happened to cause this impotence. Is it a cause or an effect of the apparent growth in openly unpleasant interpersonal behaviour? How far can we blame the rise of individualism for the acting out of impulses in the form of crime and lack of respect for other people's norms? Or should we seek underlying causes in the rise of socio-economic polarisation? Jock Young (1999: 54) discerns the influence of frustrated aspirations, the effect of individualism encountering a dead end:

> Habits of obedience, deference, of willingness to defer to family, neighbours, or the local community have all declined partly because of the system's inability to produce acceptable opportunities and partly because of an unwillingness to accept authority just because it is authority. The decline in unthinking obedience is perhaps one of the most significant changes in the twentieth century. This loosening of social ties is not a mechanistic process but a result of greater demand for individual aspiration: its roots lie not in deficit but in aspiration.

Young believes we cannot put the clock back on individualism but should strive for a society where aspirations can be fulfilled. This is rather different from the nostalgic wish for a return to a recent past of social solidarity, low crime and mutual trust, where informal social control was exercised in the street and from the doorstep. The latter view is reinforced by, for example, Robert Putnam (2000), whose writings have inspired New Labour's efforts to kick-start a new *gemeinshaft* society. He believes that individualism has eroded 'social capital', which is measured on two levels: the degree of interaction in a community on an organised basis, such as church membership, and the more informal social networks through which people relate to each other. Contrasting today's findings with the immediate postwar period, he finds a steep decline in trust relationships that has weakened communities and with it social control. Etzioni (1993), an earlier inspiration to Tony Blair, deplores the corrosive effects of a society driven by self interest and his 'communitarianism' demands a renewed moral order of society based on 'responsibilities as well as rights' embracing everything from the family to political institutions. The language, as well as the ideas, recur in Labour government statements and documents, such as the 2003 White Paper *Respect and Responsibility.*

The *British Social Attitudes* survey for 2001–2002 (Johnston and Jowell) tentatively concludes that there has not been the same decline in social trust in the United Kingdom as in the United States, and at least not the generational difference identified by Putnam. Younger people are less trusting but they found that trust increases with age. They tested attitudes towards young people by asking a sample of 2,293 people whether, if they saw an old lady who was being forced into a busy road by a group of teenagers blocking the pavement, they would ask the group to make way. Fifty-four per cent said that they would definitely do so, and 37 per cent probably would. Of course such a question is not contextually refined by such things as whether the group is very loud or drunk, or whether on the other hand the lads are known to the observer.

The first chapter indicated the broad social trends of late modernity, conducive to social exclusion and more disengaged forms of conducting our lives, and in which traditional forms of social control are spread thin. Hunter (1985) conceptualises three layers of spatial order: private, parochial and public. Private relates to family, friends and household. Family engagement can be variable in quality (Lindstrom, 1996) and extended family links are less likely today to be in close physical proximity. The public layer is the sphere of citizenship, formal institutions and the state, and spacially relates to city streets, public transport, etc., where people around are strangers. This is the sphere in which many people nowadays feel uninvolved and distrustful. At the 'parochial' level, the one which represents the home locality, or geographical 'community', where relationships (if at all) are between neighbours, there is often the least engagement, formal or informal, as people either remain largely cocooned in their own dwellings or perform actively only in distant workplaces or discrete sites of commerce and leisure facilities. In this middle layer agents of traditional social control such as park keepers and caretakers are largely absent (Jones and Newburn, 2002).

The three layers act upon each other. Families with poor quality interaction and weak attachment to norms will affect the quality of life at the parochial level if there are too many of them in one place. And if public institutions have little relevance or even presence in this middle spatial layer, then the maintenance of order becomes even more problematic. The middle classes are more likely to possess an active social life independently of their home surroundings, and may be more confident in sorting small local conflicts of interest informally (Baumgartner, 1984).

Working-class neighbourhoods used to achieve informal social control on the basis of familiarity with neighbours and workmates as well as family ties, as ethnographical studies have shown. Oral histories provide pictures of the recent past that seem another world. This is summed up by Elizabeth Roberts (1984: 192) on the basis of a rich series of interviews.

> Neighbours provided a mutual support society, but like all societies it had its rules and regulations, and it was expected that all members would obey these rules. The rules were unwritten but understood by all. Those who broke them were punished by self-appointed judges and juries. The system for controlling behaviour was an effective one. Positively, it helped to control some of the excesses of drunken behaviour, it maintained standards of cleanliness, and it tended to limit vandalism and petty crime. Negatively, the system interfered with and influenced many aspects of life which would now be regarded as matters of individual choice and decision, and it produced a very conforming and conformist class of people.

Gossip and physical chastisement were the commonest forms of this informal social control – vividly confirmed in Robert Roberts's autobiographical account of life in working-class Salford in the early twentieth century (1971).

Interviews conducted by Hood and Joyce (1999) with three generations in London's East End sought to depict the relationship of rising crime levels to the huge social changes in the area – changes which gathered pace in the years after the classic study by Young and Willmott (1957). Striking differences were recorded in the testimony from people asked about their youth in, respectively, the 1930s, 1950s and 1980s. Even allowing for the effects of nostalgia, it was clear that for the two older generations preying on your neighbours was completely unacceptable and – apart from getting into fights which did not seem to count – wrongdoing was held in check by the twin forces of trust and shame. But by the 1980s everything seems to have changed – crime was seen as commonplace, socially acceptable and primarily an easy way to get things you could not otherwise afford. The authors attribute this breakdown in norms to structural factors such as high unemployment and the related loss of work-related routines, to the break-up of social networks through local authority rehousing policies and to the emergence of a drugs market. Parental values and discipline were consciously rejected by some of the youngest generation.

These tendencies are not all confined to poor neighbourhoods, and not all poor neighbourhoods are crime ridden. But, as American research going back to 1920s Chicago (Shaw and Mackay, 1942) has often demonstrated, the effect of structural factors on social order is likely to be hardest to withstand in deprived areas with populations of mixed origin. Criminologists use the term 'collective efficacy' (Sampson, Raudenbush and Earls, 1997) to describe the ability of communities to work together to see off threats to public order and safety. High-crime neighbourhoods are shown to lack this ability. People are not necessarily indifferent, but they feel powerless. Of course, when looked at individually, high-risk neighbourhoods present a more mixed picture. Researchers on poor housing estates in multiracial Brixton found people more ready than they expected to summon the police if they saw a stranger going round the back of a neighbour's house, and to reprimand misbehaving children (Liddle et al., 1997).

A number of studies take social interaction between neighbours as a key variable in relation to local crime rates but this is hard to measure and assess (Sampson and Groves, 1989; 1988; Bellair, 1997). You can live in area with a low crime rate and have quite infrequent contact with neighbours, while some 'criminal' neighbourhoods have good social networks of their own (Walklate and Evans, 1999, Bottoms and Wiles, 2002). A simple measure is whether people say that in their local area people 'look out for each other'. This has been used in the British Crime Survey (Nicholas and Walker, 2004). In 2003/4, where people answered in the affirmative, only 12 per cent also perceived high levels of anti-social behaviour in the neighbourhood, but this shot up to 40 per cent of those who answered in the negative. Not surprisingly, people who said they enjoyed living in their area were also far less likely to perceive high levels of anti-social behaviour.

Social integration cannot guarantee social control in the face of severe structural decline and reduced public services. Rather than blaming poor communities for social malfunction, W. J. Wilson (1996) describes impoverished American black ghettos as having a high level of neighbourliness but a dearth of institutional support and opportunities for improvement. Parents felt undermined and unable to control the activities of their children.

It is easier for parents to control the behavior of the children in their neighborhood when there exists a strong institutional resource base, when the links between community institutions such as churches, schools, political organizations, businesses, and civic clubs are strong. The higher the density and stability of formal organizations, the less that illicit activities such as drug-trafficking, crime, prostitution, and gang formation can take root in the neighborhood … As one resident of a high-jobless neighborhood on the South Side of Chicago put it, 'our children, you know, seem to be more at risk than any other children there is, because there's no library for them to go to. There's no center they can go to, there's no field house that they can go into. There's nothing. There's nothing at all. (p. 64)

Elliot Currie (1997) attributes the rise in violent crime in America to the effects of what he calls 'the market society' – a society whose guiding principle is private gain. He lists among these effects: the progressive destruction of livelihood; the growth of extremes of inequality and material deprivation; the withdrawal of public services and supports; the erosion of informal networks of mutual support. As described in the second chapter, 'incivilities' and crime are symptoms of the same socio-economic causes, rather than the first being itself a cause of the second (Taylor, 2001). If one were to seek one encapsulating trend it would be that of polarisation: the growth of income, educational and areal inequalities that are so marked in Britain and the United States, and also apparent in other western societies.

In Britain, there is ample statistical evidence, mainly from the British Crime Survey, that both crime and perceptions of a range of local incivilities are most widely experienced in council estates and other poor areas. Thirty-nine per cent of people in these neighbourhoods perceive high levels of anti-social behaviour in the locality, compared with, at the other extreme, 9 per cent of people living in affluent suburbs and rural areas. Among the range of environmental and social indicators used in the survey, people living in different types of neighbourhood highlight different problems – for example, teenage groups and drug problems are of much more concern in council estates and low income areas, while people in affluent urban areas complain most about litter and vandalism. These differences reveal the inherent logical flaws in an overarching concept of 'anti-social behaviour' which embraces perceptions of such varied phenomena.

Areal comparisons are on much firmer ground when crime reports rather than something so vague as perceptions of anti-social behaviour are being measured, although in reality the two cannot be separated, as they present a spectrum of deviance. Crime measures bring out local differences much more starkly. In particular, a small proportion of neighbourhoods suffer quite exceptionally high rates of personal and property crime; it is no surprise that these are the places where poverty is also concentrated (Hope, 2001).

But not all places of a similar socio-economic character display the same relationship to crime, as work over the years by Anthony Bottoms and his colleagues in Sheffield (Bottoms, Mawby and Xanthos, 1989; Bottoms and Wiles, 2002) has shown. By measuring offender rates as well as crime rates, two apparently similar neighbouring council estates were found to have markedly different crimogenic profiles. This could be shown to have evolved through the managed public sector housing market, whereby more 'respectable' working-class tenants, whether by choice or through preferential treatment, tended to end up together in one of the two estates, in contrast to known criminal families who partially dominated the other estate and the less capable tenants placed there. This is a reminder of the micro-level differences in social behaviour between small geographical areas, also borne out by more recent work in Sheffield by Bottoms and Wilson (2004).

A detailed statistical study in Pittsburgh (Wikstrom and Loeber, 2000) tried to estimate the relative importance of the neighbourhood, compared with individual propensities, in determining youthful offending. They found that boys with low 'risk' characteristics would be most likely to be influenced into committing serious crime when they lived and went to school in very disadvantaged communities. 'Serious' offending, in recognised categories of crime, is more distinct than incidents of anti-social behaviour, usually defined as non-criminal disorder or low-level offending. But where communities apparently suffer from much of this kind of behaviour it may be even more necessary to look at the neighbourhood effect and how it is constructed. It remains a fruitful area of research for criminologists who continue to unravel the varying influences from families, schools and peer groups within the neighbourhood context (Wikstrom, 2002; Oberwittler, 2004).

There is something lacking in these exercises if they do not also include comprehension of the public service and infrastructural input, or lack of it, in different neighbourhoods. Matthews and Pitts (2001: 5) rightly point out:

> Crime is related to almost every other negative indicator in society – poor health, limited educational facilities, unreliable transport, bad housing and the more serious environmental problems. Indeed, these negative indicators predictably overlap to the extent that high crime areas also rank high on every other scale of social and economic misfortune.

The role of social housing

I propose to focus on one of these negative indicators – housing tenure. This is because so much of the focus of concern and enforcement directed at anti-social behaviour has taken place in areas of social housing, especially in council-run estates, attention has to be paid to that sector of the housing market and the changes that have taken place within it in recent years. I have written elsewhere of these changes and the effects for housing management (Burney, 1999) but the subject is so pertinent to the present discussion that the outline must be repeated. Historically, provision of houses by local councils for carefully selected and graded tenants was a welfare service which always tended to separate the respectable working class from the 'rougher elements'. That became less easy during the 1980s for a number of reasons. Changes in the law on security of tenure made it harder to evict families for bad behaviour. The introduction of the tenants' right to buy the houses they occupied at heavily discounted prices soon transformed the sector. More attractive estates became largely owner-occupied, while councils were forbidden to use the proceeds to create new dwellings or repair old ones. Any new social housing had to be provided by independent voluntary associations, who also allocated tenancies on a needs basis. As owner occupation burgeoned the social housing sector became increasingly residualised.

Meanwhile, from the mid-1970s onwards, industrial recession set in and communities that had been sustained and focused through the local factory or coalfield rapidly lost both jobs and the locus for cohesion. People who could afford it moved away to newly expanded suburban areas. Thus, despite the shrinkage of social housing from 31 per cent of all dwellings in 1983 to 23 per cent in 2003, large portions of the council domain in the old industrial areas became surplus to demand. Anxious to fill vacancies, managers could not afford to be choosy over tenants, and some of the ensuing crime and disorder can be directly attributed to unsuitable allocations. Janet Foster (Foster and Hope, 1993; Foster, 2002) explored a 'hard to let' estate where high levels of crime were associated with an unpopular high-rise block where flats had been filled with large numbers of young single people, uncomfortably juxtaposed with elderly residents, and the rise of a hard drug culture. She describes how:

> Residents became increasingly polarised between a 'stable' group (some of whom were empowered by tenant consultation and saw the solution to the estate's problems as evicting 'problem' tenants and restricting access to the estate through allocations), and the increasingly stigmatised, but highly vulnerable subterranean culture which included the young previously homeless, and families and individuals whose lives were often very chaotic and precarious. (Foster, 2002: 177)

Shifts in the character of residential neighbourhoods occur for many reasons, but the influence of local authority allocation decisions is often decisive, as Bottoms and Wiles (1986) explained when they introduced the idea of 'community crime careers'. The change from respectability to disorder is very upsetting to long-term residents and it is the reaction to change as such as well as the experience of its effects that produces some of the most heartfelt complaints about anti-social behaviour.

Stability is undermined when people come and go frequently, as they do in low-demand areas, and instability correlates strongly with disorder (Bursik, 1988; Bursik and Grasmick, 1993). The presence of a disorderly household, or the experience of threats, typically associated with drug dealing, can quickly empty nearby properties when residents find it easy to move elsewhere. A process called 'churning' has been described (Keenan, 1998) whereby people escaping some personal menace shift around within the same district. Shifting populations mean that people are less likely to know their neighbours and interact with them. They see strangers who, in a climate of fear of crime, may seem threatening. They do not know the names or families of local children and so feel less able to intervene to check misbehaviour. Boarded-up houses increase alienation and fear.

Most destructively, the presence of a few families presenting not only grossly intrusive bad behaviour but also threats and crime can paralyse local life and cow their neighbours so that they dare not complain. The traditional 'problem family' has always been a management headache but in the past it was housekeeping and rent-paying ineptitude rather than hostility to neighbours that was the main concern. The closure of large mental hospitals where many 'difficult' people were formerly housed may account for some of this change. The 'neighbour from hell' may be dysfunctional in many ways and their hostility just one manifestation (Burney, 1999: 68). People displaying these characteristics are the target of political polemics as well as supplying the *raison d'être* of the ASBO. It has taken the Labour government many years to come round to the realisation that there are only a relatively few such people, and that they need social support as well as enforcement.

The characteristics of low-demand areas were examined by the Social Exclusion Unit, a government think-tank (SEU, 2000a). They found predominantly youthful populations, with high levels of unemployment and concentrations of poverty. The level of dissatisfaction with the area was four and a half times the average. Thirty-eight per cent of people wanted to move away because of crime, anti-social behaviour and environmental dereliction and 39 per cent had been crime victims. However, despite the high correlation of low demand and anti-social behaviour, the report found no evidence of a causal link.

Low demand is not confined to council-owned property. Streets of very low-cost owner-occupied and private rented houses have been among those worst affected, especially when people evicted from council property for bad behaviour end up being housed by disreputable private landlords (Burney, 1999). Likewise the effect of the right to buy has often been that council-built estates in difficult areas have ended up peppered with private rentals or property owned by voluntary sector landlords. The control of bad behaviour in mixed tenure neighbourhoods is a particularly vexing problem (Nixon et al., 2003). With the focus so strongly on social tenants, the needs of more complex residential areas are only beginning to be addressed.

Management concerns about behaviour problems within social housing stem from the residual character of the sector. The responsibility of social landlords towards needy people, combined with the movement of more mobile and capable households into owner occupation, means that social tenants include disproportionate numbers of poor and vulnerable households: old people, young people who have been in care, homeless families and single parents. Little support is supplied to people with special difficulties such as mental disorder. Women bringing up children as lone parents form 18 per cent of all social tenants, and the majority of children are not living with both birth parents. As many as 43 per cent of households are people living alone, mainly the elderly (ODPM, 2004). Only 38 per cent of households have anybody with a job. This skewed profile helps to explain why people living in social housing are more exposed to crime and more likely to report experience of bad and uncivil behaviour.

Youth, again

Young people are often blamed for a rise in anti-social behaviour. In the eyes of the police the category is synonymous with youth (Bland and Read, 2000). Anxieties about loss of social control find their focus in loud, uninhibited, gatherings of young people in public places.

The previous section referred to research linking youthful criminality to neighbourhood effects, and similar associations can be made with behaviour that falls short of serious criminality but evokes an uncomfortable or fearful response. 'Youths hanging about' have become synonymous with disorder and public threat and are routinely used to measure the degree to which people feel uneasy in their neighbourhoods. American studies use terms like 'unsupervised teens' when presenting concepts such as social disorganisation. Social scientists thus play their part in demonising the young and presenting their behaviour as a cause of community failure as well as consequence of it.

The British Crime Survey, purporting to measure perceptions of anti-social behaviour, lists 'teenagers hanging around on the streets' as one of its eight key variables[1] (a mix of criminal and non-criminal features). In 2002/3 teenagers in the street were seen as a 'very or fairly big problem' by 33 per cent of those questioned. Asked to name which out of the eight incivilities was the biggest problem in their area, people in affluent urban areas mainly chose rubbish and vandalism, but 28 per cent of people in council estates and low-income areas said it was the teenagers. This is hardly surprising given the demographic shape of these areas, with much higher youthful populations than elsewhere, and the prevalence of crimes such as burglary and car crime associated with young offenders. But the perception is seemingly linked in less tangible ways with fears and insecurities of a more general nature, as suggested earlier.

By the following year (2003/4) all the eight features listed had fallen significantly in people's perception, and that included the teenagers (now cited by 27 per cent as a very big or fairly big problem). But government policy-makers had by then seized upon the higher figure of one third in order to justify new legislation enabling groups to be banned from the streets in designated areas and curfews to be imposed on younger teenagers (Home Office, 2003; para. 4.12).

Young people have always hung around together. What is it about today's youth – and this word is often stretched to cover anybody between 10 and 25 years of age – that apparently arouses so much unease? There are many complex factors at work and this section can only indicate some familiar ones and suggest how they interact in ways which sometimes, indeed, cause young people to behave in such a fashion as to seriously trouble their neighbourhoods, but at other times mean they attract censure merely for occupying public space and having fun together.

Behaviour which attracts censure in the young and may be labelled 'anti-social' often reflects the changing mores of society in general and cannot be ascribed to youth as such. The decline of deference is a general trend. Swearing, public drinking, drug taking and openly sexualised behaviour are more widespread and visible than in the recent past. Young people adopt these things because they are there to be copied – as emblems of sophistication, a means of 'pushing the boundaries' and a relief from boredom. Survey evidence shows that alcohol consumption by children in Britain is almost the highest in Europe (only young Danes drink more) and starts younger – more than a third of 15-year-olds report being drunk at least once at age 13 or younger, compared to about a tenth of French or Italian children (Prime Minister's Strategy Unit, 2004). There are more 15–16 year old drug users in the UK than in any other

EU country (SEU, 2002a). Habits which are a health risk to the young are also a stimulant to censured behaviour, whether it be school-age pregnancy, violence or loutishness. These things occur in many settings, including rural villages and country towns, as well as disadvantaged areas of the type described in the previous section.

It has become a truism that people are afraid to intervene with young people who are misbehaving for fear of reprisals and insults, but when attitudes are explored in particular locations the picture may be more varied. A survey of people's experience of nuisance (personal and environmental) on four housing estates in Brixton in 1996 did indeed find people who said they were too intimidated to intervene when children or teenagers were misbehaving; but 47 per cent said that, on the contrary, they had actively intervened, not only for things like playing in lifts, rudeness and making too much noise but sometimes for serious damage or harassment, mugging, drug use or vandalising cars (Liddle et al., 1997). The two high-crime areas of Sheffield studied by Bottoms and Wilson (2004), showing contrasting levels of punitiveness, also scored very differently on questions (put by the researchers in an unpublished survey) testing readiness to intervene when children or teenagers were truanting, fighting, being rude to an old lady or spraying graffiti. The more punitive area, also that with more perceived problems like joyriding and vandalism, was markedly less ready overall to say that neighbours would intervene in such circumstances.

Analysing the 'youth problem'

The Social Exclusion Unit, summarising its findings on young people (2000b: 45) reported:

> For a significant minority of young people, disproportionately concentrated in the poorest areas: family life is characterised by disrupted relationships, poverty and worklessness; education provision does not meet their needs; their way of life lacks stimulation, enjoyment and challenge; they face serious health problems and are prone to problem behaviours; they find it difficult to find a decent place to live or money to live on; they are far too likely both to be victims of crime and to offend against others. Young BEM [black and ethnic minority] people also face these problems disproportionately – not least because they live in poverty and disadvantaged neighbourhoods, as well as facing the additional effects of racism.

The following sections look at some of these issues in more detail.

Victimisation
In contrast to their popular image as predators, children and young people are far more at risk of becoming victims of crime, especially violence, theft and robbery, than older generations (Anderson et al., 1994; Aye Maung, 1995; Wood, 2005). According to the British Crime Survey, they are also more likely to meet with insulting, pestering or intimidating behaviour. A quarter of those aged 16–24 had been the target of such behaviour in the past year, compared with 15 per cent across all age groups. It should therefore have come as no surprise when a close analysis of the 2003/4 BCS findings (Wood, 2004) revealed that the respondents most likely to see 'young people hanging around' as a 'very or fairly big problem' were themselves young people. One-third (33 per cent) of the 16–24 age group reported this problem, with percentages diminishing in line with age for older groups, falling to 14 per cent of those aged over 75.

The young are out and about more than middle-aged or elderly people, meeting their friends in the open, often well into the night (Matthews et al., 2000). Encounters with rival groups, known predators, or (in the words of the BCS) 'insulting, pestering or intimidating behaviour' may be frequent. Bullying does not stop outside the school gate. Their experience has fed into the aggregate statistics of intimidatory youth, directly influencing policies designed to curb young people's freedom of movement. Had policy and legislation waited until the full analysis, the problem would surely have been seen differently. It is still true that older people are the ones that go to meetings and complain about youths hanging around or who see children in their street as a nuisance if not a threat. They also have votes. Anti-social behaviour has become a convenient peg on which to hang generalised prejudices about young people and their activities which make restrictive policies popular. It does not do anything to bridge mutual hostilities between youths and their neighbours or make things safer for the many young people being harassed by their peers – both types of problem being encompassed in the 'youths hanging about' issue.

Deprivation
Young people are proportionately more numerous in deprived areas, where they are most likely to be seen as a problem both by their neighbours and by agencies (SEU, 2002a) and where, for all the reasons associated with deprivation, they face greater difficulties in their lives. It is important to remember, however, that impoverished and socially

excluded young people are just as likely to live outside deprived areas (Stenson and Watt, 1999; SEU, 2002a) and may be therefore censured for their difference. In the 1970s one in ten children lived in poor households, whereas today it is one in three.

In rural areas the lack of facilities and transport excludes many young people from normal social activities (Meek, 2005). Affordable and accessible leisure facilities are a general problem for young people, as are the inadequate support services highlighted by the SEU. But on all counts the neighbourhood factor is particularly important in the poorest areas (Wikstrom and Loeber, 2000). Poor education coupled with poor opportunities mean fewer qualifications and less incentive to acquire them. Changes in the labour market have had particularly dire effects. Violence, including violence in schools, is more common in deprived areas (Eisner, 2003) and the numbers of teenage pregnancies are way above average. Black and minority ethnic families are more likely to live in such areas and their children are particularly at risk.

Status change

Many of these things relate to difficulties facing young people in general, but are writ large in poor neighbourhoods. Among the well-known changes affecting all young people are the weakening of family ties, including the break-up of relationships and rise of lone mother families, with the resulting absence of male role models. More general still is the changed status of the young who, instead of progressing naturally from school to jobs, remain in a juvenile role often well into their twenties. It is often forgotten that, within living memory, children left school at 14 and went straight into work, doing the kind of jobs that no longer exist (who needs errand boys nowadays – apart from drug dealers?). For many of today's school leavers, either suitable jobs are not available, or they have not acquired even the basic level of education necessary. Minimum wages are limited by age, as are welfare benefits. The difficulties are summed up by MacDonald (1997: 186):

> The institutions which have previously structured youth transitions – in employment, training, welfare, education, housing, the family, the criminal justice system – have themselves undergone dramatic restructuring in recent decades. The combined effect of these changes has been to make youth transitions riskier, more insecure and, for already disadvantaged youth, more prone to social exclusion.

All this contrasts painfully with the rise of consumer culture which stimulates desires that cannot legitimately be fulfilled – a condition originally theorised by Robert Merton (1938) as a type of 'anomie' – driving a sense of exclusion (Young, 1999) and providing incentives to crime. None of this helps to instil a sense of citizenship and social responsibility in young people.

Mental health

Mental health problems and personality disorders clearly underly some of the uncontrolled aggression and acting out that has brought down ASBOs on the heads of some individual young people. Disruptive behavioural disorders like ADHD are a significant strand in the clutch of factors associated with delinquency (Loeber et al., 1998). 'Out of control' youngsters get a poor deal from mainstream services (school exclusion being the commonest reaction). Grave mental disorders are apparent among some young offenders sent into custody because there are no hospital places for them – with tragic results sometimes in terms of suicide.[2] These may be extreme cases but probably the tip of the iceberg as far as the connection goes between some young people's mental frailty and their unacceptable behaviour in their neighbourhoods. Similar links can be made over lack of family support services. Research in Brighton showed (Chapter 5) that even children subject to voluntary Acceptable Behaviour Orders sometimes had mental health problems or learning difficulties which made it very hard for them to keep in line, yet they received little or no help.

The Social Exclusion Unit (2002) and the Audit Commission (1999) have expressed grave concern over the shortage, inappropriateness, and patchy nature, of mental health services for young people. Reform was promised in the autumn of 2004 following publication of a longitudinal study revealing a sharp worsening of emotional and behavioural difficulties of 15-year-olds since 1974, as observed by their parents (Collishaw et al., 2004).[3] In 1999, 16.7 per cent of boys had 'conduct problems' (fighting, bullying, stealing, lying and disobedience) – in other words, they were behaving badly. About the same proportion (16.9 per cent) of boys were labelled hyperactive. Girls fared better on these counts but were far ahead of boys when it came to emotional difficulties (20.4 per cent compared with 13.3 per cent). Hyperactivity had not changed much since 1974 but for the whole cohort emotional problems (up from 10.2 to 16.9 per cent) and, especially, conduct problems (up from 6.8 to 14.9 per cent) were significantly higher. (The researchers believe they ruled out any effect from over-reporting due to increased awareness or concern.) There are other proofs of the fragile mental health of the young (cited by the SEU), such as the rise in suicide and self-harm,[4] and the earlier onset of depression.

Masculinity

More general psychological dislocation among young men is sometimes discussed in the context of the so-called 'crisis of masculinity', usually meaning that males, deprived of their traditional role as workers and family providers, create new identities based on macho images and act these out in violent, loutish behaviour (Willmott and Griffin, 1996; O'Donnell and Sharpe, 2000). Beatrix Campbell (1993) saw the mass violence by young men in the estate riots of the early 1990s as a gendered response in disempowered communities where the only people with responsible roles were the women. These scenes have not been repeated in any significant way since then, possibly due to a combination of more resources and more surveillance by police and CCTV – although there are still some places seriously intimidated by very aggressive groups of young men who are also chronic offenders, though seldom 'gangs' in the American sense.[5] More often, the new generation of youths may still be alienated and disempowered, and still find destructive ways of acting out – sometimes described as a 'slow riot' – but at a level now merely labelled as 'anti-social'.

Teachers, not only in the UK but across western Europe, have long complained about worsening pupil behaviour (Council of Europe, 2003). Different influences impact more at different ages, and problem behaviour interacts with the neighbourhood when teenagers involved at school also live near each other (Pitts and Hope, 1997; Oberwittler, 2004). Exclusion from school has become a common response to aggressive and disruptive behaviour, which readily results in more neighbourhood nuisance.[6]

Families and parents

For the youngest children family influences are decisive. Increasingly parenting in the earliest years is seen as the key point where agency intervention is needed – hence the rise of Sure Start and numerous parenting programmes. Longitudinal studies (Farrington, 2002) emphasise the early individual and family characteristics associated with deviant behaviour, although others are wary of seeming to blame parents without acknowledging the structural factors that make parenting harder. There is a repeated emphasis in government publications such as the White Paper *Respect and Responsibility* on family values, parental responsibility and, if necessary, the obligation to undergo training if your children behave badly. This does not connect well with recognition that family life is under great stress: more than one in four children under 16 will have seen their parents divorce; one in five live in lone parent families; and over 75 per cent of these families are in poverty, compared with under 20 per cent of two-parent families (SEU, 2002).

Censuring parents for failing a moral standard does not sit easily with the idea that they need a helping hand. But offering help to parents can nevertheless be done without censure, and in an empowering way which gives the lie to representations of a culturally irredeemable social stratum, occupied mainly by the families of never-married mothers, such as can be found in the writings of Charles Murray (1990, 1994).

By the time children reach adolescence, the peer group rather than parents is the main influence on conduct outside the home. Bad behaviour is often stimulated by companions, especially in settings which create opportunities (Wikstrom, 2002). For this age group imposing parenting orders when offspring get into trouble makes limited sense.

Intolerance
Alienation and disengagement of the young may have increased for all the reasons mentioned above. An alternative or, more accurately, parallel explanation involves a perceived growth of intolerance towards the activities or even the presence of young people. In this context it is worth remembering that youth services are not a statutory local authority responsibility and are commonly starved of funds. There is a danger in pathologising youths who are mainly involved in normal pursuits – playing football, skateboarding, riding mopeds, playing music – which perhaps thoughtlessly cause damage or intrude on the peace and quiet of older people. There is a continuum stretching from mild nuisance to aggressive and intimidating behaviour, sometimes aggravated by mutual lack of respect between youths and critical adults. There are many complaints of foul-mouthed repartee on the part of even quite young children when ticked off by adults. The reliance formerly placed on physical chastisement has not yet been widely substituted with alternative control mechanisms favouring respect and dispute resolution.

Some situations may be exacerbated by the presence of one or two youngsters from problem backgrounds who are likely to be involved in bad behaviour and crime from an early age – but they are by definition the exception rather than the rule. Most complaints involve public order rather than crime, and solutions will often depend upon the line taken by local beat police officers – who may reach for ASBOs or dispersal orders or attempt more positive solutions such as finding a different place for youngsters to hang out.

Given the slippery nature of the concept, quantifying the amount of anti-social behaviour by young people is a hazardous exercise. What do we make of the Home Office report that '29% of young people said they had committed at least one act of antisocial behaviour in the past year' (Hayward and Sharp, 2005)? Do we feel shocked, or relieved? It turns out that, when asked, 15 per cent said they had been noisy or rude in a public place and 13 per cent had behaved in a way that caused a neighbour to complain. Only 4 per cent admitted to graffiti and 2 per cent to racial harassment (both of which are of course criminal). Figures like this are hardly the stuff of social breakdown, or even policy formation.

Contested space

It is significant that survey questions relate to teenagers hanging around *on the street*. Public space is presented as a contested arena in which adults are asked to assume that young people have lesser rights. The cultural implications of this aspect of social control have not recently received much attention from criminologists – unlike in the 1970s when studies of youth gangs, their motivations and their habitats were plentiful.[7] Geographers, on the other hand, have recently developed a detailed interest in spatial relationships as they affect young people's lives. Aitken (2001) sees a trend that confines young children to designated 'safe' play areas while denying adolescents freedom of movement – in America, curfews may mean that youths have the right to be out and about for only a few hours in the day. Matthews et al. (2000), in a study of adolescents in two poor estates in Northampton, showed how important it was to both girls and boys to create their own meeting places outside the home, normally in open spaces of various kinds. Here they might be regarded with suspicion. In the words of one 14-year-old girl asked what people thought about her group hanging around:

> They hate us. Some of them moan all the time … We've got people … who are calling us tarts 'cos we are sitting with … It's like everyone judges us on the way we look just because they think we're louts and layabouts. (p. 74)

A 13-year-old girl said:

> … say you were standing around, hanging round there, people report you to the police and say, oh they're breaking into houses and you get blamed for things you didn't do. (p. 75)

These observations are validated as it were in reverse by BCS responses indicating that adults of all ages who objected to 'youths hanging about' were most likely to refer to children aged 13–15 years (Wood, 2004: Table A7.8).

In the light of powers to curfew under-15s after 9 p.m. in designated areas, Matthews et al. reveal the extent to which in the summer holidays parental curfews of 10–11 p.m. were commonplace for young girls who went out most often, while others stayed at home more and were expected back earlier when they did go out. Sometimes adolescents were told to get out of the house and keep out of the parents' way in the evening – probably a reflection on housing conditions as much as family relationships.

The link between adult suspicion of youths in public space and general anxieties was illustrated by action research in 'Townville' on Teesside (Foreman, 2004). The project aimed through community development techniques to bring the generations together in formulating plans for regeneration in which they all had a part. In preparation for this effort, project workers first explored 'how public leisure space has become a metaphorical and an actual battleground between the generations as they seek to manage the everyday risks (for example, unemployment, financial insecurity, drugs and the fear of crime' (p. 143). Risk was managed differently by young people compared with adults. The former moved round in groups because it made them feel safer, forming their own 'community' from the peer group. The latter saw those groups as a menace that chimed with their own sense of loss and powerlessness since the disappearance of the steel industry which formerly supported them. 'The anger instilled by the apparent intransigence of young people and the visibility of a group other residents already perceived as threatening to them as individuals and as a risk to the sustainability of the community as a whole, ensures public leisure space becomes a site of conflict' (p. 147). The young people complained of the way that they were restricted in their movements by adult attitudes, such as two boys aged ten and eleven who (echoing the complaints heard in Northampton) said:

> They swear at you and say you've done things you haven't. And they chase you. They don't want you to play near their houses. (p. 147)

If this is an attitude which is increasing generally it may indeed be linked to different types of risk aversion. Those boys could be burglars, or football in the street could damage your car, or you just feel uneasy passing a group of youths who might decide to insult you, or worse, should you reprimand them for some misdemeanour. A more general culture of risk aversion, which some see has the hallmark of late modernity, helps to blight possibilities of easy interaction between neighbouring adults and local youth and increasingly confines the latter to their own peer groups, while rampant youth culture creates further barriers.

It is not only in places devastated by deindustrialisation where intolerance is manifested towards the presence of children and youths

73

hanging out in public spaces. In recent years the most revealing ethnographical study of the relationship of an English community to its young people, in the context of perceptions of crime and disorder, is that undertaken by Girling et al. (2000) in the prosperous Cheshire town of Macclesfield and the nearby village of Prestbury. A detailed and nuanced picture emerged, wherein the degree of suspicion expressed towards the behaviour of local youths varied markedly with the depth of emotional attachment to the area. Older inhabitants of long-standing, and people bringing up families, were far more likely to be concerned than childless professional couples commuting to work, who had little engagement with the community. The young people in their turn complained about adult attitudes in just the same way as those from poorer areas, and expressed the same need to enjoy each other's company away from adult oversight. For one group, a car park was their escape, where they were:

> [j]ust having fun, you know what I mean, trying to make the most of the dump what we're in, standing on a car park, what else is there. Have a laugh, tease each other, get on, you know what I mean. Maybe get a little loud, but at least we're just stood in the middle of the pissing car park, we're not in the guy's pissing car pinching his stereo. (p. 79)

In one period of two months in 1995, 14 per cent of calls to the police were about 'nuisance or suspicious youths'. To some established residents the behaviour of the young signified neighbourhood decline and loss of moral standards and could even seem intimidating.

> They seem to feel that anything goes and people just do not count, these youngsters. Some of them, not all of them, seem to have great disrespect for authority in general. They go about in these groups, and I know a lot of it is bravado, but they're a frightening sight sometimes. (p. 82)

The authors did not find equal concern about the safety of the young people themselves, apart from parents worried about what might happen to young teenagers out at night – and a widespread, seemingly exaggerated, level of worry about the availability of drugs. However, the young people were not rejected – most residents felt that they belonged to the community and adults just wished that the young could have more opportunity to get involved in 'acceptable' pastimes. The more punitive attitudes occurred in the context of generalised discussion:

Locally occurring forms of teenage mis/behaviour prompt discourse that slips away from the locality (as both its referent and locus of explanation) and accounts for 'the problem' in terms of the economic or social or cultural or moral decline of 'the nation'. Thus posed, the youth question fairly readily prompts responses that fit snugly with, and borrow terminology from, dominant media and political rhetoric on 'law and order'. (p. 93)

Other forces help to encourage age-group segregation. Aitken (2001: 156) links the trend to commodification: he claims that 'by the late twentieth century, the street was transformed by bourgeois notions of consumption from a multipurpose space for all groups and classes into space that required stricter control and regulation'. This reflects a process begun half a century earlier, described by Jane Jacobs (1961) in her classic lament for the fading heterogeneity of street life.

The resulting social distance is made explicit in semi-public spaces such as shopping malls where security guards make sure that children and young people do nothing to upset 'respectable' customers and CCTV keeps a watchful eye on their movements (Wakefield, 2003). It is assumed either that they will behave badly, or, as indeed may be the case, that their presence will seem intimidating to others. This suspicion merely arouses antagonism and may actually stimulate anti-social behaviour. Wakefield (2003: p. 177) quotes one security officer:

> you get the young 'uns that have got now't better to do, nowhere to go, coming here. Ninety per cent of the time they behave. There's just that ten per cent when they've had enough. Nothing's gone their way. So they decide to have a bit of play … They see the shops looking at 'em, and the shops call us and we have to go down. But all it does is antagonise them. They just say to me, 'Oh, they're moaning, we'll give them something to moan about'.

If the young people concerned are visibly from minority ethnic groups they may be still more likely to be viewed with suspicion. A commercial landlord was unsuccessfully challenged in the European Court for imposing lifetime injunctions against a group of black and Asian teenagers which prevented them from using a town-centre shopping mall[8] (Gray and Gray, 1999). The pejorative term 'gang' is particularly likely to be applied to groups of black youngsters, often automatically assumed by the police and others to have a criminal association. Asian youths are beginning to attract the same labels, following riots in Burnley and Oldham. Following some headline crimes, almost the first designated dispersal zone to be imposed in London, in June 2004, was in the Somers Town area behind Euston station and was said to be intended to curb the activities of Asian youth gangs.[9] Since then, dispersal areas have proliferated in the Metropolitan police area, including in some outer suburbs.

Hallsworth and Young (2004) have warned against 'accepting the idea that when youths congregate collectively, crime and anti-social behaviour somehow emerge as a consequence'. They argue that it is ecology of urban space that encourages group formation and inter-group conflict. They suggest that forced dispersal of groups is likely to cause more vandalism, graffiti and acts of expressive violence, not less, since 'smaller groups with no more than two members will perpetrate most low level crime in an area'. The more children on an estate, inevitably the more damage: it has been estimated that more than six children aged 10 to 16 per 10 dwellings caused a marked increase in vandalism (Wilson, 1978).

The assumption that youthful behaviour is 'anti-social' is pervasive and seems to be growing. To return once more to the remark of a council officer in Milton Keynes: 'Because there is so much talk about anti-social behaviour, people say: why should the children be playing ball in the street?'

Drugs, alcohol and incivilities

If one is looking for one feature of modern life not found in the past which is associated with nuisance behaviour and fear of crime, it must surely be drug dealing and use. Most other types of incivility have long been present in one form or another, but the rise of hard drug cultures over the past thirty years has introduced a new element of disorder on the streets and in residential areas. What used to be described as heroin 'epidemics' – reflecting the original health-oriented approach to control – were at first identified in very depressed areas such as Glasgow and parts of north-west England (Pearson, 1987). Drug availability and fashions have since permeated society far more widely. But heroin use is still associated with poverty and it is, yet again, the poorer neighbourhoods where people are most likely to suffer the effects of drug dealing in their midst, including associated violence.

As already described, council estates and poorer residential areas are identified in the British Crime Survey (Nicholas and Walker, 2004) as most likely to see drug dealing and use as the biggest problem in their area – 21 per cent expressing this view compared with 8–16 per cent in other types of area. When asked whether drug dealing and use was 'a fairly big or very big problem' over half (51 per cent) of dwellers in council estates and other low-income areas said yes. This rose to 64 per cent among the sub-group living in multi-ethnic low income areas, which was twice the rate reported from all households surveyed. These are the kind of areas where drug markets – as distinct from individual user-dealers – may spring up and blight whole neighbourhoods with nuisance and associated crime.

The effect of drug dealing in, say, a block of flats can be dire – constant comings and goings at all hours, discarded needles in common parts, threats from dealers, violence from turf wars and to enforce debts, and so on. Often the dealers are not tenants, but have moved in and control a flat which may be occupied by a terrified woman (who will be the one liable for eviction). A study of drug markets in deprived neighbourhoods (Lupton et al., 2002) confirmed the blight that can be caused by heroin and crack dealing, raising the level of fear and hindering regeneration. Crimes spread, particularly shoplifting from local shops, rather than burglary. However, drug markets were only one of many problems and residents mostly said that crime and anti-social behaviour troubled them more. The researchers concluded:

> In no area did a vibrant and disruptive drug market occur without the presence of other neighbourhood problems, such as anti-social behaviour, high crime, poor quality housing, lack of local employment, or a bad reputation. The impact of such factors is heightened in situations of housing oversupply, where people have a choice to move. (p. 39)

Put another way round, both anti-social behaviour and drug markets are found within a matrix of social and economic issues afflicting and defining deprived neighbourhoods. Individual dealers, frequently selling to supply their own habit, exist on the fringes of drug markets and contribute more widely to neighbourhood disorder, especially when dealing from their own homes.

There is nothing new about the connection of alcohol and bad behaviour, as historical records and more recent memories attest. Current concerns focus on two versions of drink-related problem behaviour. One is the recently developed habit of public drinking by teenagers below the age of legal purchase of alcohol. The other is the weekend 'bingeing' by young men and women attracted to the plethora of clubs and bars in town centres (Richardson and Budd, 2003). BCS 2003/4 found that drunken, rowdy behaviour was almost as likely to be observed in the respondents' own streets (48 per cent of those affected) as in the vicinity of pubs, clubs or nightclubs (50 per cent) – although of course more people will notice things in their own street than are present around nightclubs (Wood, 2004: Table A6.5).

Under-age drinking, mentioned above in connection with youthful misbehaviour, is less studied than drugs for its effect on local tranquillity, but has the effect of both enhancing public distaste for gatherings of young people and disinhibiting the latter from behaving in ways that are inconsiderate or rude. A crackdown during the summer of 2004 targeted illegal selling to under-age drinkers (often hard to distinguish from over-18s) or buying alcohol for them; it also involved arrests and fixed penalty fines for disorderly or violent drunken behaviour, and for urinating in public. Subsequently, action to curb unbridled alcohol-related nuisance and violence has become a major government policy plank.

Arguably these issues deserve more attention from the forces of law and order than the daytime street drinkers – usually homeless or semi-homeless men – who have been the object of intervention on grounds of anti-social behaviour, even receiving ASBOs for reappearing in forbidden places. Nobody wants these down-and-outs on their doorstep and they can now be moved on from designated areas or banned by by-laws from town-centre drinking. As with beggars, those who are unable to accept whatever help is on offer are likely to enter the cycle of repeat behaviour, frequent court appearances, short prison sentences – and further repetition.

Technology, noise and anti-social behaviour

Many environmental nuisances condemned as anti-social – and increasingly subject to special punitive measures – illustrate how changing technology and commerce help to create new challenges to tolerance. Motor cars driving in the street were once condemned as a new form of public nuisance. A hundred years later it is parked cars abandoned at the roadside that attract special controls and monetary penalties (Home Office, 2003b). The spate of car-abandonment (and the dumping of other large artefacts) has arisen largely because of the market slump in their value, even as scrap, attributable to global influences. (The cheapness of old cars has incidentally facilitated the 'boy racers' craze which has become a nuisance-making youth cult.) Litter of many kinds derives from packaging of goods on a scale never before seen, often involving the use of non-degradable materials. People have always dropped things in the street – the Victorians complained about orange peel – but there are now many new opportunities for littering and no improvement in human carelessness. Even the fashion for graffiti would not take the form it does if spray paint and marker pens had not been invented – Roman soldiers just carved their names.

Noise nuisance is the most frequently reported form of anti-social behaviour. Although intrusive noise comes from many aspects of modern life, domestic noise is easily the largest source of complaints. Statistics kept by the Chartered Institute of Environmental Health show that the number almost doubled in four years from 114,245 in 1998/9 to 224,502 in 2002/3. But the Institute warns that year-on-year comparisons are not reliable, because the returns made by local authorities are on a voluntary basis. No allowance either is made for double counting – more than one person complaining about the same thing. Certainly complaints will have been facilitated by the increasing number of authorities running out-of-hours services. The main remedies, if any, are mediation and informal warnings, although the figures also show that authorities are making more use of abatement notices. Seizures of equipment and prosecutions remain rare.

The most effective use of mediation is in cases of noise nuisance by neighbours (Dignan et al., 1996), which is often unwitting. People who disturb neighbours because of poor insulation or late working hours surely do not deserve the label 'anti-social' in the same way as those who refuse to turn down the music when asked. Amplified music is often the main problem. One environmental health inspector explained:

> There are so many noise-making pieces of hardware in houses, with Playstations, play CDs, TV, of course you've got the big TVs with surround sound systems. The obvious ones like radios and amplifiers, but you've also got these people who have in a small domestic flat the sort of sound systems you'd associate with a club. Great big amplifiers with loudspeakers as big as an armchair. And they would say they were DJs practising their trade, developing their trade at home.

Noise complaints, he explained, may only be a small part of a wider problem:

> Sometimes it's a feud has developed between neighbours and their complaining to us is a way of getting at the neighbour. And on other occasions it's a tale of woe involving all sorts of intimidation and harassment as well as things like noise. Noise can be one component of the intimidation that's being used.

One example started with complaints about a tumble drier being operated late at night in the hallway of a block of flats. Removing the power point would have been a simple solution, but it turned out that the family involved were creating all kinds of other unpleasantness and intimidation, to the extent that three members of the household were eventually issued with ASBOs and an eviction notice served.

Children can be noisy and are the second largest category of noise-related calls on mediation services. Noise inspectors find that dealing with things like children playing in the street late at night do not fit readily into their legal powers and negotiated settlements are more appropriate. Other kinds of street noise involving late-night car-revving and general rowdiness involve lifestyle clashes, becoming serious if it occurs on a regular basis. It can be associated with illegal activities and menacing behaviour, as in the following description:

> Young lads were renting a house in the close and they were terrorising everyone ... They would bring back stolen cars at high speed and abandon them close to their place. They would hold noisy parties and they would come back from the pub in a group and yawp about outside in the early hours and raise voices and swearing at people for parking where they wanted to park. (Environmental health officer)

Once again, disorderly youths are at the centre of a local problem for which nobody has taken responsibility – and, in this case, not openly acknowledged for fear of the effect on house prices. (p. 130)

A culture of complaint?

The citizen-consumer is a personality promoted by government since at least the early 1990s, with the introduction of the Citizen's Charter and the growing emphasis in the twenty-first century on choice and standards in public services. Service users in both public and private sectors have become 'customers', with dedicated helplines and facilities for logging complaints. In social housing, for example, the development in the 1990s of neighbourhood management offices meant that people became more able to bring complaints and grumbles to the attention of landlords (Burney, 1999; Karn et al., 1993). Service providers are increasingly expected to deal with problems that, before, might either have been ignored or dealt with between those involved. An experienced mediator spoke of 'a culture of complaint ... people are quick to pick up the phone rather than sort it out themselves'. Almost universal telephone ownership itself has facilitated converting irritants into complaints, now perceived in terms of 'anti-social behaviour'.

The 'one-day count' of anti-social behaviour arranged by the Home Office on 10 September 2003 relied upon agencies reporting the number of complaints received that day in a heterogeneous collection of categories deemed anti-social (several clearly chosen to match the various incivilities targeted in the new Anti-Social Behaviour Act). No allowance was made for double counting by different agencies receiving the same complaint and no way of telling the degree of annoyance or upset experienced by complainants. The figure arrived at – 66,107 anti-social incidents in one day – received wide publicity and was costed at a largely speculative figure of £13,500,000, further extrapolated to a putative annual total of £3.375 billion. Given that some people complain readily and others rarely or never, that recording systems vary and that there are many different ways at arriving at a money loss for each type of incivility, it cannot be held that either quantitatively or qualitatively this was a meaningful exercise. Researchers at the London School of Economics were given the task of costing anti-social behaviour (Whitehead et al., 2003) and, though able to outline an approach, ended up with so many unknown quantities that they could only report 'fundamental difficulties of definition, measurement, and interpretation'. This epitomises the problem created by presenting a range of disparate and often subjective phenomena as a finite entity, when it is really more accurate to see 'anti-social behaviour' not as the object of investigation, but rather as a convenient container into which many differing objects of complaint and affront can be packed, to be taken out and examined individually.

Notes

1 The others are: vandalism, rubbish or litter lying around, people using or dealing drugs, drunken or rowdy behaviour, noisy neighbours, racial attacks, people sleeping rough.
2 Professor Rod Morgan expressed his frustration with this situation at a public meeting at Cambridge University Institute of Criminology on 10 February 2005. He said that a group of Crown Court judges had told him that their greatest concern was the shortage of mental health facilities for serious young offenders – obliging them to use custody instead.
3 The research incorporated the findings of three independent studies, in 1974, 1986 and 1999.
4 Suicides among 15–24-year-old British males increased sharply in the 1980s but has since fallen slightly – it is less than in several other EU countries.

5 For example a group of seven youths were said to have caused 'a two-year campaign of intimidation and violence' on an estate in the London Borough of Brent. They reportedly abused and threatened estate workers, residents and visitors, destroyed lighting, threw stones from balconies, set off fireworks and stoned a police van in an encounter described as a 'mini-riot' (*Guardian*, 8 October 2004). The three juveniles among them appealed unsuccessfully against 'naming and shaming' posters (see Chapter 4).

6 In 2001/2002 there were 9,540 children permanently excluded from school.

7 As pointed out by Jock Young in a talk, 'Cultural Criminology', given to the southern branch of the British Society of Criminology in February 2005.

8 *CIN Properties v. Rawlings* [1995] 2 EGLR 130.

9 *Camden New Journal*, 17 June 2004.

Chapter 5

Legal instruments of control

People whose lives are affected by persistent nuisance conduct just want it to stop. Recent statute law relating to this problem has mainly taken the form of preventive orders, the best known of which is the Anti-Social Behaviour Order (ASBO), introduced in s.1 of the Crime and Disorder Act 1998, with extended availability provided in the Police Reform Act 2002. Courts are able to make limitless prohibitions designed to prevent repetition of the conduct in question, with no maximum length but a minimum of two years. Related legislation imposes proxy prevention on parents of offending or misbehaving children by means of parenting orders, and the extension of proxy responsibility for other people's misbehaviour is to be found in other spheres, notably in social housing. The Anti-Social Behaviour Act 2003 pushed the boundaries of behaviour control still further, with an eclectic mix of environmental enforcement and new constraints on tenants, parents, young people and groups gathering in specified areas – the latter attracting condemnation on human rights grounds.

The common thread in all these forms of social control is that civil, rather than criminal, law is the instrument, even when the offensive conduct has all the elements of a criminal offence (Paradine, 2000; Burney, 2003 unpublished). The Labour government has made clear that its reasons for going down this path relate to the perceived inadequacy of the criminal justice system in the face of repeat offences of a relatively minor nature. Prosecution is likely to result in each single offence receiving only a small punishment, and may anyway be impossible because of witness intimidation. The process is lengthy and, in the view of its critics, too heavily weighted in favour of the accused. Civil process on the other hand stems from the position of the aggrieved, even though the initiative in preventive orders comes from local authorities, police or social landlords. It is a means of providing a tailor-made response to matters of local public concern.

The process does not, however, stop there. Many preventive orders are of a hybrid nature, that is to say that although they are imposed under civil procedures, including hearsay evidence and even in certain circumstances in the absence of the respondent, any breach of the imposed conditions constitutes a criminal offence. Thus a parent who fails to observe the terms of a parenting order becomes liable on conviction to a fine of up to £1,000. More strikingly, both sex offender orders and ASBOs can result in a prison sentence of up to five years if breached. This is in contrast to the long-established sanction for disobeying the terms of a civil injunction, a maximum of two years' imprisonment for contempt of court (not a criminal offence). It is also far in excess of the maximum sentences available to magistrates in their criminal capacity[1] or even the statutory maxima for typical 'anti-social' crimes such as minor criminal damage or threatening behaviour – quite apart from the fact that the original conduct may not have been criminal at all (Krudy and Stewart, 2004).

The ASBO is intended to protect not just the individual sufferer but anyone who in future might be affected by the anti-social acts committed by the perpetrator. It is in this sense an attempt to impose a doctrine of 'communitarian protectionism' (Hopkins Burke and Morrill, 2002), in opposition to the individual rights of the restrained person. It therefore deserves particular scrutiny for its potential clash with the individual protections of human rights legislation – ironically incorporated into English law in the same year as the creation of the ASBO. Critics maintain it goes too far in its bias against the individual in certain key respects.

Professor Andrew Ashworth (2004: 289) has pointed out that, with regard to the European Convention on Human Rights:

> It is plain that in introducing the anti-social behaviour order – which has since become a model for other orders – the government intended to sail as close to the wind as possible. Its hybrid order is intended to achieve (a) the admissibility of evidence according to rules of civil evidence and procedure; (b) the assessment of evidence by reference to the civil standard of proof; (c) the making of a civil order, whose terms would not be restricted to desistance

from the conduct established in court; (d) the threat of a criminal offence for breach of the civil order, with a substantial maximum penalty; and (e) sentencing on breach that takes account of earlier conduct not proven or admitted in a criminal court.

The key element is whether the safeguards in Article 6 (The right to a fair trial) of the European Convention regarding procedures in criminal cases apply to the ASBO. As Ashworth points out, it is not permitted to get round the safeguards simply by declaring a process to be civil rather than criminal. However, preventive orders are normally regarded as civil rather than criminal. The question then is: is the ASBO solely preventative or is it in effect a form of punishment?

This was the issue upon which the appellants in *Clingham* and *McCann*[2] came to the House of Lords. The matter in dispute was the use of hearsay evidence upon which ASBOs had relied. It was argued that the nature of the orders was punitive in content and inextricably linked to the fact of criminal punishment if breached. Therefore the procedures, including the standard of proof, should be criminal. The Law Lords disagreed. In what seems a narrow approach, unanimously supported, Lord Hope said:

An anti-social behaviour order may well restrict the freedom of the defendant to do as he wants or go where he pleases. But these restrictions are imposed for preventive reasons, not for punishment. The test that has to be applied under section 1(6) is confined to what is necessary for the purpose of protecting persons from further anti-social acts by the defendant.

In addition, Lord Steyn dismissed the link between the order and the consequences of breach:

These are separate and independent procedures. The making of the order will presumably sometimes serve its purpose and there will be no proceedings for breach. It is in principle necessary to consider the two stages separately.

Critics of the judgment have questioned Lord Steyn's principle (e.g. Macdonald, 2003). When sentencing for breach, the court takes into account the course of conduct which attracted the order in the first place, not simply the action constituting the breach. Retrospectively, the whole record of anti-social behaviour becomes criminalised. Retrospective penalties for crimes – punishing people more heavily than the penalty for the original offence – are a breach of common law principles and also of Article 7 of the European Convention. But preventive measures imposed without a criminal conviction do not come within this rule, so the ASBO procedure is reckoned to be legal.

Although the House of Lords endorsed the use of hearsay evidence, it went on to impose a strict rule for its interpretation. In effect the judgment abolished the civil standard of proof for ASBOs by saying that courts must be 'sure' that the evidence supported the claims of anti-social behaviour being made and their use of hearsay evidence must reflect the seriousness of the matters in question and the implications if proven. The very low rate of rejection of applications for anti-social behaviour orders suggests that this presents no problem to the courts.

The Lords did not make any observation with regard to the appropriate-ness or proportionality of conditions laid down in the orders (which in *McCann* excluded three brothers aged 13, 15 and 16 from their home neighbourhood), merely accepting that the conditions were needed to protect people in the area from further anti-social acts by them. Lord Hutton considered:

> that the striking of a fair balance between the demands of the general interest of the community (the community in this case being represented by weak and vulnerable people who claim that they are the victims of anti-social behaviour which violates their rights) and the requirements of the protection of the defendants' rights requires the scales to come down in favour of the protection of the community and of permitting the use of hearsay evidence in applications for anti-social behaviour orders.

Ashworth (2004: 290–1) comments:

> This is not an appropriate way of determining the issues at stake in this kind of case. It is wrong in general because human rights would have no special significance if they could simply be 'weighed' against public interest and then discarded, and also because it implies that defendants are 'outside' the community. It is wrong in particular because the rights in question are those safeguarded by Art. 6: in this respect Lord Hutton repeats the error of the Privy Council in *Brown v Stott* in assuming that rights coming within Art. 6 can simply be 'trumped' by public interest considerations.

Professor Ashworth expects the Strasbourg court to have to consider further whether 'the strong sanctions for breach together with the limited range of public authorities that can apply for the order render the proceedings in which the order is made in substance criminal proceedings'. In possible anticipation of this, and more obviously in further development of the communitarian agenda, the Home Office minister Hazel Blears in the summer of 2004 described plans to allow ASBOs, curfews and dispersal orders to be initiated through local meetings, petitions or polls and rubber stamped by police and local authorities.[3]

While criticism of the form taken by anti-social behaviour orders should not distract from the misery which can be caused from repeated offensive behaviour and the way whole neighbourhoods can be blighted from it, a fundamental problem remains of how this should be defined. The definition in the Crime and Disorder Act 1998 is not very helpful. An ASBO can be imposed if it is shown (s. 1(1), as amended by the Police Reform Act 2002):

(a) that the person has acted ... in an anti-social manner, that is to say, in a manner that caused or was likely to cause harassment, alarm or distress to one or more persons not of the same household as himself; and
(b) that such an order is necessary to protect relevant persons from further anti-social acts by him.

The actions may or may not be technically criminal, although it is certainly arguable that the effect is to criminalise what Home Office guidance in 1999 described as 'sub-criminal' behaviour. An academic debate is in progress concerning the extent to which behaviour which causes offence but does not inflict harm can or should be criminalised (Simester and von Hirsch, 2000; von Hirsch and Simester, forthcoming) but this legislation does not address these subtleties. The phrase 'harassment, alarm or distress' is a cut-and-paste import from public order legislation, first introduced in 1986 when it was decided that the old definition of conduct likely to cause a breach of the peace was inadequate to protect peaceable members of the public who were passive bystanders or victims of disorderly conduct. In this case, the presence of a police officer to form an opinion of the impact of the public disorder is necessary for the offence to be established. No such rule applies in establishing the prerequisites for an anti-social behaviour order, although in practice, in accordance with the hearsay rule, police or local authority officers often supply the clinching evidence.

A similar definition is used in the Protection from Harassment Act 1997, one of the last pieces of legislation enacted by the outgoing Conservative government. This Act also adopts the hybrid format (civil with criminal penalties for breach) for the less serious form of harassment (where violence or fear of violence is involved there is a separate indictable offence).[4] Breach of the civil version becomes, like the ASBO, an offence liable to a five-year maximum sentence. Unlike the anti-social behaviour legislation, the Act lays down time limits within which harassment can be deemed a course of conduct, involving at least two occasions. Although repetitiousness was a key element used to justify the ASBO, it is not stipulated in the statute.

The non-statutory guidance on ASBOs issued by the Home Office (Home Office, 1999) nevertheless emphasised the persistent nature of the conduct to be targeted. It stated (para. 3.10): 'The main test is that there is a *pattern*[5] of behaviour which continues over a period of time but cannot be dealt with easily or adequately through the prosecution of those concerned for a single 'snapshot' or criminal event'. Examples are given of the type of behaviour which could qualify (para. 3.9).

> In broad terms an anti-social behaviour order is likely to be relevant where there is behaviour of a criminal nature which causes or is likely to cause harassment, alarm or distress to other people. This definition would include cases where people are put in fear of crime since this causes alarm or distress.

Note the definition as 'criminal' conduct. Elsewhere in the document the phrase 'criminal or sub-criminal' is used, although there is no real meaning to the term 'sub-criminal' – something is either criminal or it is not. The advice goes on:

> It should not include run of the mill disputes between neighbours, petty intolerances, or minor one-off disorderly acts. Nor should orders be used to penalise those who are merely different. Where the anti-social behaviour is the result of some underlying problem, such as drug and/or alcohol misuse, the orders should certainly be considered when it is not possible to get the individual to moderate their behaviour in any other way. The police and local authority need to care not to get involved in individual disputes which should be settled, as private matters, in the civil courts. Examples of cases where anti-social behaviour orders might be appropriate include:
> - where individuals intimidate neighbours and others through threats or violence or a mixture of unpleasant actions;
> - where there is persistent unruly behaviour by a small group of individuals on a housing estate or other local area, who may

dominate others and use minor damage to property and fear of retaliation, possibly at unsociable hours, as a means of intimidating other people;

– where there are families whose anti-social behaviour, when challenged, leads to verbal abuse, vandalism, threats and graffiti, sometimes using children as the vehicle for action against neighbouring families.

The list goes on to include abuse of elderly or disabled people, organised bullying of children in public places, racial harassment and persistent anti-social behaviour related to drink or drugs. Quite clearly the whole context is seen in relation to residential neighbourhoods, thus reflecting the origins of the order in the concerns of social landlords and complaints to MPs about 'neighbours from hell'. This was to change markedly in new guidance issued in November 2002, in conjunction with new statutory powers. Five years from its launch, in 2004, the ASBO had transcended the boundaries of the neighbourhood and the housing estate to serve a variety of different purposes, as will be shown in due course.

The use of ASBOs

ASBOs became available on 1 April 1999. Six months later the Home Secretary, Jack Straw, wrote impatiently to local authorities and chief constables urging them to use the orders – only five had been imposed at that point. He offered reassurance that human rights legislation was no hindrance, something which it was said had put off some councils. More advice, on setting up local ASBO protocols, was published in June 2000 (Home Office, 2000) emphasising that ASBO terms must be reasonable and proportionate, and giving guidance on the desirable local administrative structures for dealing with the orders. But still the number of ASBOs picked up only slowly and it was noticeable that a handful of councils, notably Manchester, were responsible for the majority. Cost and complexity were cited (Campbell, 2002). But there were other factors at work (Burney, 2002). Chief among these was the statutory obligation to consult in a multi-agency context before seeking an order. Not only could this be a cumbersome affair, but, more importantly, consultation often produced alternative solutions. Many authorities valued the case conferences and social landlords sometimes even saw the problem-solving element as the most useful part of the ASBO process (Campbell, 2002; Hunter et al., 2001). In any case, councils already had more familiar tools, notably evictions and Housing Act injunctions, together with the noise and nuisance-curbing powers wielded by environmental protection officers. The phrase was frequently heard, 'it's just another tool in the tool box'.

Many crime and disorder partnerships (the multi-agencies created by the Crime and Disorder Act 1998) were not particularly inclined to use such a drastic tool, often regarded as a confession of failure. They preferred a step-by-step approach with ASBOs as a last resort – although the government guidance specifically stated that this should not be the case. A new half-way house became available with the non-statutory Acceptable Behaviour Contracts (ABCs) pioneered in the London Borough of Islington and quickly adopted nationwide. With these, police, social landlords or schools engage in a dialogue with children and parents (the recipients are nearly always youths) and together arrive at an agreement lasting six months and involving both negative and positive elements intended to improve behaviour. The 'contract' soubriquet is somewhat misleading since there is no obligation on the authorities to take on reciprocal obligations, although help in terms of family support, access to leisure facilities and so forth is sometimes provided. Underlying the agreement is the threat of an ASBO should it be broken. Research into the Islington scheme reported mainly positive results (Bullock and Jones, 2004).

ABCs, quick, cheap and relatively benign, have been taken up with far greater enthusiasm than have anti-social behaviour orders. But they are not without problems and a lot may depend upon the way they are administered. A small action research project in Brighton (Stephen and Squires, 2003) found that ABCs were applied to families with multiple problems, who experienced considerable stress and stigmatisation as a result. They felt under great pressure to accept the contracts, even though some thought the evidence against their children was biased or even false. The mental health needs and learning difficulties of some of the children on the contracts were not recognised, so that they had limited understanding of what was involved or ability to conform. The fact that 12 out of the 13 children got through the contracts successfully has to be set against some of the strain involved – terrified of being evicted (although legally ABCs have no part in this), some parents kept their children indoors practically all the time. Only two out of eight families felt entirely positive about the experience. The researchers felt that more should have been done to link the participants to support networks and services and that restorative justice could have been tried first.

Those local authorities who most readily resort to ASBOs are those with dedicated legal teams, usually located in the housing department, who are practised in evictions and other forms of legal coercion and unafraid of wielding a big stick. The diversity of political and administrative cultures within local government and local constabularies has produced a range of responses to CDA 1998, which introduced the concept of local responsibility for dealing with perceived local problems of crime and disorder, albeit with the expectation on the part of government that it would continue to steer the agenda. This assumption was resented by local government leaders: Sir Jeremy Beecham, chairman of the Local Government Association which is often at odds with the Home Office on this issue, was quoted as saying: 'The spirit of the Act enables the use of anti-social behaviour orders to be decided locally by councils, the police and other agencies as part of the crime and disorder partnerships – not centrally'.[6] It has been commented that '[t]his story demonstrates the limitations of what David Garland (2001: 124-7) has called "the responsibilisation strategy" by which governments seek to achieve their law and order ends by relying on non-criminal justice agencies to provide the means' (Burney, 2002: 482).

David Blunkett, who succeeded Jack Straw as Home Secretary in 2001, was even more determined than his predecessor that local government and police should deliver the predetermined agenda on anti-social behaviour. A burst of legislative changes to the delivery of ASBOs, plus radically new guidance and a whole new range of other powers relating to various forms of nuisance, emerged during his first three years in office, and more was to come in the 2004/5 Parliamentary session. The measures introduced in 2002 to 2004, together with the vigorous publicity campaign described in a previous chapter emanating from the newly created Anti-Social Behaviour Unit within the Home Office, soon started to boost the number of ASBOs granted in England and Wales, which had reached a total of 2,455 by 31 March 2004, five years after their introduction – the figure having increased by some 25 per cent in the latest quarter. Yet it is worth recalling that this five-year total was under half the 5,000 *annual* rate predicted at the outset.[7] One police authority, Greater Manchester, was responsible for some 15 per cent of the total, having imposed more than twice the number of ASBOs (422) as Greater London (199). The quarterly updates on ASBO numbers provided by the Home Office showed a continued sharp climb through 2004, reaching 3,826 by the end of September. These orders were still very unevenly distributed among the 42 different police forces (see Appendices 1 and 2).

Public opinion also played its part. The idea of the ASBO has great popular appeal, boosted by media publicity, and as the existence of the order became more widely known there has often been great local pressure to use the power, pressure which is sometimes resisted by police and local officials. The British Crime Survey has consistently shown that neighbour trouble is a less widespread concern than litter, graffiti and groups of youths. The Home Office guidance of November 2002 reflects this wider range of annoyances. The examples of anti-social behaviour which local partnerships are encouraged to target are somewhat different from the conduct described in the 1999 guidance. The list is headed by graffiti 'which on its own can make even the tidiest urban spaces look squalid'. It goes on to include 'abusive and intimidating language, too often directed at minorities; excessive noise, particularly late at night; fouling the streets with litter; drunken behaviour in the streets, and the mess it creates; dealing drugs, with all the problems to which it gives rise'.

This list demonstrates concern for incivilities affecting public space in general, in place of the earlier focus on the residential neighbourhood. This was possible because, as the document says, 'anti-social behaviour has a wide legal definition'. Further paragraphs discuss the linkage between ASBOs and ABCs, the latter being presented as a lower level of social control but seamlessly connected with the enforcement-oriented ASBOs. Conduct which might attract either of these sanctions include both the criminal, e.g. criminal damage, vehicle crime and assault, and the merely deviant, such as substance misuse and under-age smoking or drinking. Begging, prostitution and kerb-crawling are also listed, a sign that 'cleaning up the streets' is not confined to litter and graffiti. Some local authorities have needed little encouragement to focus on this sanitising agenda, as a later chapter will show.

This new focus was accompanied by legal changes which significantly affected the use of ASBOs. The Police Reform Act 2002 included provisions designed to make the orders more widely available and easier to obtain. Probably the least significant was that which allowed ASBOs to be made applicable anywhere in England and Wales rather than simply in the issuing local government area and those adjacent to it. The wider the area the less likely are breaches to be identified – even though ASBO details are available on the police national computer, somebody prohibited from spitting and swearing in a London borough will probably spit and swear with impunity in Aberystwyth. Police have welcomed the power in s. 50 of the Act to obtain names and addresses from people 'acting in an anti-social manner'. Additionally, the right to apply for an ASBO was extended to British Transport Police and registered social landlords (RSLs). The latter have become responsible for large swathes of former council housing and their full integration into the process was overdue.

Section 65 of the Act provided a new interim order – a fast-track way of imposing immediate controls without a full hearing and even, in emergency, without the presence of the accused. In such a case the interim order would not be effective unless served upon the recipient within seven days. Despite there having been no opportunity to dispute the allegations, interim orders carry the same penalties if breached as full orders. The Court of Appeal ruled in the case of *Kenny* v. *Leeds Magistrates' Court*[8] that an interim order made without notice to the defendant did not contravene Article 6 of the European Convention on Human Rights.

The Police Reform Act also introduces new ways of obtaining ASBOs. They can be applied for in county courts, where they may be imposed in conjunction with evictions or injunctions. Social landlords feel more at home in this tribunal. Potentially the most important provision, in s. 64, extends the right to impose ASBOs on top of a criminal sentence if there is evidence of past anti-social behaviour. Post-conviction ASBOs have, for example, been given to chronic shoplifters and persistent burglars. Courts may do this on their own initiative, but often orders are imposed at the request of the police. Post-conviction ASBOs carry no requirement for wider consultation – particularly worrying where young people are concerned.

This procedure has been the subject of one of the few successful appeals against an ASBO, by way of judicial review. In *C* v. *Sunderland Youth Court*[9] magistrates had imposed an ASBO as part of a sentence when a month before they had refused one when sentencing the same youth, the second sentence for matters pre-dating the first appearance. Meanwhile the defendant was said to be making good progress on an intensive supervision and surveillance programme. No reasons had been given by the magistrates for this change of tack, and the judges decided the process had been unfair and the order should not have been made. The case also revealed confusion over the use of the new power, and also uncertainty as to whether a post-conviction ASBO was civil or criminal. It has also been established, through *R* v. *P*,[10] a juvenile, that post-conviction orders should not be made where custody has been imposed if the offender is not persistent and a period on supervision will follow.

The increased number of ASBOs – though still insignificant compared with any common sentencing figures – is due both to wider availability and also to the expanded view of their suitability. It is not possible to assess the relative impact of these twin forces together with what seems to be greater public pressure to deal with perceived anti-social behaviour and the stimulus of government publicity. Multiple ASBOs are being used by police to deal with trouble-spots, as in the *Kenny* case. Social landlords are more at home dealing with county courts and use ASBOs in combination with evictions where they think the ex-tenants will return and make trouble. And the interim order will have encouraged applications in cases where previously the process was deemed too lengthy.

Most importantly, it is clear that some police forces – the writer has information to this effect from Manchester and Nottingham for example – are making very active use of the post-conviction facility as a means of controlling persistent offenders. The figures indeed show that it is the post-conviction ASBOs that are mainly responsible for the increase in orders. In the period between the end of November 2002, when the facility first became available, to 30 September 2004, orders on conviction accounted for 71 per cent of all ASBOs issued in England and Wales.

Increasingly, then, the procedure is becoming simply another sentencing add-on – a far cry from the original vision. Hopkins Burke and Morrill (2002) believe that the ASBO is best used to reinforce the strength of a criminal sentence since those concerned are already proven lawbreakers. But for this to be acceptable, the elements of disproportionality in the orders have to be addressed. In short, nothing less than a drastic revision is called for, as the following discussion indicates.

Prohibitions

Apart from a requirement of 'reasonableness' there is no limit on the conditions which can be attached to an ASBO in order to prevent further acts of anti-social behaviour. Conditions are appealable, but there are no figures on how often this happens or how successfully. Some courts merely demand avoidance of the original conduct or specify a geographical area within which anti-social acts are banned. But very detailed, excessive or simply unenforceable prohibitions are not uncommon. A youth given a two-year night-time curfew receives four times the maximum permitted in an ordinary sentence (Burney, 2002). Spitting and swearing anywhere in public is a typical ban – hard to enforce, yet a profoundly deaf girl ordered not to spit was remanded in custody when she did so (Statewatch, 2004).[11] Manchester police prohibited gang members from riding bicycles (used for drug deals) and wearing gang-related clothing such as balaclavas for the rest of their lives[12] – justified as reasonable on the grounds of the violent, lethal activities of gang members.

A burglar with 258 offences targeted on old people received seven years in custody to be followed by a five-year ASBO in which he was forbidden to call at or telephone any residential premises in the country without permission.[13] A potentially harmful ban was that forbidding a prostitute to carry condoms (see p. 101). Many young people are banned from streets around their homes or only allowed along certain routes.[14] One 18-year old banned from congregating with three or more other youths breached his order when he attended a youth club – where the evening session was about anti-social behaviour (NAPO, 2004). In an extreme case,[15] a boy of 11 was banned from all streets in a large neighbourhood except his own, and forbidden to go to the town centre. He could only visit his grandmother in the company of a named relative – all this when, according to his mother, he was awaiting a place in a residential home. Other cases involve bans which effectively prevent visits to the Connexions service or the Jobcentre. In every case, normal, legal activities are made criminal for the individuals concerned, in violation of the rule of law which says that criminal laws should apply to everyone equally.

Enforcement

The survey conducted by Campbell (2002) on a sample of 40 orders found that 14 (36 per cent) had been breached within nine months to a year. Hunter et al. (2001) found social landlords reporting similar figures. By the end of 2003 the breach rate had risen to 42 per cent, and that does not include multiple breaches by the same person (see Appendix 2). Bearing in mind that orders must last for at least two years and some detailed prohibitions may be hard to police, one would expect there to be a large number of undetected breaches.

Police will admit to seeking ASBOs instead of prosecution, in the expectation that breach will subsequently lead to prosecution by an easier route (personal information). Breaches occur whenever one of what are usually multiple conditions is broken, and this may not involve a repeat of any bad behaviour but could be simply a technical violation of, say, a geographical boundary. It would not be surprising if a majority of ASBOs were breached in one form or another. That is not to say that most are likely to be 'failures' in the sense of failing to modify behaviour, but change may be short term and probably not achievable by this means in the case of persistent perpetrators.

Courts are likely to vary in their response to breaches according to the nature of the violation. The Magistrates' Association recommends custody as the sentencing starting point, and 23 per cent of people given ASBOs do end up in custody (see Table 5.1), sometimes after several previous breaches and usually only for a short time. Given the recognition that short sentences are of no value in terms of reform, and

Table 5.1 ASBOS by age, breach, and custodial sentences resulting from breach.[16] (England and Wales: 1 June 2000–31 December 2003)

	Number*	%	% breached	% breaches given custody
All ASBOs issued	1,892	100	42 (n = 793)	55 (n = 437)
at age 10–17:	991	52	40 (n = 392)	46 (n = 179)
at age 18 plus:	861	46	47 (n = 401)	66 (n = 258)

*Age not known = 40 (2%)
Source: Home Office.

longer sentences would be disproportionate, these punishments must be regarded as purely symbolic.

Young people were less likely than adults to be punished with custody, yet the numbers reaching young offender institutions by this route increased sharply during 2004, to the concern of the Youth Justice Board. In many cases the local Youth Offending Team (YOT) had not been consulted, even though most of those involved were known to them. Indeed many had already been punished for serious offences. Had ASBOs not been available, it seems likely that they would have faced prosecution for further offences (Morgan, 2005). The availability of the ASBO as a means of fast-tracking persistent offenders into custody suggests that this is what is driving the process.

Publicity

One of the more controversial aspects of the procedure is the local publicity used to inform neighbourhoods than someone in their midst has been dealt an order which restrains his behaviour in specific ways, including often banishment from the area. This may take the form of posters with photographs, notices through letterboxes or local newspaper announcements – which may infringe rights under Article 8(1) of the ECHR. The practice was exonerated in *Stanley* v. *Metropolitan Police Commissioner* [2004][17] on the grounds that it was necessary to inform residents of the details of the order so as to assist enforcement and to deter others as well as the recipient of the order.

The practice becomes much more controversial where children are involved, given the traditional anonymity of court proceedings afforded by s. 39(1) of the Children and Young Persons Act 1933, under which the court may, and usually does, prohibit publicity of personal details and photographs. There is often great demand for exemption from s.

39 where ASBOs are concerned. The youth court dealing with ASBO breaches is specifically exempted from the normal anonymity of young defendants in s. 86 of the Anti-Social Behaviour Act 2003.

The main judgment on this issue, *R (T)* v. *St Albans Crown Court*[18] states that disclosure of relevant details of an ASBO must involve a balance between the interests of the community and the welfare of the recipient, but concluded that enforcement considerations, and the public interest in knowing what was going on, were influential. However, no court is prevented from refusing to apply s. 39 in an ASBO case.

More recently, three juvenile defendants, members of a larger gang that had been terrorising an estate, appealed against the publicity distributed by Brent Borough Council when ASBOs were made against them – leaflets not only gave photographs and addresses but listed the criminal convictions of each. The appeal was lost.[19] To eliminate qualms on this score, in March 2005 the Home Office issued guidance stating that the names and photographs of young people given ASBOs should be published.

The practical arguments in favour of publicising ASBOs notwith-standing, the practice is likely to be particularly harmful where young people are involved, as well as unwise. 'Naming' cannot be separated from 'shaming', and shame by itself, without any reintegrating process, is likely to be counter-productive, resulting in rejection of the ethical standpoint of the accusers (Ahmed et al., 2001). It enhances the outcast aura which can be very damaging to the personality and prospects of a child. It may increase defiance and bravado, with the ASBO as a macho badge (Willow, 2005). It may also encourage acts of hostility against the families of the children concerned, as some personal stories have revealed. The mother of the 11-year-old boy described on p. 95 above received hate mail from all over the country when his case was publicised.

Who receives ASBOs?

Children

The most striking feature of ASBO statistics is the extent to which they have been applied to children and young people. Since June 2000, when age breakdowns were first available, up to the end of September 2004, there were 991 orders given to 10–17-year-olds, representing over half (52 per cent) of the total in that period. It must be remembered that social landlords pressed for the power because under-18s could not be subject to a civil injunction[20] and the alternative might be the eviction of a whole family. At first the government was unwilling to encourage the use of ASBOs against juveniles, but following local government protests the 1999 guidance was only restrictive with regard to children under 12 (para. 2.1):

> It is unlikely that there will be many cases where it would be appropriate to apply for an order against a 10–11 year old although the order may be the right response where the juvenile has been involved in anti-social behaviour with adults. Applications may routinely be made for the middle and older age groups of juveniles and young people (e.g. 12–17 year olds) as experience has shown that such individuals may commit serious acts of anti-social behaviour without adult encouragement or involvement.

Social service departments and Youth Offending Teams (YOTs) should be consulted if an order is contemplated against anyone under 18 (though in a two-tier authority SSDs are unlikely to take part in the final decision). But the degree of YOT involvement appears to be variable, and the Youth Court is not involved at all except for breaches – children appear before the adult magistrates' court sitting in its civil capacity. Although the guidance reminds users that there is a duty on local authorities under s. 17 of the Children Act to provide for children in need and mentions the possibility of care and supervision orders for children out of control, there is in practice little work in this field by SSDs, who are almost exclusively focused on child abuse.

This does not, it seems, prevent local authorities from applying for ASBOs against children who are in the care of their own social services (Ashford and Morgan, 2004). There is a clear conflict of interest, noted in *R (M)* v. *Sheffield Magistrates' Court*,[21] where the judge noted that, whereas in applying for an ASBO a local authority was discharging its duty to the people affected by the conduct, without any regard for the welfare of the perpetrator, the Children Act 1989 requires an authority, in consultation with others, to promote the welfare of any child in its care. In principle, therefore, said Judge Newman, social workers should prepare a report on the child for consideration by the panel considering whether to make an ASBO application, but the same social worker should not participate in the panel. A court should not make an order against a looked-after child unless it had heard in person from a social worker. This advice places a very thin layer of protection against a conflict of interest – especially when, in practice, people looking after the child may have reasons themselves to welcome an ASBO.

The media have been particularly keen to report stories about out-of-control children being slapped down by orders. One of the earliest stories making national headlines concerned a 14-year-old boy from Nottingham who became the first person to be given custody for breach of an ASBO. He already had 67 criminal convictions and came from a very troubled background.[22] It is now agreed locally that this if anything made his behaviour worse, and that the ASBO was counter-productive (personal information). Another headline case concerned 13-year-old so-called 'terror triplets' from Gillingham, Kent (Burney, 2002). They were said to have been involved with others in theft, abuse and violence in shops. Their ASBOs were breached when they again acted aggressively in a shop, and national newspapers, including *The Times*, confidently predicted custodial sentences. This was actually impossible, for at their age they would have to be classified as persistent offenders to qualify for custody, and in fact they only had one previous conviction and two cautions between them (they were given supervision orders). A *Guardian* investigation found that the family had many difficulties and had received little help from statutory authorities.[23] (Although Home Office advice on the use of ASBOs (Home Office, 2002) reminds local authorities of their duty under s. 17 of the Children Act 1989 to promote the welfare of children in need, it also says that the welfare of the child is not the first consideration in an ASBO hearing.)

These and other like stories reveal depressingly similar features: family difficulties from an early age result in troublesome and some-times persistently criminal children, and the public feeds on media representations which reflect in exaggerated form the general tendency to demonise young teenagers. There is seldom any public attempt to link the behaviour with family needs, and indignation which could be directed at failures to resource appropriate services is instead solely focused on punishment. The ASBO has provided a convenient vehicle for these emotions. The exaggerated nature of some of the restrictions express an almost boundless desire to restrain the young people concerned, sometimes for apparently trivial annoyance. Ten-year-old twins given ASBOs preventing them from looking through the windows of other people's flats; a child forbidden to use the word 'grass' in public; others forbidden to wear 'hoodies'; a family of three siblings and their cousin forbidden to appear in public in a group of more than three – these are some of the cases known to Carolyne Willow of the Children's Rights Alliance (2005). No wonder the media, when not in vengeful mode, finds comic relief in ASBO jokes.

People with mental disorders and other problems

Campbell (2002) found that over 60 per cent of the ASBO cases she examined involved people with obvious mental or social problems, mainly linked to alcohol or drugs. These are always going to be difficult cases, where mere prohibitions are unlikely to have a permanent effect on behaviour. Examples cited by Krudy and Stewart (2004) included a 14-year-old boy with ADHD who had been out of mainstream education since aged 11, a prostitute with severe psychiatric problems and a drug addiction, and an alcoholic woman given to sexual exhibitionism.

Failure or rejection of services may often be involved where mental or personality disorders cause troublesome conduct, involving some of the most recalcitrant nuisance neighbours – but welfare considerations are involved on both sides. There is explicitly no bar on ASBOs being given to mentally ill people (Home Office, 1999), but in housing law there is a potential clash with legislation protecting disabled people. In *North Devon Homes*[24] the judge found that the law meant that a woman who had a psychotic condition could not be evicted even though her abuse was causing misery to neighbours. Contrasting judgments in favour of Manchester City Council later established that disability protection can be overruled when the health of victims is an issue – the behaviour of the two women, one with a depressive illness and one with a personality disorder, had made their neighbours mentally ill too.[25]

Concern is mounting about the use of ASBOs on people who are obviously in need of treatment for mental disorders (Mason, 2005; NAPO, 2004). The National Association of Probation Officers (NAPO) cites the case of a woman who made 700 emergency calls from public telephones. She continued to do so despite an ASBO banning her from kiosks – and was imprisoned for two weeks for breach. A man upset his neighbours by shouting, swearing and banging on windows, and standing on a windowsill holding a Christmas tree and 'moaning'. Not surprisingly an ASBO did nothing to stop his bizarre conduct. He got four months in prison.

Alcoholism is another route to an ASBO. A woman in Lincoln, frequently drunk in the street and displaying troublesome behaviour, breached an ASBO seven times. Unusually, as she faced a Crown Court sentence, she attracted quite a lot of public sympathy. The local paper, the *Lincolnshire Echo*, questioned the need for a jail sentence. The judge heeded these messages, and gave her a community order with a condition of alcohol treatment.[26]

Social tenants

There are no statistics on the distribution of ASBOs among different housing tenures but everything suggests that, although one reason for creating the orders was that they could be applied to residents of any tenure, in practice council tenants remain the prime target for local authority-initiated ASBOs. It is no surprise that over 80 per cent of Acceptable Behaviour Contracts in Islington were given to the children of council tenants. This is because the mechanisms and resources exist within this sector to apply enforcement and threat, whether by means of eviction, injunction or ASBO.[27] Registered social landlords have had the power since 2003 to apply for ASBOs themselves, and can do so in the County Court in association with related actions, usually evictions (Hunter et al., 2003). Most ASBOs are given to males (85 per cent), in contrast to evictions where women tenants are often those expelled for bad behaviour by themselves or their children (Hunter and Nixon, 2001).

Prostitutes and beggars

Prostitutes are among the female recipients of ASBOs – not a class of person originally envisaged as falling within the anti-social behaviour remit, but along with beggars and increasingly 'moved on' by the orders, especially where drugs are also involved. In *Chief Constable of Manchester* v. *Potter*[28] it was established that even if an individual prostitute was not causing 'harassment, alarm or distress' she contributed to the 'red light' character of the neighbourhood which collectively did cause such feelings to residents, and therefore she could be removed with an ASBO. NAPO cites the case of a prostitute banned from carrying condoms in the area of the drugs clinic which supplied her with free condoms.

The street cleansing function of the ASBO is in the historic tradition of using whatever legal tools are at hand to rid communities of undesirable groups. It has been applied in places, like Kings Cross in London, where ASBOs have been among the methods used against drug markets. In Leeds the police obtained interim ASBOs without notice against as many as 66 people in the Little London area, which had become notorious for drugs and associated violence and acquisitive crime (the subject of the *Kelly* case referred to above).

Thus we see the ASBO moving into the sphere of direct crime control. This is especially apparent in Manchester where police have used ASBOs to curtail the activities of violent street gangs. The orders include detailed, lifetime prohibitions about clothing, such as balaclavas and golfing gloves, associated with gang membership. In one case short sleeves were banned because they revealed the wearer's significant tattoo. Frequently, the orders are expected to be breached and become a short cut to custody.

When we contrast this with the attempt by Camden Council in London to obtain ASBOs against directors of companies responsible for fly-posting, it is apparent that the orders have become all purpose instruments, adaptable to any type of crime or disorder, far beyond the neighbourhood problems originally envisaged. Within high-crime neighbourhoods, it is primarily outright criminal behaviour, rather than mere nuisance, that is targeted, and police welcome the power that it gives them to use hearsay evidence in place of formal witness statements, nailing what one police officer described as their 'targets' and yet bypassing the criminal justice system altogether.

The question is often asked: do ASBOs 'work'? There are frequent examples, such as those presented on the Home Office website, where peace and quiet has prevailed after the imposition of an order and the relief expressed by former sufferers is genuine and profound. But we know little or nothing of the longer-term effects on perpetrators or of the extent to which problems like drug dealing and prostitution have simply been exported elsewhere. It does seem that ASBOs can have a counter-productive effect on some young people, and their families. The order provides nothing positive to improve behaviour or meet underlying needs, although there is now a provision in s. 322 of the Criminal Justice Act 2003 for Youth Courts to be able to give Individual Support Orders on conviction for an ASBO breach, similar in content to action plans meted out to other young offenders. Given that ASBOs on conviction are seemingly regarded as part of the sentence (Madge, 2004) the 'civil' nature of the orders looks increasingly meretricious. And to a young person already deeply involved in the criminal justice system it may simply be another formality with little meaning.

The unsatisfactory aspects of this experiment in social control have to be seen against the sometimes intolerable situations in local neighbourhoods which gave rise to it in the first place. The shocking case of *Hussain v. Lancaster City Council*[29] illustrates that doing nothing is not an option, but the choice of legal instrument is sometimes difficult. The principle of a preventive order is not objectionable in itself – after all injunctions have been around for a long time. But the ASBO rests on a wholly imprecise definition of proscribed conduct; it is unique in the unlimited scope it affords for restrictions only tangentially related to the original misbehaviour; and it imposes an order with a minimum of two years but no upper limit. The penalty for breach is disproportionate, especially given that custody may result from a mere technical violation relating to original conduct which is not itself imprisonable. A more modestly drafted sanction, closer to a conventional injunction, might have served the purpose just as well. Indeed the order might not have been created at all had it not been for the perceived need for an instrument that, unlike an injunction, could be used against children. The growing concerns about its effects on individual juveniles and on the youth justice system are beginning to make themselves heard. Local government is divided on the efficacy, and the Local Government Association argues for prevention to take precedence over punishment (LGA, 2004).

Pressure is mounting against the inappropriate use of ASBOs, their often excessive consequences, and the uneven way that the orders are used in different parts of the country. It could be that the political heyday of the ASBO is on the wane and the enthusiasts will find themselves reined in.

The Anti-Social Behaviour Act and the White Paper
Respect and Responsibility

A new phase in the Blair government's campaign against bad behaviour was introduced in March 2003, with the publication of the White Paper *Respect and Responsibility – Taking a Stand Against Anti-Social Behaviour*. As the title implies, this was a rallying call to people to get together and take matters into their own hands where government action could not reach – a demonstration of what has been dubbed 'the limitation of the sovereign state' (Garland, 2001). It looked dangerously like a call to vigilantism, although the bulk of the paper, and the subsequent Bill, concerned a range of new and often quite petty powers conveyed to police and local authorities.

Many of these powers concern environmental eyesores – graffiti, litter, abandoned cars – assessed as contributing to fear of crime. Others convey more control over parents and young people, most controversially in the police power to establish 'dispersal areas' within which group bans can be imposed and curfews enforced on under-16s. The police also get sweeping new powers to close down premises where hard drug dealing is causing trouble. There are amendments to housing law giving landlords even more power to curb the behaviour of social tenants – already subject to more controls in their home lives than any other group. The White Paper and the Act focus on a range of new types of petty enforcement, such as the extension of fixed penalty notices (FPNs) for environmental violations, with new powers for civilian community support officers. It introduces FPNs and 'contracts' for parents of truanting or misbehaving children, where teachers are to be used as the enforcers. In spite of its mainly petty detail, the effect of this legislation is to extend the range of social control and recruit more classes of people authorised to exercise it.

The police rapidly adopted the most draconian of the new powers – those concerning the closure of 'crack' houses and the establishment of 'dispersal areas'. Premises where the use, production or supply of hard drugs is causing disorder or serious nuisance can be rapidly closed for a specified period of time, owners and residents having been identified and the local authority consulted. The closure notice must be authorised by a police superintendent or above and magistrates must issue a closure order within 48 hours. Bona fide residents will be allowed back in, but concern has been expressed about the effect on their living conditions, especially where children are involved (Padfield, 2004a).

A police officer interviewed who has used this power was enthusiastic:

> Crack house notices are brilliant. I'm really impressed. People were complaining nothing was being done – it was, but eviction is so lengthy it looked as though nothing was being done. We went to court that morning and closed it in the afternoon and people were mightily impressed.

Dispersal of groups (Part 4 of the Act) give extraordinary extra powers to the police to control the presence of 'groups' (a group can be only two people) within specified areas. As Padfield (2004b) asks: 'Do the police need more powers? Not only do police already enjoy wide statutory powers under the Public Order Act 1986, the Criminal Justice and Public Order Act 1994 and the Criminal Justice and Police Act 2001, they have the common law power to take such steps as are necessary to prevent a breach of the peace.'

Under s. 30 a senior police officer must have reasonable grounds for believing:

(a) that any members of the public have been intimidated, harassed, alarmed or distressed as the result of the presence or behaviour of groups of two or more persons in public places in any locality in his police area (the relevant locality), and
(b) that anti-social behaviour is a significant and persistent problem in the relevant locality.

On the basis of this belief a geographical dispersal area can be designated for up to six months (renewable), and within this area a uniformed constable can order any groups who he believes are behaving in a way which is or may cause intimidation etc. to disperse, to go home if they do not live in the area and/or not return for up to 24 hours. Bad behaviour by just one person in a group means all are subject to the order. Any contravention becomes an arrestable offence.

What is more, there is the option to impose a curfew on children under

16 who are out and about unsupervised after 9 p.m. in a designated area. The police constable may take the child back to his or her home unless there is reason to believe that the child would thereby suffer significant harm. (Officers have complained at the idea of providing a children's taxi service). It is notable that a similar curfew power given to local authorities in s. 14 of CDA 1998 in relation to children under 10 was never used. The Home Secretary undertook to review the system, including age limits. Now that the police, and older children, are involved, curfews have taken off. One of the first designated areas was near London's King's Cross, where (in obvious emulation of American practice – see Chapter 2) it was claimed to be necessary in order to prevent trouble by Asian teenage gangs during the summer holidays. Since then dispersal areas have spread all over London, including the outer suburbs. But a test case in Richmond in July 2005 resulted in a High Court ruling that enforced removal of children from the streets was illegal. This may spell the end of curfews, but not dispersal zones.

Children's charities and human rights groups have vociferously criticised the provisions of s. 30. Critics cited Articles 5, 8 and 11 of the ECHR (right to liberty; respect for family life; freedom of assembly). The UN Convention on the Rights of the Child also protects children's right of assembly and recreational activities. The Parliamentary Joint Committee on Human Rights was scathing:

> We consider that the potential intrusion on family life and liberty is so extensive, and the benefits in any case to be so speculative, that it might be difficult to establish (either in general or in specific cases) that the powers [granted under this section] will or would not be used only when it was proportionate to a pressing social need. A constable or community support officer who considers using these powers will be in a difficult position, without much guidance from the legislation as to when and how he or she should exercise them.[30]

The effect of s. 30 is to provide yet another strand in the increasingly seamless web of control and surveillance instituted in a succession of legal changes under New Labour. Anyone who thought that vagueness or lack of guidance would inhibit police use of the powers was mistaken. This is well illustrated by the following conversation with a sergeant in charge of a high-crime neighbourhood.

> I've done quite a bit of dispersal. I did a dispersal at [X neighbourhood] and that was good. That's good legislation that is.

If you use it in conjunction with the power to get the name and address.[31]

Q. What were they doing?

A. You can trawl the [incident report] system, you can have groups of youths throwing stones, breaking windows, fighting, chasing other people, causing problems of damage. And it may be as well that it's just a group outside a shop, they may not be doing anything but the fact that they're there in a group is itself intimidating ...We have a police system and we can identify a number of calls where people have complained about groups of youths.

Before we had a problem if they stood in a group they might be causing damage but residents wouldn't give you a witness statement for fear of reprisals ... So we hardly ever took statements from witnesses.

Q. So how did you prove what they were doing?

A. Obviously you can't prove the criminal damage but you know who's done it because they've told you. A lot of the civil legislation you use hearsay evidence. The main problem was as I said before all the ones in the group we didn't know who they were, they were anonymous, they were safe. Once you know who they are you're 90 per cent there aren't you? You can give them acceptable behaviour contracts, you can ASBO warn them, you can go to the parents and if they're council tenants their tenancy's in jeopardy. So actually at X we only had two arrests [for coming back into the area] in the first week but we'd identified 38 youths which I think is more of a success than the actual arrests.

Q. So you're saying all these 38 youths were causing trouble?

A. Yea, they would have been, yes ... What you've got to realise is that you apply common sense to it and just because there's a dispersal notice it doesn't mean you've got to disperse a group if they're not doing anything and they're no threat ...

Looking at anti-social behaviour you identify targets on the estate and these targets they're actually making residents' lives a misery ... Now we know who they are and a lot of the time you can't take criminal action because you haven't got witnesses to take statements. They'll tell you who's doing it and that's fine because as long as we know who's guilty, who's the offender we'll do it, we'll employ the legislation and we'll act as professional witnesses and we'll get the evidence ourselves.

Q. How do you get the evidence against them?

A. We might do surveillance, we do various operational orders, we'll get a dispersal notice and go out on high visibility patrol ...

CCTV has been a great help to us ... so you know who the people are driving cars around and burning them out and they've got no documents so they become disqualified with power of arrest ... The CCTV operators are very good, they'll provide us with tapes of some of our targets.

This discussion illustrates precisely the tension between the need to protect neighbourhoods from corrosive crime and disorder and respect for principles of due process and civil liberties. There is no doubt where the balance now lies. The police are in their own eyes doing a better job of containing troublemakers and their job does not extend to establishing preventive schemes which might perhaps channel youths' activities in legitimate ways – let alone does it extend to long-term social causes.

Alternative remedies under previous legislation

The publicity attached to the ASBO has obscured the range of more long-standing remedies against bad behaviour available to local authorities. Public nuisances can be prosecuted under common law or dealt with under the Environmental Protection Act 1990 or specific noise legislation. The Local Government Act 1972, although it ultimately failed to control crime in Coventry, was used to good effect against drug dealing on an estate in Hackney, and subsequently in Nottingham. Most of of all, councils have large powers over their own tenants, who historically have been controlled in the way they conduct their lives and use their homes through a variety of formal and informal means (Burney, 1999; Hughes, 2000).

The residualisation of the council housing sector (see Chapter 4) meant that tenants were drawn increasingly from low-income, economically inactive families with a disproportionate numbers of very young and very old people and of female headed households. This rise in inequality coincided with the sharp rise in crime in the 1980s and 1990s, and was not unconnected with it (Hope, 2001). Housing managers were recruited into the ranks of crime prevention and surveillance (Clapham, 1997), and housing law developed into an instrument of behaviour control.

The longest-standing civil law controls are the contractual obligations set out in tenancy agreements, breach of which can result in eviction. Where formerly these were normally confined to rules relating to the upkeep of houses and gardens, plus general prohibitions on criminal or 'immoral' activity within the house and disturbance to neighbours, latterly many tenancy agreements have been rewritten in more specific ways with regard to anti-social behaviour (Burney, 1999: 98–100). One typical example has a clause banning 'Anti-Social Behaviour, Nuisance, Harassment (including Racial Harassment) and Domestic Violence' and it prohibits nuisance behaviour not only in the immediate neighbourhood but throughout the city. It spells out the tenant's responsibility for bad behaviour by family, friends and visitors to the home, and by anyone incited by the tenant to act for them.

Proxy responsibility by tenants for the misbehaviour of others passed into statute law in the 1996 Housing Act (Part V, Conduct of Tenants), which introduced an extraordinary new array of powers adapting housing law to crime and disorder control. The anti-social conduct not only of people residing in the dwelling but also of visitors could bring action, including eviction, against a tenant. Moreoever, the offending conduct could take place anywhere in 'the locality' of the dwelling – a large leap into social control throughout whole estates and beyond (the extent of this control was argued in *Manchester City Council* v. *Lawler*[32]). Conduct justifying a possession order was newly defined as that 'causing or likely to cause' nuisance or annoyance to residents, visitors or anyone engaged in lawful activity in the area (this would, of course, include housing officials). Evidence could be supplied by 'professional witnesses'– variously interpreted as hired observers or officials or police with knowledge of events. Any household evicted under these terms is liable to be regarded as intentionally homeless and therefore not eligible for statutory assistance.

As an alternative to eviction the Act introduced strong injunctive powers against anti-social tenants, including the power of arrest where violence was used or threatened. These powers were replaced in the Anti-Social Behaviour Act 2003 to cover (s. 153A) conduct *capable of causing* [emphasis added] nuisance or annoyance to any person and which directly or indirectly affects the management functions of a relevant landlord'. (The latter phrase was devised to deal with the effect of the judgment in *London Borough of Enfield* v. *D.B. (a minor)*,[33] which said that the landlord did not have sufficient nexus under the former legislation to bring an injunction against somebody who had violently attacked staff in a council housing office.)

The Housing Act 1996 also enabled councils to use 'introductory tenancies', whereby no security of tenure was available for the first year and bad behaviour could result in eviction without appeal (except by judicial review). ASBA 2003 applies the same principle to secure tenants of social landlords who behave anti-socially. They can be 'demoted' to lose security of tenure and the right to buy. The Act also provides exclusion orders in association with injunctions carrying the power of

Table 5.2 Social tenants as perpetrators of anti-social behaviour

Risk factors	Women tenants (39)		Male and joint tenants (28)		Total sample (67)	
Out of control children	16	41%	5	18%	21	31%
Physical/sexual abuse	10	26%	2	7%	12	18%
Alcohol problems	5	13%	2	7%	7	10%
Mental health problems	7	18%	5	19%	12	18%
Drug related problems	4	10%	4	15%	8	12%
Physical disability	3	8%	3	11%	6	9%
% of sample in which one or more of the above risk factors was recorded on file	30	77%	15	54%	45	67%

Source: Hunter and Nixon (2001).

arrest (i.e. where violence has been used or threatened) – so that in fact a tenant could be excluded from their own home.

This huge range of powers in many ways foreshadowed the ASBO and helps to explain why the orders have been used less frequently than was originally anticipated and also why, because an injunction can rarely be used against a minor, the focus of ASBOs has been on the children of tenants rather than their parents. Evictions or injunctions are the more likely sanction against social tenants who do not control their children's bad behaviour – and mainly it is women who suffer, as research in social landlord's files has shown (Hunter and Nixon, 2001) – see Table 5.2. This research also showed how multiple risk factors lead tenants to be labelled seriously anti-social. It bears out Brown's point (2004) that housing management *creates* anti-social behaviour.

Injunctions are civil prohibitions with no criminal outcome – breach counts as contempt of court and is imprisonable for up to two years, although a few weeks is the usual length. However, committal requires proof to the criminal standard. Practitioners say injunctions are mainly effective, and quicker and cheaper than an ASBO. The plaintiff must have a direct nexus with the respondent. In the Local Government Act 1972 s. 222, this is interpreted in a novel way to give local authorities the power to bring an injunction to protect the interests of the inhabitants of their area. It was this power that was invoked in the case of *Coventry City Council* v. *Finnie* (see pp. 20–21). More recently it was allowed on appeal to be used, in combination with the Highways Act 1980, in

Nottingham City Council v. *Zain*,[34] to ban a drug dealer from a particular estate. Subsequently in Nottingham further use has been made of this combination to ban beggars and prostitutes as well as drug dealers.

Reliance on nuisance laws primarily created to control social tenants has left a weakness when it comes to dealing with neighbourhoods of mixed housing tenure. The fragmentation of council tenancies through the right to buy has resulted in many areas where owner occupiers are alongside both social and private tenants. A study (Nixon et al., 2003) considered the best approach to anti-social behaviour in such places: essentially, a multi-agency one using all the powers available in the various circumstances, but with strategies based upon strong local data, problem-solving and developing services for vulnerable households. A potentially powerful system became available in the Housing Act 2004, ss. 55–100, whereby in designated problem areas strict licensing controls can be imposed on private landlords, explicitly with the intention of preventing anti-social behaviour.

Fixed penalty notices, Noise Act and by-laws

Instant fines and fixed penalty notices (FPNs) were favoured in various pronouncements by the Prime Minister Tony Blair in the lead up to the Anti-Social Behaviour Act 2003, on the grounds that they bypass the criminal process if paid and avoid a criminal record. An experiment with police handing out instant fines to drunk and disorderly people was pronounced a success, and new forms of fixed penalty were introduced in the Act. For example, they can be issued by education authorities to parents of truanting children in lieu of prosecution – the amounts and other details being left to regulations. Fixed penalties for litter and waste dumping, graffiti and flyposting paid to local authorities can be retained by them, a change in the law which has stimulated much more activity in these areas by local councils. Civilian community support officers can issue fixed penalties along with other powers delegated to them that were formerly confined to police constables. Penalty Notices for Disorder (PNDs) have been pronounced a success and there is a power to apply them to children (see discussion in Chapter 2).

Local authorities have power under the Act to temporarily close licensed premises on grounds of noise. The Noise Act 1996 now applies to every local authority, not just those few which have chosen to adopt it. It places a duty on them to take reasonable steps to investigate complaints of night-time noise (previously resisted because of the resource implications). Once again, encouragement is given by allowing the councils to keep receipts from fines.

The Victorian remedy of by-laws (local laws creating criminal offences) has been revived as a useful concept.[35] The government has pointed out that it can be used to ban modern intrusive behaviours such as loud music and skateboarding, and that the penalties can now range up to £500. As a response to the minutiae of nuisance it makes local sense – while adding yet another layer to the mounting heap of public protection against disorder.

Among the legislation rushed through Parliament at the end of the 2004–5 session was a Clean Neighbourhoods and Environment Act spelling out further minutiae of enforcement against abandoning vehicles, repairing them or exposing them for sale on the road, and against litter, stray dogs, graffiti and noise nuisance. The appetite for anti-social legislation is apparently never satisfied.

Protection for victims and witnesses of anti-social behaviour

Victims of nuisance behaviour receive more consideration under the Anti-Social Behaviour Act 2003. Injunctions can be sought by social landlords to stop behaviour affecting a wider range of people, and courts, when deciding whether it would be reasonable to grant a possession order, must consider the impact that anti-social conduct has had in the past and even what it might be in future. This gives extremely wide discretion and trades reduced security for the tenant against the peace of mind of anybody who might be affected by conduct that has not yet occurred.

In more general terms, the question has been raised as to how far local authorities, especially but not exclusively in their role as landlords, have a duty to protect victims of anti-social behaviour (Bright and Bakalis, 2003). The main case that gives rise to this question is *Hussein* v. *Lancaster City Council*.[36] Mr Hussein lived above his corner shop, and over a period of years was subjected to regular and very severe harassment by local youths. He was not a council tenant but some of the offenders were. The council repeatedly refused to take any action against them and the police failed to prosecute. A series of appeals resulted in the conclusion that the council had no duty of care towards somebody who was not their tenant even if people causing the trouble were. This confirmed the finding in *Smith* v. *Scott*[37] that a landlord could not be liable for nuisance caused by his tenants.

A victim who is also a council tenant might have more chance of forcing the landlord to take action by way of judicial review against an administrative decision, but Bright and Bakalis (2003) argue that neither this nor expectations based on tenancy agreements are very likely to provide relief. They suggest that the Human Rights Act 1998 is the most promising basis for a victim, who could argue that by not resolving the problem the council had infringed his or her right under Article 8 for respect for private and family life.[38] The trouble with this approach is that perpetrators too have rights. Eviction, for example, could certainly be said to infringe family life. Bright and Bakalis conclude:

> There is an imbalance in the law at the moment in that the perpetrators of anti-social behaviour have the right to complain if their rights are infringed by ASBOs, possession proceedings or injunctions, and yet the victims of such anti-social behaviour are restricted to the use of uncertain and limited private and public law remedies to air their views. Unless judges use the opportunity afforded to them under Human Rights Act 1998 to redress this imbalance by giving victims an effective voice, our legal system cannot guarantee that the victim's interests are given the same weight by the authorities as is given to the rights of perpetrators and to the interests of society. (2003: 334)

The trouble with this argument is that in practice the Human Rights Act has so far given precious little protection to people being sanctioned for anti-social behaviour either. It is one thing to have a right in theory, but another to find the judiciary willing to interpret he law so as to enforce a right in favour if either victim or perpetrator.

Another area where victims and those who bear witness for them deserve even more protection – and this means often literally physical protection – is in connection with courtroom evidence. The preceding pages have described the problem, which underlies the entire legal apparatus of the ASBO. It is now almost taken for granted in connection with anti-social behaviour that perpetrators will turn on anyone they can identify who gives evidence against them, to the extent that hearsay evidence has become the norm. Witness intimidation has long been a crime in criminal cases, and the Police Reform Act extends the same protection to civil case witnesses. It still takes a determined and sustained system to persuade witness to testify and to ensure their safety and that of their families and property both before and after the court case. Alarm links to the police station, mobile video cameras, and provision of mobile phones and fire-proof letter-boxes may all be necessary. Police and neighbourhood wardens can step up their presence. Safety in numbers is reassuring: the more people who can be persuaded to give evidence the better and they can be confidentially given each other's phone numbers to keep in contact. Fast-track injunctions can put restrictions on the perpetrator before and after the case. Unfortunately the higher the risk the more expensive the protection, so that it is not surprising that the alternative of hearsay evidence has become so popular.

Hunter, Nixon and Parr (2004) point out that witnesses in civil cases do not receive the support from victim and witness services that would be available to them in a criminal case, although they may be just as intimidated giving evidence for an eviction or injunction as for a prosecution. They argue that the full emotional and practical support network, before, during and after the case, should be available to these witnesses and victims too. Not surprisingly they found that fear of reprisals was the greatest barrier to testifying, especially considering the very local nature of cases involving anti-social behaviour, and that the experience of being a witness was often nothing but an ordeal which could have lasting ill-effects. Rather than simply treating every case individually, Hunter et al., see the way forward in building up confidence and cooperation within communities afflicted by bad behaviour (as has already been achieved in some places) – in other words, to foster the collective efficacy now much promoted as the long-term answer to most of the behaviour in question. It might be added that had witness protection been given the priority it deserves at a much earlier stage, the introduction of procedures that evade the normal rules of evidence might never have been necessary, and had civil law not been relied upon in place of criminal prosecution, witnesses to the bad behaviour of their neighbours would already be better served.

Notes

1 *The Economist*, 5 February 2005, reported the case of a prolific shoplifter in Cardiff. He received a normal month's custody for one offence, but the next one, for breaching an ASBO, received 18 months.
2 *Clingham* v. *Royal Borough of Kensington and Chelsea LBC; McCann* v. *Crown Court at Manchester* [2002] UKHL 39.
3 *Observer*, 4 July 2004.
4 This Act is amended in s. 12 of the Domestic Violence, Crime and Victims Act 2004, to permit a restraining order against harassment to be imposed after an acquittal.
5 Emphasis in original.
6 *The Guardian*, 7 September 1999.
7 Hansard, HOC, 25 January 2001, col. 718W.
8 [2004] EWCA Civ 312; [2004] 1 WLR 2298; [2004] 1 All ER 531.
9 {2003] EWCH 2385 (Admin) 9 October 2003.
10 [2004] EWCA Crim 287.
11 From a website tracking ASBO excesses: www.statewatch/org/asbo/ ASBOwatch.

12 *Guardian*, 30 January 2004.

13 Statewatch.

14. A long feature article by Fran Abrams in *The Guardian* of 16 March 2004 described the exclusionary effects of this type of order on a group of street-corner youths in Bootle, Merseyside.

15. *Guardian*, 7 December 2004. The boy could not read or write and was under permanent school exclusion. He was said to be notorious in the neighbourhood for arson, thieving and racial abuse.

16. For full statistics see Appendix 1.

17. EWHC 2220 (Admin) 7 October 2004.

18. [2002] EWMC 1129, applied by *K.* v. *Knowsley MBC* [2004] EWMC 1933; [2005] HLR 3.

19. *R (Stanley and Others)* v. *Metropolitan Police Commissioner* [2004] EWHC 2229 (Admin) 7 October 2004.

20. In *Harrow LBC* v. *G* [2004] EWHC 17 (QB) this principle was upheld. The sanction for the contempt of court involved in breaching an injunction is a fine or imprisonment. The 14-year-old in the case, as a minor, could not be imprisoned, nor could he be expected to have the funds to pay a substantial fine.

21. EWHC 1830 (Admin), 27 July 2004.

22. *Guardian*, 14 March 2000.

23. 27 March 2002.

24. *North Devon Homes* v. *Brazier* [2003] EWHC 574; [2003] HLR 59.

25. *Manchester City Council* v. *Romano and Samari* [2004] EWCA Civ 834; 18, 19 May, 29 June 2004.

26. *The Guardian*, 20 October and 10 November 2004.

27. It is relevant that over 80 per cent of Acceptable Behaviour Contracts in the London Borough of Islington were given to the children of families living in council property (Bullock and Jones, 2004).

28. [2003] EWHC 2272 (Admin).

29. [1999] 31 HLR; [2000] QB 123. Mr Hussain lived above his corner shop and was subject to gross racial harassment for years on end by local youths. Neither police or local authority took effective action. See Bright and Bakalis (2003) for discussion of the failure of nuisance law to provide a remedy, and further in this chapter, p. 111.

30. Cit. Padfield (2004a: 37).

31. Section 50, Police Reform Act 2002 states that anyone behaving in an anti-social manner must give their name and address to a police officer if asked.

32. [1998] 31 HLR 119.

33. [2000] 1 WLR 2259.

34. [2001] EWCA Civ 1248; [2002] 1 WLR 607.

35. See ODPM website: www.local-regions.odpm.gov.uk/byelaws/index.htm.

36. [2000] QB 1.

37. [1973] Ch 314.

38. This was successfully argued in the European Court of Human Rights against Valencia city council, Spain, in *Moreno-Gomez* v. *Spain*, App No 4143/02, 16.11.04. The case, which involved non-enforcement of noise control, is likely to have repercussions in the UK (Mitchell, 2005).

Chapter 6

Enforcement and problem-solving in the local context

In recent years local government has been put in the forefront of controlling bad behaviour through a combination of new obligations and new powers. On the one hand, primarily in their role as housing landlords, councils have moved into realms of enforcement far greater than those traditionally imparted through housing law, using a growing array of legal powers to bring perpetrators to heel. Ironically this has been happening at the same time as their part in the provision of social housing has been severely curtailed in favour of other providers.[1]

On the other hand local authorities have taken on quite new statutory duties with regard to crime prevention. Rather than hands-on powers, they have to work through and with others. Their job is that of coordinator, negotiator and opinion-seeker within the context of a multi-agency Crime and Disorder Reduction Partnership. These two quite different roles, that of enforcers and that of coordinators, do not always fit together smoothly. Each will now be considered in turn.

Crime control by local housing departments

As previous chapters have explained, council house managers during the 1980s became reluctant policemen in the face of increased crime and disorder on their estates, especially where job and population losses had destabilised communities and made it hard to fill empty properties.

The normal means of enforcement through tenancy conditions were considered insufficient and were significantly extended in the Housing Act 1996.

Among other things tenants were made answerable for the behaviour not only of themselves and other household members but for that of visitors who caused nuisance or annoyance or were convicted of arrestable offences committed in the dwelling or its 'locality'.[2] Grounds for repossession of the property were thus extended to include crimes which might have no connection with the property itself. If tenants or their visitors behaved violently or threatened violence to residents or others in the locality, injunctions with power of arrest could be obtained by the landlords. (Probably the first use of the term 'anti-social' in a statute occurs as the heading to Part V, Chapter III of the 1996 Act which contains this power.[3]) On top of all this, tenancy agreements became increasingly prescriptive concerning bad behaviour, including in some cases clauses seeking to extend prevention throughout the whole local authority area. Quite clearly, crime control was being built into housing law and practice in a far more general fashion than the traditional prohibitions against using the property for 'immoral or illegal purposes'.

Having started down this path, managers realised that they could not use injunctions against anyone under 18, yet young people were often blamed for aggressive nuisance behaviour. The alternative of evicting the entire family was sometimes applied, but was obviously unsatisfactory. They would either be judged 'intentionally homeless' and left to fend for themselves in the private sector or the council would have to rehouse them elsewhere. Hence, as has been shown in a previous chapter, the ASBO was created. These orders were also welcomed because they are not tenure-specific, and were seen as an answer to the problem created when, as is often the case, estates built for council tenants become peppered with owner occupiers and private landlords as the result of the right to buy.

Other owner-occupied or mixed tenure areas and rented housing run by housing associations and other registered social landlords (RSLs) can all potentially attract ASBOs where behaviour warrants it, and since 2002 RSLs have had the right to apply on their own behalf rather than going through the local authority or the police. Yet it is clear that the shrinking number of council estates remain the chief focus of the orders, and this is likely to be so because council housing departments can feed information directly to their own enforcers (Brown, 2004).

Dedicated anti-social behaviour units have been set up by many councils, but these tend to be located within housing departments, staffed by former housing managers sometimes jointly with police, so it is not surprising that their attention is largely drawn to behaviour on the council's own estates. Some of these units do work under contract for RSLs and in Manchester (there may be other examples) the enforcement team also works when requested in difficult mixed tenure areas. The Housing Act 2004, which provides for the licensing of private landlords, making them responsible for the bad behaviour of tenants, plunges councils into a wider enforcement role, previously only accessible through health and safety violations. With Whitehall approval areas affected by disorder and anti-social behaviour can be identified for this purpose.

All housing managers will say that enforcement – whether it be in the form of notices seeking possession (the first stage of eviction), eviction itself, injunctions or ASBOs – is at the end of a long line of warnings and other informal actions which deal satisfactorily with the vast majority of unwelcome behaviour. Mediation services, where available, are sometimes under contract to housing departments and RSLs to deal with neighbour disputes. Where these are caused by noise or other physical nuisances, the regulatory and enforcement powers of environmental health officers are available to any household. The range of other support from service providers is in theory at least quite varied, but many housing officers will say that they cannot rely upon it and do not place much faith in multi-agency approaches. More optimistic views are also to be heard, and local perceptions may well depend upon the degree of integration achieved within different crime and disorder partnerships. Enforcement units located within Neighbourhood Services rather than departments devoted exclusively to housing are more likely to see the merits of inter-agency working, and are more likely to extend enforcement into general public space.

Local authorities and crime prevention

Duties relating to crime prevention, previously embraced by some leading authorities and endorsed by the 1991 Morgan report (Home Office, 1991), became statutory in the Crime and Disorder Act 1998, ss. 5 and 6, which laid joint responsibility on councils and the police to cooperate with probation, health authorities and others in creating and implementing a crime and disorder reduction strategy for the local government area. To drive the message home that local authorities are now in the forefront of crime prevention, s. 17 of the Act lays a duty upon them to consider the effect in all their functions on crime and disorder and to do all they reasonably can to prevent these twin scourges. Housing allocations, planning decisions and liquor licensing are among the more obvious functions which should be affected.

Foster (2002: 190) is sceptical about local authorities' capability to deliver community safety, given their 'massive failings … in relation to public housing and quality of life in high crime areas', and given their subordinate relationship to the police in practical terms. But s. 17 offers creative possibilities when viewed holistically, and should open the way for socially inclusive policies that at the same time address underlying inequalities and malfunctions which feed directly into crime and disorder. It would suggest, for instance, the importance of focusing social support and youth services in deprived estates, and many other ways in which mainstream services might (and often try to) adopt priorities concerning social justice as well as efficiency. As Adam Edwards has pointed out (2002) the seminal Morgan Report made this linkage. Unfortunately the message has been blurred by the increasing emphasis on exclusion and enforcement which now dominates so much of the community safety agenda, and is anyway probably harder to deliver amidst the welter of performance targets governing service delivery.

Crime and Disorder Reduction Partnerships (CDRPs) are themselves not immune from the latter. The statute lays down a step-by-step process for partnerships to follow, involving objectives, performance targets and monitoring, thus ensuring that bureaucratic structures and managerialist systems are put in place to deal with supposedly concrete, measurable and, by implication, manageable local problems. CDRPs are required to publish their strategies, with objectives and performance targets, but they have no responsibility for managing the detail. They devise their own objectives but there is no guidance in the statute as to the type of problems to be addressed or how performance is to be measured. This absence was especially obvious when it came to strategies for dealing with anti-social behaviour. The only point of reference in the Act is that which describes behaviour in subjective terms as behaviour which causes, or is likely to cause, harassment, alarm or distress. Some authorities attempt to distinguish 'anti-social behaviour' from crime, a rather difficult exercise considering the large range of actions capable of being classified as criminal. Many merely adhere to the statutory definition.

It was expected that the mandatory audit of crime and disorder would throw up concerns which could then be translated into policy objectives to suit the needs of the local community. Research commissioned for the Office of the Deputy Prime Minister (ODPM), which holds the housing portfolio, found much confusion (Nixon et al., 2003: 6):

'Although 'disorder', 'youth nuisance' and 'anti-social behaviour' were often identified as priority themes in local Crime and

Disorder strategies there was lack of clarity as to what behaviours were being referred to. Indeed the terms 'crime', 'disorder', and 'anti-social behaviour' were frequently used interchangeably with respondents referring to a whole range of activity from low level nuisance to criminal behaviour under the umbrella term 'anti-social behaviour'. Any behaviour could be classed as anti-social depending on a number of factors, including the context in which it took place, the location, the tolerance levels of the local community and expectations about quality of life ... [I]t was rare to find a working definition which was shared by all members of a Partnership and which had permeated down from the central coordinating body to all strategic and operational levels.

By the same token different agencies operated different recording systems and it was unusual to find a centralised system for coordinating and analysing information and tracking cases.

Six years after the passing of the Crime and Disorder Act, the Home Office, through its Research, Development and Statistics Department, at last provided some practical guidance on defining, measuring and tracking anti-social behaviour (Home Office, 2004). It set out a typology based not on perceived reactions to behaviour, but on specific phenomena garnered from a survey of CDRPs, listed under the four headings: misuse of public space; disregard for community/personal well-being; acts directed at people; environmental damage (for detail see Chapters 1 and 5). It listed three types of data source – reports to service providers; incidents witnessed through street audits of, for example, abandoned cars, graffiti or begging; surveys of public perceptions – and gives advice on their use. This document could at last go some way towards resolving problems of disparate and poorly focused strategies.

A report on anti-social behaviour from the Social Exclusion Unit (SEU, 2000a) stressed the importance of specialist teams and dedicated officers to lead policy and coordinate action in this field. By November 2002 the Home Office found that 90 per cent of authorities had a named person in this role. Structures and job descriptions vary, but dealing with anti-social behaviour is now enshrined in municipal bureaucracies and provides a new career path in the town hall. This alone will ensure that more local government activities will be viewed and labelled as part of the same endeavour.

In contrast to the confused and overlapping parameters of anti-social behaviour within CDRPs, the enforcement arms of local authorities, often serviced by specialist legal teams, have much more clear-cut briefs and rules, and little obligation to consult other agencies when dealing with cases. For several years – often before the introduction of partnerships – many housing officers have worked closely with police at a neighbourhood level (Burney, 1999). Outside this sphere, operational partnership with local government is less likely to occur and the police will still pursue their own priorities, independently of other agencies potentially able to contribute to crime prevention (Edwards and Benyon, 2000), despite their statutory involvement with CDRPs.

The survey of 62 CDRPs by Nixon et al. (2003) confirmed that when it came to dealing with complaints about anti-social behaviour (however defined) police were seen as the main resource (identified by 97 per cent of respondents), followed by housing departments (74 per cent). The authors comment that

> [i]n developing operational responses to anti-social behaviour it was apparent that many CDRPs are still in their infancy ... and [they] had not yet developed methods of co-ordinating initiatives with action being taken by other relevant agencies such as mental health services, mediation schemes, youth services, drug and alcohol abuse schemes or neighbourhood warden schemes. (Nixon et al., 2001: 33)

Although the partnerships often reported formal membership of other statutory agencies, such as health, probation, housing and social services, that did not guarantee joint engagement: indeed some representatives never attended meetings. Case studies identified lack of support by senior management as a main cause of difficulties in multi-agency working (p. 71).

There are in any event significant cultural barriers to be overcome before people from different agencies share a common purpose in the field of crime prevention, although Crawford (1997) argues that even where tensions exist, practitioners can work round them to achieve common ends. But the power balance in multi-agency arrangements is always likely to be uneven, as discussed by Pearson et al. (1992). Inevitably the police, with their superior resources in terms of both information and personnel, and their ability to act quickly, are always likely to dominate (see also Foster, 2002).

Any hope that CDRPs will transcend their crime and disorder reduction role to address wider 'safety' and social justice concerns (Hughes, 2000) seems fairly remote if they cannot even enrol the more socially-oriented public services in the cause of alleviating anti-social behaviour. Initiatives such as resettlement and multi-agency support for difficult tenants come from social landlords rather than CDRPs (Nixon et al., 2001: p.117).

However, some matters of principle may gain recognition if incorporated into partnership strategies – the Milton Keynes commitment to mediation being an example (see below p. 138).

Such is the volume of the enforcement message being delivered from central government that it is not surprising if the problem-solving approach is often drowned out. Yet defining the nature of a problem must be a first step towards a solution. In a policing context the so-called SARA model (Scanning, Analysis, Response, Assessment) (Lea et al., 1996) has been adopted, and the Home Office research department has recommended this method for use by practitioners who want to reduce anti-social behaviour (Home Office, 2004). Agencies should first identify problems through scanning information sources, including electronic mapping; then analyse through hunches and IT sources; then plan a solution if possible and if necessary with the help of the community; and finally assess the result. While this by no means guarantees a solution that goes further than conventional enforcement, if applied in a multi-agency context there is more likelihood that social prevention methods will gain acceptance.

The Local Government Association (2004) is at odds with the government over its monotone enforcement message, and argues instead for 'sustainable solutions'. It highlights the many roles exercised by different departments, especially those involved with children and young people, in preventing bad behaviour. It admits to a problem of achieving a united focus when faced with a plethora of single issue initiatives introduced by Whitehall. Many examples are cited of local councils doing work that has a more direct bearing on behaviour improvement than mere enforcement – including some better known for the latter. The Borough of Camden has imposed more ASBOs than any other in London but it also runs a Families in Focus project which combines a range of educational and recreational activities in needy neighbourhoods with intensive individual work with children displaying problem behaviour and their families. In truth most authorities combine prevention and enforcement in varying degrees. Millie et al. (2005) found a mixed approach even in authorities where they had expected stronger contrasts at one end or the other of the enforcement/social prevention spectrum. It would need another book to describe the range of relevant projects – many of which, unfortunately, do not last beyond the initial funding stage.

Stenson (2002) has described the contrasts and conflicts of interest in matters of community safety within the large, mainly affluent Thames Valley police area. Hidden from general view is the segment of the population most adversely affected by changes in the farming and industrial economies, where deprivation and exclusion can be as bad as anywhere in Britain and whose needs are neglected when local politics are dominated by the concerns of the well-off. Their misbehaviour is likely to be seen by local councillors as a matter for enforcement only.

A countervailing influence is to be found in the work of the Thames Valley Partnership (TVP), a voluntary organisation promoting restorative and problem-solving methods to deal with anti-social behaviour. They are proactive throughout the region, promoting early intervention as essential, coupled with multi-agency solutions. Their 'Mending Fences' project aims to promote good practice among agencies in the Thames Valley CDRPs, aiming at 'greater awareness of the potential for mediation, conflict resolution and restorative justice techniques in making communities safer' (Hedge, 2002; TVP, 2004). One objective is that ASBOs should be a last resort and that there should be no significant increase in the use of legal orders or punitive sanctions in Thames Valley. Their pro-active approach is facilitated by the fact that the Thames Valley police force is a notable pioneer in the use of restorative justice – although there is room for argument about whether police officers themselves should be involved in community mediation.

Techniques such as those advocated by Thames Valley Partnership may be easier to 'sell' to the professionals involved in CDRPs than to the population at large or their elected representatives. Practitioners still complain that MPs and local councillors tend to think only in terms of the number of ASBOs imposed. Police officers dealing with troubled neighbourhoods often face community demands for far more extreme action than they would contemplate. Enforcement is an easier concept for people to grasp than negotiated solutions. One practitioner quoted by Nixon et al. (2003: 102) said: 'At residents' meetings that's all I ever hear about is "why isn't the borough doing more ASBOs?" and so I talk about ABCs and then they say "we don't want that soft crap, we want ASBOs".'

Talking to practitioners in the course of my own study, the question was put as to whether they felt that they were under political pressure to deliver particular kinds of action. Pressure from central government is evident, but locally the relationships between elected representatives and officers varies. One response indicated somewhat impatiently that practicalities made it impossible to accede to every demand from ward councillors to clear up graffiti. Another saw political pressure from councillors as a justified and democratic reflection of popular demand to deal with things like begging. There are still places, within the diminished world of local politics and power, where committed local leadership can make a difference to priorities on anti-social behaviour

– and these may be the places where government money is more likely to be attracted to fund those priorities. Kevin Stenson (2002: 114) has argued that determinist views of crime control as a uniform expression of late capitalism ignore the importance of local 'political agency, conflict, and choice'.

Different cultures in both police and local authorities underlie some very different approaches to issues of policy and enforcement in different areas. Practices and power centres strongly entrenched since before the existence of CDRPs continue to fuel the action. This is particularly the case in places where strong legal teams service housing departments and are practised in applying enforcement on their tenants. Manchester's is the most obvious example of an enforcement-driven policy, and it is a combination of keen senior policemen and keen local authority officers that has given Greater Manchester the dubious distinction of imposing by far the greatest number of ASBOs of any area in the country – 608 by end-September 2004, 67 per cent more than Greater London and between eight and nine times the 69 imposed in the Thames Valley police force area. Tony Blair, in electioneering mood after his summer holiday in 2004, urged other authorities to follow Manchester's example. Bill Pitt, Manchester's housing enforcer, was sent round the country by the Home Office to preach the gospel, with the somewhat ambiguous title of 'Anti-Social Behaviour Ambassador' – although there was nothing ambiguous about his performance as an advocate for enforcement.

In fact a great deal of the growth in ASBOs in Greater Manchester has been initiated by the police. Because the processing is done through the city's legal department, the hand of Greater Manchester constabulary is not visible. Two senior police officers who had worked the system in the city subsequently took up posts in other authorities within Greater Manchester where, finding that ASBOs were not being used, set about promoting them (personal information). At the same time the police were making use of the post-conviction ASBO facility which became available in December 2002. By September 2004 nearly 70 per cent of all Greater Manchester ASBOs had come from this source.

Manchester city's enforcement trend was evident soon after the Housing Act 1996 brought new powers to council landlords. Its 'Neighbour Nuisance Strategy Team' quickly made use of the strengthened facility for bringing injunctions against unruly tenants. While council tenants have therefore felt the full force of the law this has left large parts of the city untouched. Under a new initiative the services of the city's neighbour nuisance team have begun to be contracted to troubled mixed tenure neighbourhoods as well. The thousands of housing law injunctions obtained in council estates dwarf the city's much-publicised

ASBOs. Injunctions are favoured over evictions because the former does not involve displacing a family – with possible implications for social services if children are involved. It is recognised that eviction may simply shift the trouble elsewhere, often into the private rented sector where the council has little control. With this in mind, Manchester has one of the country's few intensive resettlement projects for families facing eviction, run by National Children's Homes.

Two places, two worlds

In order to illustrate in more detail how different CDRPs and their constituent agencies may vary in their approach to anti-social behaviour, some interviews were carried out in two contrasting urban authorities of fairly similar sized populations: Milton Keynes in Buckinghamshire, pop. 216,000 (within the Thames Valley police area), and the city of Nottingham, pop. 267,000. Both have the advantage, when it comes to multi-agency working, of being unitary authorities.

Nottingham is, of course, a historic city with a rich industrial past, now bearing the scars, and the emblems, of the shift from a manufacturing to a service economy. Milton Keynes is a prosperous new town in the booming south-east, with a young and growing population. Set out on a planned level grid, with segregated residential neighbourhoods and a vast central shopping mall, it is a bland contrast to the irregular, hilly, multi-faceted nature of Victorian Nottingham (which also, however, has its share of antiseptic central shopping malls). In both towns, the most concentrated disorder takes place around late-night bars and pubs at weekends, but there the likeness in behavioural terms ends. Despite its youthful population Milton Keynes has a low crime rate and little evidence of hard drug use. Nottingham has a reputation for violence, enhanced recently by drug-related gun crime. Crimes of violence against the person recorded in 2003/4 were, per head of population, nearly twice those of Milton Keynes. Domestic burglary rates were five times higher and car thefts per head of population more than twice as high.

Despite its prosperity, Milton Keynes does have pockets of deprivation, with a few wards reckoned among the 5 per cent most deprived in the country, containing the neighbourhoods most known for environmental mess, domestic violence and noise. Two of these neighbourhoods were the subject of a two-year experiment in neighbourhood policing (Singer, 2004) – see p. 128. Nottingham has much larger and more obvious areas of deprivation, mainly the neighbourhoods that historically have been known for poverty and disorder. Some estates built forty years ago to replace Victorian slums are now in such decay that they in turn are due for demolition.

Not surprisingly containment of anti-social behaviour has fallen to Nottingham council's housing managers, who for some years have forged a partnership with the police to control and survey the actions of tenants on the most deprived estates. Recently, however, in response to local political pressure and government encouragement, the focus of defining and combating anti-social behaviour has shifted beyond the housing neighbourhoods to environmental and social incivilities perceived in the city centre and the general public domain.

Enforcement is the response of first resort in terms of behaviour control in Nottingham. 'We've traditionally a reputation for going in hard', explained a senior housing officer. A specialist anti-social behaviour team was first set up in the housing department in 1994 and dealt essentially with the worst cases of endemic misbehaviour in council housing estates. It was later known as the 'Group Disorder Unit' (GDU) reflecting the growing concern over gang activity. Police officers working in a civilian capacity were seconded to the GDU. Less serious problems were dealt with in traditional ways by housing managers assisted by nine dedicated 'nuisance officers', one in each main housing office. By 2002 the central team had been joined by a roving task force, with a stronger police involvement, sent in to crack down on troublemakers on 'hot-spot' estates for six months at a time. In 2004 both were being replaced by four enlarged task force teams covering the four police command units within the city, plus another team dealing city-wide with prostitution. A housing official explained how police and housing worked together in the original team, in a graphic picture of the involvement of the housing department in crime control:

> The original task force was a mixture of police and housing. The idea was that the kind of things the police officers would do would vary, so it could be high visibility patrols or at the other end of the spectrum it could be covert surveillance. It could be community intelligence gathering. I know they executed a lot of warrants, made arrests. And then, from the housing department point of view, we would follow up with possession proceedings, injunctions, anti-social behaviour orders, whatever was appropriate … It was visibly joint working to the point where a housing officer will actually go on the raids – some of the drug raids etc. Get in there, take photographs of anything that was found. Then in a day or so, following the arrests being made, they'd have a notice seeking possession served.

One of the things that improved dramatically was the speed with which information could be shared between the police and civil officers. We've had a protocol since 1998, since section 115 of the Crime and Disorder Act ... but the speed of it was sometimes the delaying factor. Now what happened was the taskforce based here, and we actually had a PNC [Police National Computer] terminal here, so I could literally go to the sergeant and say 'have you got anything on this individual?' and within a matter of minutes ... he could give me information on that individual.

The four new teams were being generously manned, each with two police constables, two police community support officers, two 'anti-social behaviour officers' seconded to the police from housing, a community drugs worker and a detached youth work facility to serve all four areas. Close working with housing enforcement continued, but it became more of an overtly policing system. Home Office funding was covering most of this but for a limited period, after which it was assumed (if proved successful) that the system would be supported by mainstream budgets. These task forces, together with the housing department's nuisance officers, represent a very substantial resource for controlling crime and disorder on housing estates. It may be that the need for this is justified by the large drug-related gang and gun culture in the city, but it was evident from the discussion with a police sergeant on the current task force that much action is concerned with less serious youth crime and nuisance. New powers and opportunities available to the police in the shape of Anti-Social Behaviour Act 2003, S. 30 dispersal zones and the post-conviction ASBOs introduced in the Police Reform Act 2002, have been taken up with enthusiasm (see Chapter 5), and the focus is on targeting known individual troublemakers.

The task force was expected to remain on this site for six months, but the effects might not be expected to last long after its departure. It was admitted by police that a previous task-force location in Nottingham was already reverting to its former ways. Moreover, because the nuisance control by housing officers was confined to city-owned estates, there was no regular resource for dealing with trouble stemming from other households. Other social landlords lacked the means, and disorder from property owned by private landlords was a particular source of frustration. The housing department had no remit to spend its money dealing with any of this.

At the time of the research Nottingham was at the stage of trying to improve the working of the Crime and Disorder Reduction Partnership, coordinated from within the Neighbourhood Services department. The main thrust against anti-social behaviour was the tough 'Respect for Nottingham' campaign, a highly publicised effort to sweep environmental and human detritus from the streets. The plan states:

> The aim of the 'Respect for Nottingham' strategy is to clean up the City's streets, taking an uncompromising stand against begging, street prostitution and drug dealing and restore civic pride in the City. The strategy will demonstrate that Nottingham is not a soft touch for those bent on criminality and damaging the quality of life in the City.

Cleaning up the city is primarily a matter for better performance by the responsible council services, with enforcement as a by-product. Results are easier to demonstrate than for more complex and subjective aspects of anti-social behaviour. Dealing directly with personal behaviour may require more joint working across departments and a longer-term view on problem-solving. In Nottingham, shared solutions would have to bridge the divide between the two key directorates of Housing and Neighbourhood Services.

The latter department was beginning to develop a coordinating role with regard to problem behaviour outside the realm of council tenancies, where most of the action against anti-social behaviour by known individuals took place. The question of what tasks the new neighbourhood wardens should undertake and at whose behest had thrown up various interim arrangements between police and local authority services. On top of all this, nine area community safety working groups were being developed to help identify local problems and help work out solutions. Greater youth service provision was promised. The problem-solving approach would be unlikely to become the norm within the CDRP until a culture of joint working, such as was already being achieved in the city's Youth Inclusion and Support Project (YISP), was generally established. Meanwhile the enforcement culture, epitomised in the 'Respect for Nottingham' strategy and in the four new task forces set up to deal with problem estates, still supplied the strongest theme.

Given that crime and anti-social behaviour are often two sides of the same coin it is no surprise that behaviour control has a much higher profile in Nottingham than in Milton Keynes. This is evident both from the way that crime and disorder reduction strategies are presented and the manner in which they are carried out. Milton Keynes's community safety strategy for 2002–5 has five aims of which the first is 'To promote quality of life'. 'Reducing anti-social behaviour' comes within this stream, as does promoting neighbour mediation, good parenting and 'a culture of community living'. Reducing abandoned cars and vandalism – especially graffiti – are quality of life aims. Although vandalism is defined separately from anti-social behaviour, on the grounds that it is a criminal offence whereas the 'anti-social' label is supposedly applied to non-criminal incivilities, in practice the distinction is not maintained when it comes to an organised response. Complaints to the council of 'anti-social behaviour' in the years 1998–2001 were dominated by domestic noise, but dog fouling leapt up to second place after a publicity campaign. The aim of the strategy is to reduce repetition of the same anti-social behaviour.

The experiment in neighbourhood, or what is now termed 'reassurance', policing took place in two very deprived neighbourhoods and was a three-way enterprise between Milton Keynes council, the local parish councils and the police (Singer, 2004). The aims were to promote engagement with the public by police and civilian ancillaries employed by the parish, to improve feelings of safety and security among residents, and to increase satisfaction with and confidence in policing. The results were only moderately successful. For example, the outreach did significantly diminish fear amongst minority ethnic residents, but measures of general social cohesion, or 'collective efficacy' actually worsened – this was attributed to structural factors, notably in one neighbourhood with a high population turnover and a large number of houses in multiple occupation. Worries about drugs, drunkenness and teenagers were somewhat reduced. But despite the visibly improved environment following intensive clean-ups of rubbish and graffiti more people thought these were 'a very big problem' at the end of the two-year period. This surely illustrates the difficulty of achieving success against the shifting sands of public perceptions, which are likely to be enhanced rather than reduced by local campaigns such as this. It also provides a clear example of local improvement being hampered by structural and global influences, in so far as the multi-occupied houses were the result of market forces and their inhabitants included migrants of different origins.

Over the time of the project the importance attached to enforcement against anti-social behaviour moved up in popularity – 9 per cent put it top out of six priorities at the end of the period compared with 3 per cent at the beginning. Was this due to the activity around them or to political and media publicity on the subject? It still came a poor fourth to the constant first choice of around 30 per cent of respondents – more police on the beat.

Undeterred by the mixed messages from the neighbourhood experiment, Milton Keynes CDRP has continued to develop new structures. In what is regarded as an innovative development, a 'Safer Communities Unit' was set up in 2003 to manage the delivery of the aims relating to anti-social behaviour. This involves bringing together the work of departments dealing with the 'quality of life' environmental issues, overseeing the new community wardens and helping to refocus the work of housing management. Four police officers are seconded to the unit. The restorative justice techniques favoured by the Thames Valley force have been applied to offences which affect the community through actions such as vandalism and graffiti-spraying. One constable is a designated 'anti-social behaviour coordinator' – working with council employees to deal with troublesome behaviour as it emerges and sifting complaints through a three-tier system of referrals.

The first call is on the appropriate agency, be it housing, education welfare or environmental health. Mostly problems can be dealt with informally at this level. Failing this mediation may be called upon, notices seeking possession issued or acceptable behaviour contracts agreed. A joint visit between a uniformed police officer and the relevant agency official is often effective. Only if the problem remains unsolved does it come before an 'Anti-Social Behaviour Team', a group of representatives from all relevant services who meet monthly and consider cases that have not been resolved at a lower level. Using their joint knowledge and resources they devise a response which may or may not be punitive.

Originally called the 'ASBO team' this group has developed in ways which involve problem-solving more than anti-social behaviour orders. Interviewees from the group unanimously declared that the orders were regarded negatively, even if sometimes necessary:

> Personally, I think of an ASBO as a bit of a failure. It's a failure of all the other interventions really. I don't class it as a feather in the cap. The only good thing is that we have received some quite positive press coverage. (Police officer, coordinating ASB group)

At the time of the research in Milton Keynes in spring 2004, a total of seven ASBOs had been imposed since 1999, only one of which was on a minor. Six months later the number of orders had doubled, suggesting that, despite its professed unpopularity, the ASBO was occasionally recognised as a convenient tool for excising chronic bad behaviour. It was pointed out that whereas exclusionary Housing Act 1996 injunctions require an element of violence or threat and were rarely used in Milton Keynes (it was thought that the amended version of injunctions provided in the Anti-social Behaviour Act 2003 might be more useful) ASBOs can be used without any violence requirement. The increase in ASBOs was chiefly generated through the council's housing department, where reorganisation had recently placed more responsibility for dealing with nuisance behaviour with estate management teams, although their main aim was stated to be early intervention to prevent situations becoming unmanageable. A council lawyer suggested that a measure of success should not be the number of ASBOs obtained, but the number prevented through effective action.

The ASB group is composed of senior officers, including representatives from environmental services, educational welfare, children's services, health and the legal department – though not all were regular attenders. The relationship with the Youth Offending Team was unclear and sometimes fraught. The YOT manager was outvoted in one case where he opposed an ASBO on a boy, but in another case YOT workers successfully headed off a potential ASBO and obtained a referral order instead.

Most interviewees spoke very positively about the usefulness of a group with several different perspectives being able to consider problem cases jointly.

> What I've found with the group is really useful is that maybe we have a family where we're really concerned, there's all these things going on and we're trying to effect a change and not effecting a change and then all of a sudden somebody else comes along and says well actually this and this ... It gives it a fuller picture ... it's more helpful 'cos it helps you to plan ...
>
> A case will come up and everybody will be asked if they have any information and we'll talk around issues, maybe I've got an educational issues, they're not atttending, maybe their behaviour is poor in school ... There might be housing issues, there might be environmental health issues and then we talk around what's the best way to address this and it might be Dave issuing an ABC. (Education welfare officer)

At the time of the research social landlords outside the council-run sector (representing 6 per cent of households) were not well integrated into the anti-social behaviour strategy but their formal involvement was being planned and expected to bump up the caseload. Owner occupiers might be under-represented as complainants for different reasons. One official explained how a mixed tenure close (typical of many housing areas in the town) was plagued by rowdy and offending behaviour late at night but no house-owners made official complaints because of the fear of the potential effect on the sale of their properties when the problem might have to be revealed.

On council estates the emphasis on managing 'quality of life' rather than just repairs and arrears was a new departure. The presence of community wardens in the most disorderly neighbourhoods was also a new feature. In addition the police officer coordinating anti-social behaviour referrals was heavily engaged on the ground, helping estate managers to prevent problems escalating.

> Prior to my coming into post and for those initial few months the referrals I was receiving had been problems that had been going on for months and months, sometimes even years where things had been developing and no real intervention had been tried. And it takes an awful lot of manpower, an awful lot of time, to get people out of an entrenched attitude. Now I'm trying to get in at a very early stage and get everyone to identify problems or potential problems, so we can use earlier and earlier intervention. Such as even literally a joint visit between a housing officer and a police officer can send a powerful message that can stop the behaviour ...
>
> [Or] I send out a series of warning letters and they go on Thames Valley headed paper and it goes out in conjunction with [letters from] Milton Keynes Town Housing or the social registered landlord. [And] Acceptable Behaviour Contracts: they do work. I was very sceptical about two pieces of paper actually solving a problem but we've used them for youths and adults alike. We've had a couple of breaches. But those breaches have subsequently gone on to add evidence for eviction proceedings and an anti-social behaviour order.

The officer was asked about how he dealt with groups of youths causing problems. He cited an example where a group had been hanging around a shop, being rowdy, lighting bits of paper and throwing them about, putting off elderly customers and being abusive and threatening damage when shop staff asked them to move on. Having got names and addresses from area beat officers he then sent headed letters out to parents.

> Fifteen letters went out and fifteen irate parents phoned me up saying it couldn't be my son or daughter, and after speaking to them fifteen children were grounded. So that is obviously a very low intervention but it solves a problem ... You've got to have an element of parental responsibility ... It was one of the nicer areas of Milton Keynes. Unlike other letters I've sent out to other areas and get no reaction whatsoever.

Some parents welcome the boost to discipline imposed by outside authority, as was evident from the account given by a senior environmental health officer. He sometimes became involved with restorative cautioning and referral orders dealing with young people responsible for damage or graffiti, and evidently appreciated this unusual aspect of his work.

> It gives me a very good chance to say in a formal situation what the problems caused by the action of an individual is on the community in general. I find them extremely useful. They're a good sort of learning curve for me and I hope they're a positive thing for the offender, because it gives us as the council to have a chance to have a say in what sort of reparations that person's got to do ... I've had some quite positive response. Especially funnily enough more from the parents than the children involved.

An example of parental enthusiasm for punishment was shown in the case of three 12- and 13-year-olds caught 'tagging' the bus station. On top of a restorative justice conference and a police caution they were required do some street cleaning – an outcome viewed as highly successful although the description suggests that proportionality was not a concern:

> The punishment was actually suggested by one of the children's fathers. I was a bit concerned about health and safety issues but the parents of the three assured me that they would supervise and everything would be done ... We supplied them with the health and safety gear and the brushes and gloves ... I think what made it worse for the three offenders was that the parents insisted that they do the street sweeping and litter picking in the area where they lived. So all their peers would see them. It was done on a Saturday morning so they missed all their Saturday morning television and swimming lessons and football training and everything else and it was a great success.

Nottingham's strategy for reducing crime and disorder includes an anti-social behaviour stream which specifically sets out to target known individuals. Kerb-crawlers and city-centre beggars are also in the frame. Cleaning streets and dealing with graffiti and damage are intended to reduce fear of crime and increase a sense of community. Therefore, although these environmental aims are similar to those in Milton Keynes, the more personalised approach to the concept of anti-social behaviour is rather different. The overall aim is to reduce incidents of anti-social behaviour by 3 per cent a year from a 2002/3 baseline but the hugely disparate range of environmental and personal incivilities involved renders comparisons problematic, to say the least. The Milton Keynes aim of reducing repeat incidents is somewhat more focused – although still posing problems of reporting and measurement.

Despite the many contrasts, there are a number of likenesses in the actions of the two CDRPs in relation to anti-social behaviour. Unexpectedly one of these is lack of enthusiasm for ASBOs. In Milton Keynes this stems from a strong preference for problem-solving over enforcement – although this did not prevent a jump in the number of orders imposed during 2004. Nottingham, for all its reputation for toughness, has not gone down the ASBO route to any great extent. The explanation appeared to be twofold. In 1999 Nottingham was the first authority to give an order to a 13-year-old. The case gained national publicity, not least because of the defiant attitude displayed by the boy who was already a persistent offender. Soon he was in custody for breach of the ASBO and other offences, and his criminal career continued thereafter. It was generally acknowledged that the ASBO had if anything made him worse. There have been very few ASBOs on juveniles in Nottingham since then. However, more recently the police in Nottingham have taken the initiative in the use of post-conviction ASBOs for adults and youths.

The city has made little use of Acceptable Behaviour Contracts (ABCs) for young people either. However, it pioneered the Youth Inclusion and Support Programme (YISP), a multi-agency method of short-term intervention with youngsters seen as at risk of becoming offenders, run by the Youth Offending Team. For this purpose the YOT works closely with the Anti-Social Behaviour team in the housing department, receiving referrals from them as well as from schools, youth workers and police. There can be a culture clash, in that the YISP is firmly a voluntary engagement, not seen as part of the enforcement effort. Unlike an ABC, failure carries no punitive consequences.

As far as adult misbehaviour is concerned, the city's housing lawyers have long favoured the use of injunctions over evictions and ASBOs. These are seen as cheap, quick and effective. In mid-2004 a housing official reckoned that they had used around 400 Housing Act injunctions compared with about 90 evictions and only 25 ASBOs (apart from those obtained by police).[4] The city made legal history when it used a combination of an injunction under s. 222 Local Government Act 1972, and s. 130 of the Highways Act 1980, to ban a drug dealer from an estate.[5] The s. 22 injunction (which empowers the local authority to act for the good of the population in its area) was later employed against beggars and soliciting prostitutes, although some of these received police-initiated ASBOs instead.

Another similarity found in the two CDRPs was enthusiasm for environmental enforcement, assisted by the greater powers and financial incentives in the Anti-Social Behaviour Act 2003. The senior officer in charge of that department in Milton Keynes saw the work as an important response to public demand that also had wider social effects:

It's become much more a sort of environmental quality issue, and an anti-social behaviour thing rather than just purely the waste issue it used to be.

[*Interviewer*] Why do you think that is?

I think that people in general are becoming much more aware of the environment they live in, and in consequence they are demanding that local authorities and others actually do more to improve the quality of life for them and their neighbours ... There are some areas where the work that's been done has been most obvious in the sort of improvement in the appearance of the estate in general, the general quality of life of the residents ... and consequently there's the lessening of anti-social behaviour ... I am convinced that it does have a sort of knock-on effect because for example if you remove graffiti and improve street lighting or something like that, then the residents of an area are less affected by, not necessarily crime per se, but the fear of crime ...

Litter, graffiti and abandoned cars were being targeted alongside the anti-social behaviour strategy. It was acknowledged that fixed penalty enforcement had become much keener since the change in the law allowing local government to keep the proceeds. Milton Keynes was runner-up in a national prize for innovation for its very effective method of dealing with abandoned cars, which are cleared away within 12 hours of the expiry of the warning notice. Graffiti pose a tougher problem, as the cleaning teams cannot get everywhere fast enough, but some new approaches have been tried with perpetrators, including restorative justice and reparation, as described above. Local campaigns to report known graffiti offenders are run from time to time through the voluntary organisation Crime Concern, a technique also applied in Nottingham. The introduction of neighbourhood wardens was expected to keep a check on these and other incivilities – although likely to stimulate an increase in complaints. The wardens have no enforcement powers and act rather as caretakers. They are supposed to alert the authorities to litter or graffiti and keep an eye out for bad behaviour – passing an informal word with children or parents and warning housing managers or police if necessary. This compares with the rather more hard-edged profile of Nottingham's neighbourhood wardens, who can issue fixed penalty notices for litter or dog-fouling, demand the removal of abandoned cars, move on beggars, patrol with an eye to discouraging drug dealing and confiscate alcohol and cigarettes from children.

In Nottingham, keen political leadership helps to drive the enforced clean-up campaign. Planning was based on a telephone survey of 1,000 households from which priorities were drawn (repeated every six months with a different random sample, to monitor changed perceptions). Only a few people complained of beggars and drunks in their own neighbourhoods but many more thought they were a problem in the city as a whole. By combining answers that described begging as a 'large-scale' problem with those that described it as only small scale, it came top of the priorities which shaped the 'Respect for Nottingham' strategy. Surveys like this always pose the dilemma – what is more important, things that bother a lot of people a little or a few people a great deal? And is a problem seen as affecting the city in general more or less important than one affecting people in their local areas? On the whole, people generalise more readily when asked about problems in the city as a whole, but are likely to be more precise about their own neighbourhoods.

In the survey of March 2004, noisy neighbours and loud parties were a large problem for only 5 per cent of Nottingham people in their local area, but these may have included some very acute cases. Drug misuse and drug dealing were described as large local problems for one-fifth of respondents. Over half thought these were large-scale problems in the city as a whole, and increasing. One of the biggest local problems, perceived as large by 29 per cent, was speeding vehicles and 'boy racers' – youths tearing about in cheap old cars or stolen vehicles – a new phenomenon since the original strategy was devised. About the same proportion of people saw litter as large local problem – but how does this compare qualitatively with some of the 27 other, extremely varied, personal and environmental phenomena all listed under 'anti-social behaviour'? Perhaps a better guide is the breakdown by neighbourhood, where policy-makers might decide to concentrate on those areas that score high on a few key indicators. The nine new community safety panels being set up across the city ought to help determine priorities as perceived by residents in their own localities.

Nottingham's beggars were reckoned by the authorities to be largely hard-drug addicts. Individuals were offered assistance through multi-agency case conferences and efforts were made by the Drug Action

Team to engage them in treatment. A few persistent beggars under injunctions or ASBOs continued to breach the orders and were briefly imprisoned. Most just disappeared, no doubt to friendlier places. Following complaints, a challenge was mounted through the Advertising Standards Authority against the poster proclaiming that 90 per cent of money given to beggars went to drug dealers. After competing evidence was considered the challenge was upheld, though the leader of the city council remained defiant, claiming that whatever the exact percentage most of the money was spent on drugs.[6] Meanwhile the focus of the 'Respect for Nottingham' campaign had moved on and the posters in the city centre changed to messages reminding people of the potentially heavy fines for dropping litter. Regular surveys are done of street activities in the city centre with a view to protecting the public from what might be unwelcome advances or spectacles.

Witnesses and evidence

At the heavy end of neighbourhood nuisance, practitioners in both Milton Keynes and Nottingham said fear of being a witness was easily the greatest problem and welcomed the facility for civil procedures using professional witnesses as a way round this obstacle. Courts vary in their readiness to rely upon indirect statements and this affects the way cases are presented. In neither city did officers favour the use of hearsay evidence alone to gain a civil order.

> You have to have absolutely clear evidence to show that those events occurred. So you really need, not hearsay, you need to come along and say 'I saw him do that'. And my biggest problem is that when you get an individual on an estate everybody knows, any time anything happens, he is blamed without anyone actually seeing the person do it ... Hearsay helps for background, but you still need someone to get up and say that I've seen one event. I mean you could do it all on the basis of hearsay, serve them notices and if they don't object you're there, but in terms of actual evidence before I proceed I wouldn't go purely on hearsay. I don't think it's fair ...
>
> In terms of the noise nuisance element I can have environmental health there with tape recordings. Or a police officer who's just come to the scene and music, come up in the lift and he can still hear the same music going ... it's how you construct it but you don't always need a victim, there are other ways of doing it. But when you've got someone in court, the victim ... to the bench they come across because they're the ones affected by it ...

A lot of times when people do a witness statement and they say at the bottom they're willing to attend court but then when the crunch comes down to it say they don't want to … In those sort of instances I've got a housing officer to say 'well I've looked at the file for this particular person, there are a number of complaints, people have given me evidence but are unwilling to come forward'.

I think that quite a reasonable thing to say, it's quite right. They don't need to give any more evidence as what happened, it is all hearsay but they can say 'This is the situation'. So, you know, there are always ways around it, it's just that it would be better to have people directly affected. (Legal officer, Milton Keynes)

Similar scenarios were recounted in Nottingham by a housing spokesperson:

We would normally use hearsay to supplement other evidence. It's more like a scale tipping. I'd be very surprised if we ever went to court purely on hearsay.

[*Interviewer*] How do you define a professional witness and what do they do?

It could be me, or a member of my team … It could be a police officer, it could be a neighbourhood warden doing a patrol. It could be a private investigator that we employ to sit in a house five days solid and film everything that happens through the security grille … I think this year we've already had about three. But they don't come cheap.

We've also got a lot of street CCTV so that yields good evidence as well … And it's surprising how once people get used to the cameras being in the street they will behave in an anti-social way in front of the cameras.

[*Interviewer*] Apart from the private investigator with this very concrete visual evidence, do you simply make statements about what you've heard from the victim?

No … we class that as a hearsay statement, but we wouldn't class that necessarily as being a professional witness, although technically I suppose it is. We tend to do more of our own surveillance operations, but not for as long as the private investigators. We probably go in for an evening or whatever and film … we do use hearsay, but to a limited extent.

It was also remarked in Nottingham that the fear that prevented people going to court as witnesses might well be justified during the criminal justice process, but that it was rare for a witness to suffer reprisals after the case was over. There were a number of support measures on offer, in terms of better house security such as fire-proof letter-boxes, security locks and panic alarms, together with personal contacts and court escorts. A council tenant witness – but not anyone from another tenure – could if necessary be relocated. An injunction could provide temporary protection during a lengthy repossession process, and it was now possible to obtain an ASBO on eviction to prevent the former tenant returning to the same area.

For purposes of civil enforcement, officers in both towns needed to get the courts on their side. Early on with new noise legislation magistrates in Milton Keynes became more willing to take bad cases seriously after some training on the issue from the environmental health department. They were said to be supportive of anti-social behaviour orders but it was suggested that their attitude might change if too many were applied for. Interim ASBOs were particularly easy to obtain, as they do not require the perpetrator to be present and can be slotted quickly into proceedings at short notice. Nottingham's lawyers had clashed with the magistrates' court over the requirements for ASBOs, only settled in their favour after 'clarification' had been obtained from the Home Office and the Lord Chancellor. On the other hand Nottingham police seem to have found little difficulty in obtaining post-conviction ASBOs when they wanted them.

The role of mediation

Mediation is still the poor relation – financially and in terms of influence – among agencies concerned with anti-social behaviour. As Crawford (1997: 128–130) describes, community mediation schemes are totally dependent on their sources of referral. Many have contracts with social housing providers but have no other regular source of referrals – or may need to steer clear of inappropriate 'dumping' of cases by the police. Neighbour noise and clashes over children's behaviour are often well suited to mediation and, as Dignan et al. (1996) show, can be resolved cost-effectively compared with legal remedies. But the availability and quality of mediation services throughout the country is very varied.

Milton Keynes is unusual in placing mediation at the heart of its strategy for anti-social behaviour. The local scheme has a high profile and strong leadership. It is said to achieve agreement between both parties in over 70 per cent of referrals. Noise and children's behaviour provide the bulk of neighbour disagreements successfully dealt with.

Much depends on getting appropriate referrals. Mediation is generally regarded as unsuitable where problems of mental health or alcoholism are involved (Brown et al., 2003). And there may be no point in trying mediation if a disagreement has become too deep, or one or other party sees themselves as victims. Practitioners in Milton Keynes came up against this problem, or had to deal with cases where mediation agreements had broken down:

> We send out a noise pack which says you've made an allegation of noise nuisance, have you considered mediation? … People don't like to use it. Much to our frustration because they feel they've been wronged and they don't see why they should give ground to the perpetrator. (Environmental health officer)

> It has to be a willingness by both parties and in a lot of cases that's just gone out of the window … At the [anti-social behaviour] group we actually ask has mediation been tried and normally the person who's referred it will be able to say well we did try it last year and obviously it worked up to a point and then things have broken down again sort of thing. But the key to the whole thing is getting in there early. And anything you can do to make that happen has got to be for the good. (Legal officer)

Nottingham also has an active mediation service, but without a strategic role in prevention of crime and disorder. Contracted to the city housing department, over half its users are council tenants, although 39 per cent of referrals come from a range of other sources. A growing minority of users are owner occupiers or tenants of housing associations. The Milton Keynes service has a more mixed range of clients but still 44 per cent are council tenants, although this group forms only 14 per cent of households. Nottingham Mediation Service deals with only about half the number of referrals handled by Milton Keynes, possibly reflecting its more marginal status in a culture where enforcement is prioritised. By its own reckoning it also has a much lower success rate. On the other hand it may have more difficult cases – certainly a higher proportion of its disputes involve harassment, abuse and threats. A key to 'success' must lie in the type of case chosen for referral, and that depends upon the awareness of referring agencies (see Chapter 7).

Both schemes agree on the vital importance of getting in early, before formal steps have been taken by official agencies. The practice of encouraging complainants to keep diaries of incidents, often encouraged by police and council officers, is seen as unhelpful as it builds up a sense of victimhood inimical to mediation. However, there are plenty of examples of situations where one side is indeed the injured party, and where the neutral stance of mediators does not fit very easily (Brown et al., 2003).

Discussion

It is clear from the two study areas that a 'one size fits all' approach when dealing with bad behaviour through legal and administrative remedies is not sustainable. Given the lack of consensus as to what the term 'anti-social behaviour' means in practice, it comes down to local responses to local problems. In the case of Nottingham, this means a focus primarily on activities that are clearly criminal, but also on street disorder such as begging and prostitution. In Milton Keynes, with its much lower crime rate, 'quality of life' is central to the strategy rather than ancillary to crime control, and enforcement is approached in a more circumspect way.

Environmental 'clean-ups' have gained favour in both authorities, and despite contrasting rhetoric there is similar enthusiasm for tasks which yield visible results and are geared to meeting public demand. For longer-term results, Milton Keynes places more emphasis on social education, including the use of restorative justice techniques to reduce graffiti. Nottingham remains in the enforcement camp in this as in many other ways. In November 2004 it was chosen as one of the government's showpiece authorities for yet another initiative: find 50 examples of anti-social behaviour in your area and show how you have dealt with them (an exercise which seems to treat local councils like competing school-children).

Perhaps the recent enthusiasm for dealing with environmental mess under the guise of anti-social behaviour and community safety has partly been generated by local authority managers who see enhanced importance for a traditional local authority role. It is no new discovery that the community safety agenda has been often dominated by police, with local authorities as unequal partners. Foster, for example (2002:190) remarks that:

> It is an interesting irony that while the inclusion of local authorities in the community safety framework was intended to broaden accountabilities, in practice the local authorities have generally allowed their community safety strategies to be directed by the police (who have presented themselves as 'experts' and many of

whom feel deeply defensive about the possibility of some of their responsibilities being wrested from them).

In the two CDRPs described in this chapter, there were clear examples of the extent to which the police have penetrated the activities of local government through the field of behaviour control and the different forms their influence takes. This is encouraged by 'Partnership' arrangements but may develop independently. In Nottingham the well-established connection with housing officials to control criminal and quasi-criminal activities on council estates has evolved into a firefighting 'Task Force' format in which police are clearly in charge and have a range of new powers which they can exercise independently, notably within 'dispersal zones' and at the point of conviction when they can obtain ASBOs on offenders over whom they still want to exercise control.

Milton Keynes is within the Thames Valley police force area and some initiatives take their tone from the restorative justice culture uniquely developed within that force. Problem-solving as opposed to fire-fighting was at the core of the Reassurance Policing effort, an approach which embodies the idea of cooperative working with local councils. Subsequently police officers have been seconded to work within the department dedicated to delivering the targets of a community safety strategy couched in terms of quality of life. A police constable allocated to reducing anti-social behaviour sees it as his job to help housing officers nip nuisance behaviour in the bud, although he also helps to provide evidence for tough enforcement measures. It is he who decides which cases go forward each month for discussion by the multi-agency anti-social behaviour team, filtering and prioritising so that the group is not given more than it has time for. However helpful his role – and there is a limit to what one officer can cover – it does symbolise the extent to which a mild version of policing can in its way become as firmly woven into local government action as that of officers, such as those in Nottingham, dedicated to crime control on tough housing estates.

Notes

1 Local authorities owned 11 per cent of dwellings in England and Wales in 2003; other social landlords owned 7 per cent and owner occupiers 71 per cent.
2 The case of *Manchester City Council* v. *Lawler* [1998] interpreted locality to extend to streets outside the perimeter of an estate.
3 Sections 152 and 153, containing the injunctive powers, were significantly altered in the Anti-Social Behaviour Act 2003, s. 13. p. 108).

4 By 30 September 2004 Nottinghamshire magistrates had imposed 67 ASBOs of which 30 were issued following criminal convictions (separate figures for Nottingham City are not given). The Crown court had issued a further 9 on conviction.

5 *Nottingham City Council* v. *M.Z. (a minor)* (2001) EWCA Civ. 1248. Although the offender was 17 years old, and therefore a minor, it was ruled permissible to use an injunction against him because he was a persistent offender and anyway approaching his eighteenth birthday.

6 *Inside Housing*, 10 October 2004.

Chapter 7

Cultures of control – a European dimension

Exercises in comparative criminology are relatively rare, especially in the European context. David Nelken (2002) has indicated the difficulties of understanding and explanation, even in a seemingly straightforward area like policy research. There is no field unaffected by the specifics of history, culture, legal tradition and politics. Similarities in such things, as well as a common language, have meant that both comparisons and policy borrowings have flowed abundantly from west to east between America and Britain, with further influences from other parts of the Anglo-Saxon world, especially Australia and New Zealand (Jones and Newburn, 2002). Recently, observers have perceived some harsher aspects of crime control associated with 'the Anglo-Saxon model' penetrating European jurisdictions, usually in conjunction with a rightward political drift (van Swaaningen, 1997, 2005; Tham, 2001; Nelken, 2002).

Earlier chapters in this book have noted some strong American influences in the British Labour government's focus on anti-social behaviour and some of the associated policies. The amorphous and ill-defined nature of the problem has also been highlighted. It might therefore seem especially difficult to make it the subject of any comparative policy research in other western European countries. Yet the relevance is encapsulated in a document published by the European Commission (Commission of the European Communities, 2000) entitled *The prevention of crime in the European Union – Reflections on common guidelines and proposals for*

Community financial support. A definition of crime includes not only 'offences defined as such in national criminal laws' but also 'anti-social conduct which, without necessarily being a criminal offence, can by its cumulative effect generate a climate of tension and insecurity' (p. 4).

A critic (Hornqvist, 2004) points out that the EU Council of Ministers had decided in 2001 that crime prevention was to include measures to reduce citizens' feelings of insecurity and that this standpoint justifies combating public order without resort to criminal justice. In the cause of 'security', he argues, '[t]he law has been ruptured in two directions simultaneously: upwards, through the erasure of the line between crimes and acts of war [in the wake of 9/11]; downwards through the same thing having happened to the line between criminal offences and minor public order disturbances' (p. 5).

Insecurity and risk awareness are also themes running through earlier chapters of this book, both as a feature of modern western society generally, as theorised by Giddens (1990) and Garland (2001) among others, and as a mark of widely differing experiences and attitudes in different localities. While government policies are increasingly concerned to reduce people's sense of insecurity, the roots of such feelings are widely diffused and culturally determined, in ways which may make them vulnerable to manipulation (Crawford, 2002). Levels of insecurity vary greatly across place and social groups but the extent to which different communities and individuals suffer, or not, from insecurity are lost within systems uniformly designed for the 'risk society' and what has been described as 'the safety utopia' (Boutellier, 2004). Local differences suggest that economic and welfare infrastructure are vital elements in the maintenance of trust and feelings of security.

A case in point is the city of Vienna. As part of an EU-funded research project on 'Insecurities in European Cities', which looked at Amsterdam, Budapest, Hamburg, Krakow and Vienna, the Austrian capital seemed to buck the trend towards awareness of living in a risky or insecure society (Sessar et al., 2004; Hanak, 2004). Despite rising crime rates, levels of fear were low (though higher among women) and even some (moderately) disorderly neighbourhoods did not evoke in residents a sense of moral decline. People were not particularly neighbourly but reported a sense of trust in the local institutions providing housing, health care, welfare and urban infrastructure. Though foreigners were sometimes blamed for crime, the xenophobia evident in Austrian political life was not expressed by Viennese respondents, and the significant changes at national level with the breakdown of consensus politics and the intrusion of global influences had not affected the citizens' sense of living in a comparatively safe society. Viennese 'exceptionalism' may not, of course, remain unchanged but for the time being a rather old-fashioned contentment seems to prevail, resting on old-fashioned consensus and public services.

The extreme opposite of Vienna on the various measures of insecurity was Krakow, probably reflecting the degree of change experienced in Poland following the collapse of communism. The survey concluded that insecurity was created by much wider influences than perceptions of local crime and disorder, although these also counted. It looked closely at the relationship between fear of crime and the presence of large numbers of minority ethnic residents. The study of neighbourhoods in Amsterdam and Hamburg showed that the fears of indigenous residents were high where poorly integrated minorities (Moroccans and Turks) were present, compared with better integrated groups:

> It is much less the concentration of migrants which makes the native residents insecure or fearful; it is rather an interplay between the concentration of poorly integrated and very often marginalised ethnic groups who thus appear as a threat to the native population in the respective districts. (Sessor et al., 2004: 106)

Vienna does not suffer from marked socio-economic polarisation of neighbourhoods, which is another part of its difference with many other cities. Paul Wiles (1999), in a paper presented to an international conference on Public Safety in Europe, spoke about 'troubled neighbourhoods'. He defined these as places where socially deprived groups were geographically concentrated to the extent that the neighbourhood becomes socially excluded and reliant on the black economy and where crime flourishes (often organised through family groups) and wider norms of social control are challenged or ignored. Such areas become impacted high-crime locations within nationally receding crime statistics. He suggested that these conditions were present in western European cities but that comparative research was lacking. Since then, Sophie Body-Gendrot (2000) has published her book contrasting styles of control in turbulent city neighbourhoods in America and France. She shows the vital differences arising from political cultures and institutions.

Clearly France is not alone in western Europe in its 'troubled neighbourhoods' where social exclusion is strongly associated with minority ethnicity. In the Netherlands, as the survey referred to above indicates, there are significant concentrations of visible and marginalised minority groups in the main cities, and even Stockholm has developed similar patterns of settlement as the indigenous population has deserted the large peripheral housing blocks built in the 1960s.

I decided to go to Holland and Sweden to get some idea of the perception and treatment of what in Britain is known as anti-social behaviour. The two countries currently have different political climates, Holland having acquired a much more right-wing and overtly xenophobic slant and Sweden maintaining a centrist position, though with modification of its liberal welfarist traditions. Viewed from England, however, both countries appear substantially welfare-oriented. This affects the way that troublesome people are dealt with.

As time was very limited, interviews (15 in number) were largely confined to practitioners, municipal officials, civil servants and police. Official and academic publications filled in some of the gaps – in particular I am grateful for the critical insights of Rene van Swaaningen (2004, 2005) whose wide-ranging analysis of recent Dutch trends extended my understanding of some of my own observations. The aim was to find out how far interpretations of insecurity had penetrated policy formation and what the legal and institutional arrangements were for dealing with incivilities and disorder. In one Amsterdam neighbourhood a closer investigation of the institutions of social control was undertaken. Specific types of disorder – unruly youths, neighbour disputes, manifestations of street disorder such as begging, drug dealing and prostitution – were used to provide examples of official or semi-official intervention.

Populist politics and public safety in the Netherlands

It is well-known that the assassination of the populist politician Pim Fortuyn in May 2002 marked a turning point in Dutch politics, leading to the election of a right-wing coalition with Fortuyn's party as the second largest. Fortuyn had taken the lid off some simmering discontents which seemed to validate a more politicised and tougher line against crime and nuisance. Indeed, well before 2002 it had been acknowledged in official circles that the criminal justice system was in disarray and informal social control had broken down (Downes, 1988) and at first this took the line of social programmes as a means of local prevention. But soon neo-liberal ideology emerged and actuarial techniques of crime control were adopted, with penalties matched to risk-profiles (van Swaaningen, 1997: 177). The 'responsibilisation' strategy was adopted in the Ministry of Justice, which demanded that all relevant agencies should play their part in crime control (Boutellier, 2001). According to Baillergeau and Schaut (2001), social workers in poor neighbourhoods should now focus on social cohesion and diversion of juveniles from the street – so participating with police to reduce feelings of insecurity and promote social control.

In the twenty-first century the traditional Dutch tolerance and leniency described by David Downes in 1988 seems to have disappeared, and something of a backlash has occurred, especially as regards illegal drugs (as Downes predicted might happen). A sharp reversal in the use of custody, beginning in the 1980s, has pushed Dutch imprisonment rates up in a way that mimics, rather than contrasts with, trends in England and Wales (Downes, 1998; von Hofer, 2003). A backlash against perceived laxity in crime control and code enforcement (the latter fuelled by two spectacular disasters) helped to create a new mood of anxiety and punitiveness (Pakes, 2004).

The mantra of *veiligheid* (safety) has become the cover for a surprising number of controlling and excluding laws and practices, mainly aimed at already stigmatised groups. Van Swaaningen (2005) presents a vivid account of the way in which the safety discourse has taken over the Dutch political agenda and become translated into sweeping measures against visible public nuisances which are in no way dangerous but are seen as a cause of public unease. At the same time, it has to be recognised that those most likely to feel insecure, for whatever reason, are poorer people most affected by the downside of globalisation and by the reduction of welfare programmes (proven in the case of Sweden by Nilsson and Estrada, 2003).

Official concern about 'crime' (which in recent years has been falling) has been displaced by concern about social norms, informal social control and urban planning, all seen in the context of prevention. The current political slogan '*normen en waarden*' (norms and values) can apply equally to demands for a remoralised justice system, complaints about bad manners and litter on the streets, and the open criticism of Muslim minorities for not adopting Dutch ways.[1]

Among the many similarities to developments in Britain, the 'broken windows' thesis was explicit in a White Paper of 2002, entitled Towards a Safer Society, and has been adopted to justify crackdowns on minor misbehaviour:

> The penalisation of nuisance is motivated with preventive arguments. It is argued that tolerating or accepting such misconduct will worsen the problems. By causing inconveniences, playing truant, or urinating in the park, the criminal of the future announces his coming. (van Swaaningen, 2005)

From 2002 politicians of all persuasions shifted to a populist line, away from the traditional 'expert-led' approach in which criminal policy was largely left to the administrators and opinion led by a liberal elite (to the open distaste of public servants of the latter persuasion). The populism

147

is strongly tinged with xenophobia, since foreign immigrants, variously labelled as refusing to adopt Dutch norms, are widely blamed for crime and nuisance – especially where youths are involved. Any conversation about youth trouble typically turns, in particular, to Moroccans, and it is plain that there have been genuine difficulties of accommodation with this group. Moroccan youths are strongly associated with street crime, and suspects from this background figure disproportionately in police crime reports (Blom et al., 2005).

Rotterdam's social control

The city of Rotterdam, Pim Fortuyn's base, epitomises the new approach. As in many British cities, the municipality carries out regular audits of community safety (the *veiligheidsindex*) showing crime and other problems district by district. Nuisance/annoyance (*overlast*) regularly features as problematic or unsafe, especially in the city centre. On the strength of this (as in Nottingham – see Chapter 6) begging was banned in two areas of the city in 2003 – it had been a very prominent feature, especially around the central station, and it is claimed that aggressive begging was on the increase. Zero tolerance is applied to the presence of other unorthodox people, such as the homeless.

Now, anyone begging, especially if drug addicted, is subjected to quasi-compulsory treatment through the multi-agency community safety bureau. A case conference considers their problems and a care plan is devised. However, anyone who does not comply will go to prison. Addicts may be dealt with by a combination of detention, training and treatment, in a system which is still in the course of evaluation. Seven hundred non-compliant drug addicts have been processed through Rotterdam's *Persoons Gerichte Aanpak* or PGA (Personal Directed Approach). Troublesome youths and illegal foreigners undergo other versions of the PGA. The town hall keeps personal dossiers on anyone causing a persistent nuisance in the public domain, including youths. Prostitutes (forbidden to solicit on the street) are also among those now viewed as possibly in need of help as well as control – for drug addiction, psychiatric disorders, etc. Dutch law in general favours the tough/tender approach – you will not be prosecuted/punished if you agree to do as we say to put yourself to rights.

The Rotterdam authorities have also cracked down on nuisances through code enforcement – against bad landlords and noisy bars, for example. Each district can set its own standards for things like bar licences and opening hours. This is likely to appeal to middle-class areas, but the real problem neighbourhoods are typically places where poor immigrants are exploited by slum landlords, rubbish goes uncollected and illegal drugs are rife. A determined multi-agency effort turned round one such area (Het Oude Noorden) with a combined drive against nuisance behaviour, environmental mess, tax evasion and benefit fraud. Now, nationally, there is a 'safety' programme for 50 similarly troubled neighbourhoods, due to end in 2006.

Large-scale drug dealing and slum property ownership (a form of money laundering) are seen largely as the domain of 'immigrants', and the poor exploited slum dwellers are often illegal migrants – they welcomed Rotterdam's housing inspectors but may of course find themselves on the receiving end of the government's declared intention to repatriate 26,000 asylum seekers.

For reasons presented as a means of public order and safety rather than specifically crime control the mayor and the police may declare a crowd control zone (such as the environs of Rotterdam central station) where not more than four people are allowed to foregather. A member of the public commented to the author 'The Rotterdam authorities don't want you to do anything in the street except just walk along'. The impression now in central Rotterdam is indeed of a much-regulated city, although it is said that the drug scene has simply dispersed to other districts. The safety drive launched by the mayor in 2001 initially pushed perceptions of violent and property crime up sharply, but by 2004 people's crime-awareness had dropped back to earlier levels. This echoes national surveys showing fear of crime dropping slightly in the years 2003 and 2004 – which may or may not be linked to reduction of 'nuisances'.

The demand for tougher measures

In specific areas set by the mayor, usually town centres, Dutch police can give fixed penalty tickets for begging, sleeping rough, drinking, urinating and other street misdemeanors. A police sergeant explained:

> We're just chasing them. Obviously they can't pay the ticket. After a while, we have a thing on our computers which tells us about this guy who we know because we see them all the time. You can arrest him and then he goes to prison for a few weeks. And then they come back and it starts all over again.

Mayors and police can also agree zones where police can stop and search, without need for suspicion, looking for weapons and drugs. This power, used in high-crime areas and often involving Moroccans, is intended to show that the police are reclaiming control, after a long period during which detections declined. Reports go to the prosecutor who in the Netherlands has always had extensive diversionary powers and now has increasingly wide discretion to impose fines or conditions in lieu of prosecution. Judges can make injunction-type orders which for a limited period can ban individuals from streets where they might cause trouble – mainly used in domestic violence cases, but also applicable to young people. Individual curfew orders can be imposed but there are no blanket curfews. The hardened mood is epitomised by a law introduced in October 2004 by which anyone in a group on the street committing persistent offences may be banished from the town for two years. They may be sent to a recidivists unit for drug rehabilitation or, if they refuse, to prison for two years.

This is the nearest to the 'three strikes' law demanded by populist politicians. Opposition to such proposals comes strongly from the prosecution service. This was sharply demonstrated during the week of my own visit to The Hague. There was pressure in parliament on the Minister of Justice for adoption of the British anti-social behaviour order. Extra heat had been engendered by a widely publicised case in which a couple had been forced out of their house by harassment from a group of Moroccan youths. When the chief prosecutor realised that the Minister was inclining towards the ASBO he hastily wrote to him pointing out the possible dire consequences for the already bulging prisons. The Minister (whose CDA party stands for 'norms and values' more than repression) drew back from the idea – although political pressure continues for similar powers to control the youths, especially Moroccans, who are said to intimidate certain neighbourhoods. Instead of the ASBO it was decided to run an experiment using another British import, the voluntary Acceptable Behaviour Contract (a version of which had already been run in a couple of Amsterdam schools – see below). This is a rare example of a direct Anglo-Dutch policy transfer, and it is revealing that Britain's most controversial anti-nuisance policy was the one chosen for consideration, even though a milder version (at least for the time being) has been adopted.

Street wardens

The only other well-known example of Anglo-Dutch policy exchange was in the other direction and in a quite different mode – neighbourhood wardens in Britain (Jacobson and Saville, 1999) have been inspired by the Dutch *stadswachten*, or city wardens, introduced from 1989 onwards in order to supplement the perceived weakness of informal social control with a uniformed civilian presence in the city centres (Hauber et al., 1996). The wardens have no formal police powers but they are there to inform and reassure the public and to intervene by reprimanding people committing minor offences, such as cycling in pedestrian areas.

Subsequently another level of control was introduced in the form of civilian police auxiliaries, patrolling with limited powers of arrest – again a model adopted in Britain as 'community support officers'. A separate force of public transport inspectors, drawn from among unemployed youth, was recruited to limit fare-dodging, although the role soon became an arm of drug enforcement, which has been largely responsible for the doubling of local by-law criminal cases in five years.

Hauber et al. (1996) concluded that, on the whole, informal supervision by officials was effective in terms of prevention, though it did not make any difference to people's fear of crime. There was some pressure for wardens to be given formal powers. At this point they were beginning to be introduced into residential neighbourhoods and Hauber et al. suggest that in this context the use of formal powers would jeopardise the trust that wardens were intended to create. Even the civilian police patrollers had been advised to use formal powers in neighbourhoods as little as possible for that very reason. The Dutch experience needs to be watched closely as different versions of 'the policing family' (Crawford et al., 2005) proliferate in Britain.

The community court

Another recent innovation in Britain is the first 'community court', now operating in part of Liverpool. This is directly copied from New York's Red Hook scheme. But the innovators could have looked closer to home since both France and the Netherlands have versions of the same thing. The Dutch *Justitie in de Buurt (JiB)* or 'Justice in the Neighbourhood' reflects the social concerns linked to dissatisfaction with traditional criminal institutions. It also demonstrates that welfare considerations, especially as regards young people, have not been jettisoned despite populist rhetoric. The description that follows, however, may soon be a thing of the past, as the JiBs are undergoing a change of character that will diminish their community basis (Terpstra and Bakker, 2004).

First introduced in 1997, the JiBs are multi-agency offices led by the prosecution service, located in high-crime neighbourhoods. They formed part of a general focus of action in 'communities', seen as the answer to urban problems including crime and safety (Terpstra and Bakker, 2006: 377), and were intended to restore trust in the criminal justice process. To different degrees the JiBs co-ordinate individualised programmes, especially for youth, and prosecution is often avoided. The JiB premises visited in Bos en Lommer, a poor, multi-ethnic area of Amsterdam, were located on a main street where people could easily drop in – and so they did, often telling of fears that they would not report to the police directly. Representatives of all relevant agencies – probation, police, victim support, youth welfare – all spent some time every week in the JiB office and there were frequent joint meetings to discuss individual cases and local problems and to agree action.

This will change with the relocation to a new site and a larger neighbourhood which was due to take place in January 2005. Terpstra and Bakker report a general change of direction whereby the JiBs are withdrawing from such close contact with the public and becoming simply a venue for agency cooperation in matters of child welfare. Moreoever, in 2004 central government funding was cut off on grounds of inefficiency, judged on managerialist targets, and the JiBs left to the mercies of local authorities and other agencies.

However, the Bos en Lommer prosecutor thought that changes in the system to something more like the English Youth Offending Team might mean the possibility of preventive work – it was a cause of frustration to her that she could only deal with youths who had already committed crimes. (According to Terpstra and Bakker, some JiBs do actively warn 'at risk' individuals.) She did not prosecute cases herself, but with the help of multi-agency meetings would recommend a course of action to a centrally-based prosecution officer, usually a combination of punishment and care, but for a first offender sometimes only the latter. She kept track of youths on community programmes or curfews and would deliver serious warnings if they were not compliant. The individualised approach was emphasised: 'We don't take care of the case but we look after the person.'

Terpstra and Bakker (2005: 390) conclude that:

> [t]he main effect of the introduction [of JiB] is that problems are handled that previously received insufficient or no institutional attention. It is not so much a top-down imposition of juridical solutions to problems or of a criminal law approach as an answer to the needs and requests of citizens for more visible and explicit reactions by the authorities to the problems of insecurity in their neighbourhoods.

However, there is clearly now some doubt whether the citizens will continue to enjoy this relationship with the forces of law and order. To the community safety workers in Bos en Lommer district authority, it is a matter of regret that the feedback from the public on matters of immediate concern, which worked well through the JiB, will no longer be available.

Children's misbehaviour and youth trouble

Despite the harsher tone and legislation of recent years, low-level offending by young people is still often dealt with by HALT (Het ALTernatief), a diversionary scheme whereby police refer youths to social services for reparative programmes rather than to the prosecution (which may be favoured by the latter for sparing court time). HALT deals with 'anti-social' matters such as vandalism, graffiti and public disturbance, although petty theft is the main offence (Junger-Tas, 2004: 320). More recently, a similar voluntary scheme, STOP, has been introduced experimentally as the result of increased concern about infractions by children under 12, the age of criminal responsibility. Junger-Tas (2004: 330) sees this as effectively lowering the age of responsibility to ten, paralleled by an increase in the numbers of youths aged 16 and 17 referred to the adult court. Compulsory parenting orders are now available, with fines for non-compliance, just as in England.

Practitioners and police say they wish for more preventive work among younger children, especially those likely to emulate criminal siblings. One small project, introduced in two schools in Amsterdam by a woman police officer who had been given the opportunity to seek innovative models, was a version of the English ABC (Acceptable Behaviour Contract). The difference was that to avoid stigmatisation of 'at risk' children, every pupil in the primary school adopted a good behaviour contract, structured after discussion with the children, and relying on rewards rather than punishments for compliance. Some children unable to comply suffer from behavioural disorders; these would normally be referred to social or psychological services at an early stage. A new agency has also developed home visits to families of children displaying disturbed behaviour.

Junger-Tas (2004: 313, 329) notes that boys from Turkish and Moroccan backgrounds come into contact with the police at an earlier age, and are more likely to end up in the criminal justice system rather than receiving social care, compared with indigenous Dutch youths. She shows the huge disparity in numbers of ethnic minority juveniles in penal institutions.

At the heavy end of the scale of youth trouble, it is undeniable that in some neighbourhoods a sense of menace is engendered by groups of youths of mainly Moroccan origin. In Bos en Lommer, as in Dutch cities generally, such groups are a frequent source of public complaints and of feelings of insecurity. This can occur even if all that is happening is noise or merely the presence of a group outside a shop. Police in Amsterdam claim to know all the youth groups (who are not gangs in the American sense) and say that most are not criminal at all. Yet the police themselves are intimidated by the way some Moroccan youths convey, perhaps only by gesture, that they will retaliate if interfered with. A police sergeant explained that convictions are hard to obtain: 'You come to court with a judge and say "He threatened me" and he says "What did he say?" "He said 'Well I come back to you'." And then the Moroccan guy says "Yeah I'll come back to you to talk to you, I didn't mean a threat ...'"

Threats and insults to police are arrestable, but the police say they often cannot identify individual offenders within a group: therefore they are demanding more powers to deal with groups as a whole and seeking restraining orders or any other available sanction against individuals.

Neighbour problems

The heterogeneity of many Dutch city neighbourhoods provides textbook examples of the lack of 'collective efficacy' leading to inability to withstand bad behaviour. Officials in Bos en Lommer find that differing anxiety rates are directly related to the level of social problems in different localities. They do their best to encourage mixing and understanding by various community schemes. They try to mitigate the effects of neighbour friction arising from personal problems. Troublesome neighbours involve the intervention of the district authority before the landlord can evict them. Social landlords have none of the specific powers of nuisance control available to their counterparts in Britain. In Bos en Lommer it was explained to me that if a tenant is causing persistent aggravation the landlord must have a police report to take to court but also the local authority must first try to arrange an appropriate social or mental health intervention to reduce the problem – only if this fails may the tenant be evicted.

At the time of writing mediation schemes were being piloted in three Amsterdam neighbourhoods, including Bos en Lommer, but in Rotterdam, despite the city's tough image, there is a large, well-established and seemingly successful city-wide mediation service, active in neighbourhoods where both inter- and intra-cultural conflicts arise. In one such district (Delfshaven) where 97 per cent of the population originates from outside the Netherlands, volunteer mediators come from Turkish, Moroccan and many other backgrounds. There is little communication between people of different ethnic groups and nuisance behaviour such as prostitution is commonplace. The mediation scheme in Delfshaven (pop. 100,000) handles about 300 cases a year, roughly one a month for each volunteer.

Social services, housing officials and police are all trained in the principles of mediation, which helps to cut down inappropriate referrals and therefore raise the success rate. The schemes seem to work very closely with these agencies, and information sharing is not seen as a problem. People are in the habit of complaining to the authorities about anything, but mediation aims to get them to take responsibility for their own problems. They are helped to come to their own resolution and a written agreement is not insisted upon; it is felt that a piece of paper too easily becomes a weapon. If an agreement breaks down, people are encouraged to return again to the mediators. Activities like mediation suggest that the pragmatic, consensual Dutch tradition is still alive at the local level.

What about Sweden?

Swedish Social Democrats, along with other European centre-left political parties, show a rightward drift in matters of criminal justice and welfare provision, although their position is relative to the traditionally liberal and welfare oriented system long regarded as the hallmark of Swedish government (Tham, 1995, 2001). At the same time, surveys have depicted Swedish neighbourhoods displaying similar localised patterns of disorder, victimisation, incivilities and fear of crime (Wikstrom, 1991; Wikstrom and Dolmen, 2001) as in America and Britain. Of course these things too are relative – the intensity and polarisation of 'unsafety' may objectively be less in Sweden, and the fact that insecurity is a smaller national issue would suggest that the impact is relatively mild. National surveys show only small increases in fear of crime, despite media presentations and American-inspired use of the crime issue by political parties (Tham, 1995, 2001).[2]

International comparisons indeed show that the people in Sweden, in common with other Scandinavian countries, suffer less victimisation and are less afraid in comparison with other industrialised nations (van Kesteran et al., 2000). This would seem to be borne out by the annual audits carried out jointly by the police and the city authorities in Stockholm, asking samples of about 4,000 people about their concerns about crime (personal information). It is rare for fear of crime to show up strongly, but one year a particular neighbourhood did register an unusually high level. Further investigation found that this stemmed from one small area where a group of youths regularly gathered beside a pond. Social welfare agencies, schools, police and others worked together to resolve matters informally and the police spoke to the few 'hard core' youths and calmed them down. In the whole of Stockholm the police reckon there are fewer than a dozen spots where youths are regarded as a problem, plus the somewhat intimidating behaviour of loud groups on the underground.

Youth problems

Minority ethnic youths are sometimes seen as a threat, such as in the street robberies of mobile phones and coveted clothing by groups from the poor suburbs who come into central Stockholm. But a more general concern about youth crime has long been led by media presentations rather than evidence of an increase, and has had a political impact (Estrada, 2004). Reports of youth violence have increased, but this seems to be due to a growth in reporting of minor incidents. Many secondary schools now automatically report playground fights to the police (Estrada, 2001).

Since 1999 the traditional social services responsibility for offending youths has become more closely aligned with prosecution procedure and the social interventions are supposed to observe principles of proportionality. Social programmes, including a new requirement for community work, have replaced much of the former institutional care, but a court-ordered assessment will still mean remand to secure accommodation for many weeks, often beyond the time allocated for the court process. At the 'heavy end', a sentence which takes the form of social services care – for youths or problem adults – may mean years of compulsory treatment. Community sentences can be quite intensive, with education, social programmes and physical exercise occupying the whole day.

Outside the criminal justice system, young people up to the age of 20 can be taken to a state-run treatment centre (LVU) through an administrative order if home conditions or their own behaviour puts their health or development at risk. Most of those in care for behaviour problems are in the 15–17 age group (Janson, 2004: 416) – this may be influenced by the fact that criminal responsibility in Sweden only begins at 15. It was explained to me at one social services youth team, in the poor multi-ethnic Stockholm suburb of Botkyrka, that a prime principle is to work closely with families, and a youth would not normally be sent away if the family was supportive. The parents of misbehaving children are not stigmatised or punished in any way, but they are involved in the care plan. Families may be consulted through New Zealand-style family group meetings, and sometimes decide that eight weeks in residential care followed by a return home under supervision would be the best solution for the child. A popular form of support for problem children is a form of mentoring for five hours a week, during which time the worker will introduce them to interests and activities which may divert them from crime. Behaviour short of offending which suggests a family problem in the background would attract social service engagement, voluntary wherever possible. A young person in a situation where there is serious risk to health or well-being must be taken home by a police officer, or to social services in the absence of parents. A child showing anti-social tendencies would be far more likely to be identified and provided with help at an early stage than is generally the case in England. The Swedish system is plainly quite interventionist, often involving referral to social services for quite minor acts of delinquency. But a purely negative measure like the ASBO would be unthinkable.

Drugs and alcohol

Neither of these common causes of anti-social behaviour is particularly identified as such in Sweden, apart from drunken scenes outside bars and, at the hard end, violent turf wars between drug dealers. Extremely tough anti-drug laws criminalise all non-medical narcotics, with no distinction between 'hard' and 'soft' drugs. Any possession is treated as proof of supply, and evidence of usage alone can result in a prison sentence for up to six months for repeat offenders. The police may take blood and urine samples, by force if necessary. The intention of these measures – which have, controversially, become tougher with successive legislation – is to send a message of total unacceptability, especially to the young. Young people, and older known users, have been the main targets of police testing, yet increasing numbers of 16-year-olds admit to using drugs in the past 12 months (Lenke and Olssen, 1995, 2002; National Council for Crime Prevention (BRÅ), 2000).[3]

There has been criticism at the focus of police attention on demand rather than supply. Nevertheless police believe that demand has been stemmed and that drugs are becoming unfashionable – the main exception being in cocaine use among prosperous clubbers at weekends. Heroin addicts are relatively few, and ageing. Few new addicts are being created and the police say that drug-related nuisance is not significant in residential neighbourhoods. Botkyrka social services youth team received only 14 police reports (7 per cent of the whole) concerning drug use in the period January–October 2004 – but it must be remembered that exposure of this crime is entirely dependent upon police initiative. The youth team does occasionally have to deal with young addicts.

Alcohol, though very heavily taxed, is socially acceptable. Cheap bars have helped to shift drinking out of the home – more people are drinking socially but fewer are problem drinkers; again, the latter are likely to be found in poor areas of social housing. Noise nuisance in domestic settings has reduced with the drop in heavy home consumption and rowdiness has shifted to the street outside bars. Unsurprisingly, crimes of violence continue to be predominantly linked to alcohol.

Swedish law allows rehabilitation in residential care for drug and alcohol addicted persons instead of a sentence – this is voluntary, but can be compulsory if the court so orders.

Public order

Minor public order has moved up the Swedish agenda, although in a less extreme fashion than in Britain and the Netherlands. Private security enforcing codes against begging and drinking is visible in semi-public space such as a large shopping centre outside Stockholm (Hornquist, 2004). In law there is almost no conceivable public order problem that remains uncovered either by the Swedish Penal Code or by the separate law governing police powers, together with minor matters, such as public drinking, covered by local by-laws. Chapter 4, section 7, of the penal code concerns violence that does not cause injury, called 'molestation':

> A person who physically molests or by discharging a firearm, throwing stones, making loud noise or other reckless conduct molests another shall be sentenced for *molestation* to a fine or imprisonment for at most one year.

It is perhaps a sign of the times that molestation has only recently been added to the criminal statistics. Reported molestation of adults increased between 2000 and 2003 by 17 per cent for men and 11 per cent for women victims. Reports of disorderly conduct are not listed, but the law (Chapter 16, section 16, of the Swedish Penal Code) resembles English public order law in potential scope, covering not only being noisy in a public place but also behaving 'in a manner apt to arouse public indignation'. However, the penalty is merely a fixed fine (all fines in Sweden are expressed as day fines). Chapter 5, section 3, covers insulting behaviour – also punishable by a fine, with imprisonment only if 'gross'. (Swedish law has recently adopted more severe punishments for offences involving racial aggravation.) Fines may also be imposed for the crime of 'breach of domiciliary peace' which involves unlawful intrusion into someone's home or garden – again, prison of up to two years is available for 'gross' crimes of this nature.

Thus nearly all types of behaviour which in a neighbourhood in Britain might be deemed 'anti-social' and treated accordingly, often under civil law, in Sweden would involve breaches of the penal code and relatively mild punishment, if any. Persuasion and warnings would usually precede any formal process and mediation might be called upon. Social landlords have no special powers in law but any landlord, or residents of a block of flats, would need a police report to back up an application for eviction. 'Noisy neighbours', for example, can be reported for molestation. However, serious cases can involve intimidation of witnesses, and people need much persuasion and reassurance to testify. If necessary the police can offer protection or even relocation; as a last resort the prosecutor can proceed on the basis of a police report alone.

In the public domain police have carefully calibrated powers to deal with tiresome behaviour and minor criminality. The police code lays down the manner in which they can disperse a group. With troublesome young people they should first use persuasion, then order them to leave. If the youths ignore the order they can be removed from the area in police cars, as commonly happens with football disorder. A final step is to keep them in detention for up to six hours – which used to happen quite often until limited by a parliamentary directive.

Neither begging (unless it involves molestation) nor soliciting by prostitutes is illegal in Sweden, but another controversial law, passed in 1998, made it a crime to buy the services of a prostitute (Pettersson and Tiby, 2002). This was presented as an issue of sexual equality rather than a matter of control of street nuisance. As regards the street environment, litter and graffiti are efficiently removed by local authorities and have therefore not been adopted as signifiers of insecurity as has happened in Britain and the Netherlands. Even in poor neighbourhoods there is nothing like the environmental degradation to be seen in problem housing estates in Britain.

Signs of polarisation?

As long ago as 1989 P.-O.Wikstrom's research identified significant differences between suburban neighbourhoods in Stockholm on measures of socio-economic status, ethnicity and family structure, attachment to neighbourhood and interaction with neighbours, and perception of problems with litter, vandalism, gangs of youths, fighting, molestation and so forth. The social housing areas stood out as having the most problems and also suffered the most from theft and vandalism; in two of them, there were significant numbers of people afraid of one or more persons living in the vicinity. These findings mainly follow familiar patterns of difference found in residential areas in Britain and America.

Income inequality has increased in Sweden in recent years, though again it is still low by comparison with many other western countries (Tham, 2001; Palme et al., 2002). Polarisation is beginning to become a political issue. In December 2004 the (right-wing) Liberal party published a list of 136 housing estates throughout the country where, it said, levels of reliance on income support, low educational achievement and political disengagement were particularly serious, compared to only ten such places ten years earlier. Some of the measures chosen were subject to criticism but the exercise did reflect, or arouse, unease. Ethnicity was included as a problem, mainly seen as a matter of poor integration on the part of immigrants.

Yet the isolation from mainstream Swedish life experienced by many people of immigrant origin is a combination of unemployment and geographical separation in poor suburbs. In Stockholm, increased residential segregation is a matter of concern to the authorities. The more that this happens, the more the remaining families of indigenous Swedish origin are likely to leave. Minority ethnic youths are clearly involved in crime, but officials carefully point out that this reflects the culture of their poor neighbourhoods rather than innate criminality. No one minority group is blamed, as the criminal youth groups are heterogeneous (Pettersson, 2003) so there is not the stigma on any particular ethnic group that, in the Netherlands for example, is attached to Moroccans.

In the suburb of Botkyrka served by the youth welfare team already mentioned, the families left behind are mainly of various African and Middle Eastern backgrounds, speaking any number of languages other than Swedish. It is said that parents want their children to be able to integrate and lament the loss of opportunity to do so – it has even been suggested that Swedish families should be able to live rent-free in order to reduce the isolation. In this, Botkyrka resembles many city neighbourhoods in western Europe affected by global population movements. Poverty, thanks to still relatively generous welfare systems, may not be so great as in some other comparable places – will this prevent problems spilling over as they have in parts of France, the Netherlands and Britain?

Discussion

Britain, the Netherlands and Sweden are in different degrees exposed to, or protected against, the elements which contribute to perceptions of insecurity: poverty and joblessness, heterogeneity, disturbing behaviour by young people or neighbours, environmental incivilities, drug markets, etc. Reactions are tamed or enhanced by political and legal cultures, as Body-Gendrot (2000) found in France and the United States. Sweden is easily the 'tamest' of the three. The rightward political drift has been milder, welfare still provides a barrier against extremes of poverty despite growing signs of polarisation, and heterogeneity, although talked about, has not become a political issue. Ethnic ghettos are making an appearance, but not on the Dutch scale, and it is not deemed politically acceptable to blame crime upon these minorities – unlike the scapegoating of new minorities evident in several other European countries (Albrecht, 2002).

Social-welfarism in Sweden is far from dead and, in ways which to an outsider may even seem intrusive, misbehaviour by the young or by unconforming adults such as alcoholics is quickly picked up by social services, either directly or through the police, and control imposed – this is largely voluntary but compulsion is nearly always available. An extremely comprehensive penal code covers practically every conceivable misdemeanour, although punishment is usually in the form of a modest fine, calibrated to means. Street incivilities are treated in contrasting ways: drug laws are extremely tough; soliciting is not a crime but buying sexual services is; beggars, of whom there are few, are tolerated as long as they are not too demanding. The streets themselves, and even poor housing neighbourhoods, are generally clean and well-maintained, no doubt reflecting well-funded municipal services.

In this well ordered country of only 9 million people some of the familiar expressions of insecurity are discovered by academic interviewers, and crime plays a familiar tune in the media, but things have not got to the point where repressive measures (apart from drug control) are demanded. It is a matter of astonishment to Swedes when told of the extent of powers deployed in England and Wales against politically defined anti-social behaviour.

It is equally surprising, coming from England to the Netherlands, to find how far and how rapidly in the latter country social control in the streets through legislation and municipal decree has developed in the early twenty-first century, although this varies according to local politics. An upsurge of openly expressed suspicion of ethnic minorities, especially Moroccan youths, has stimulated demands for still more controls – on asylum seekers, on street gangs – and a demand for Dutch 'norms and values' to be respected. One outcome has even been political pressure for adoption of the British anti-social behaviour order.

The crisis of concern over the presence of poorly integrated Muslim communities is something new in Holland, and its once-taboo expression has been legitimised through politics, as well as being stimulated by events, particularly the gruesome murder of the film-maker Theo Van Gogh, who deliberately rode roughshod over Muslim sensitivities. This Dutch cultural crisis exceeds anything equivalent in Britain, where the response to 9/11 has been an erosion of civil liberties rather than widespread Islamophobia, although there is a growing concern about cultural divergence and ghettoisation. One difference perhaps is that Britain's large cities, and London especially, are home to so many different cultures that no one group stands out: the most ghettoised Muslim areas are to be found in northern mill towns.

In some Dutch neighbourhoods the fear engendered by groups of

Moroccan youths on the street, perceived as predators and sometimes openly threatening, echoes the experience in British problem neighbourhoods. A difference, however, lies again in ethnicity. Although there are long-standing perceptions about the criminality of black youths, the British government's drive against anti-social behaviour mainly targets poor white young people in old areas of industrial decline. Both the street corner Moroccans in the Netherlands and the 'youths hanging about' on housing estates in deprived areas of Britain are socially excluded groups largely untouched by support services; for both, further exclusionary measures are applied or advocated, with custody at the end of the line.

More recently, the much more widespread culture of yobbish young binge-drinkers has attracted British government attention. By definition Muslims are not involved. It is indeed likely that the powers taken by the mayor of Amsterdam to punish street drunkenness and urination in the city's centre are intended to curtail the unattractive habits of British binge-tourists (although Amsterdam's Moroccan youths drink beer in the street too).

Control of street behaviour in Dutch cities, especially in Rotterdam, closely resembles the British government's campaign (through exhortation and legislation) to rid the urban landscape of both human and environmental nuisances. Beggars and chronic drinkers are swept away from city streets in both countries, graffiti cleaned up and rubbish removed in a conscious effort to reduce the public's sense of insecurity. There is a marked similarity in the way that instruments of control are increasingly exercised through administrative rather than judicial functions (Rotterdam's PGA system being a prime example). The power to declare zones of special control, used by Dutch mayors, resembles the dispersal zones established by the police for purposes of public order in selected areas of English towns.

Despite the highly authoritarian nature of many recent developments in the Netherlands, there remains a publicly funded social support structure which can be relied upon (at least for the indigenous population) to prevent problem behaviour, especially by young people, from developing into the chronic neighbourhood plagues that have been the target of anti-social behaviour orders and other repressive measures in Britain. In this, the Dutch have more in common with the Swedes than they do with the British. This is perhaps the main lesson to be drawn from a comparison of behaviour control in the three countries – that, and the simple fact that efficient street cleaning makes for a more contented population. Expenditure on public services, rather than repression, is surely a more promising way for governments to make a lasting impact on anti-social behaviour and feelings of insecurity.

Notes

1 The murder by a Muslim of the provocative film director Theo van Gogh in November 2004 produced much hand-wringing as well as serious acts of hostility against Muslim targets.
2 In 2003 16.9 per cent of Swedish people said that they stayed at home at night for fear of being attacked, robbed or otherwise molested, slightly fewer than the peak of 18 per cent ten years earlier. This compares with 7.5 per cent who had actually experienced violence or threats in the previous year (Statistics Sweden).
3 Other information on drug trends from personal meeting with Stockholm chief of police operations.

Chapter 8

Conclusions

There is indeed a symmetry, as identified by Hornquist (2004), between the erosion of civil liberties and the rule of law in the context of terrorism, and the same process at the opposite end of the scale of seriousness, involving control of disorderly and anti-social conduct. In the early twenty-first century Britain displays the syndrome to an unprecedented degree. *The Economist* (5 February 2005), in a leading article entitled 'Taking Britain's liberties', noted that '[t]he state has given itself new powers to deal with minor offences and other crimes which are scarcely less draconian than those to deal with suspected terrorism'. At least there was a public outcry and strong political resistance to the Home Secretary's intention to use executive powers to impose house arrest and other significant restrictions on terrorist suspects. There was little protest when a 13-year-old boy was subject to similar restrictions following his admittedly insupportable behaviour in his neighbourhood. In this case a court was involved, but acting in a civil capacity as it always does in such cases. The procedure has become so commonplace, and so similar to other adaptations of civil law to suit the purposes of crime control, that objections do not make headlines. In any case, the government knows that clamping down on neighbourhood pests is always popular and critics who raise principled objections are cast as enemies of community well-being.

This is a pity, because it has been important, and overdue, to recognise the more painful effects of the erosion of the quality of life in neighbourhoods that have borne the brunt of civil and economic decay. Labour politicians have been one conduit for channelling this awareness into policy-making circles. There had to be a response, but the form it has taken, and especially the accompanying rhetoric, consistently relies upon blame, enforcement and exclusion, as well as dubious adaptations of the law. One label – 'anti-social behaviour' – is used to cover any number of different troubles and annoyances which in reality require quite distinct and focused responses graded and tailored to the matter in hand, be it an aggressive alcoholic neighbour, a crowd of young people gathering outside a shop, a drug-addicted beggar, a flat used for prostitution or a vandalised playground. 'Tough action on criminal neighbours' goes beyond the particular: it has a deeply symbolic meaning combining a law and order message with the creation of a powerful and disturbing image of the enemy within.

Seeing a social problem, the gut instinct in Whitehall is always to add to the statute book. Yet social action, rather than legal action, has always been the main need – sometimes, of course, backed up by legal powers, but these were already plentiful prior to 1998. As Hughes (2000: 191) remarks:

> The 1998 Act stands in a well-established British tradition of passing new legislation to deal with each perceived public order problem as it comes along, so that the law is a series of uncomfortable accretions lying, in geological terms, frequently uncomfortably one on top of another. This is because there is rarely [an] examination of what existing law can do to deal with the problem, how much existing law is relevant, and whether there is anything particularly new in the situation which actually makes a tailor-made response imperative.

Since the Crime and Disorder Act 1998 there have been, as described in previous chapters, still further statutory accretions in the name of dealing with anti-social behaviour, and the process continues. The emphasis forcefully projected by central government at local authorities and police is that by neglecting to use all the new powers they are failing to serve the public in the manner that people are demanding. Making the authorities more responsive to local needs must be a good thing – New Labour has rightly picked up on failures in dealing with long-standing disorders in vulnerable communities. But to assume that the right way to reverse these failures is to focus legal enforcement on a few individuals whose behaviour is itself often the consequence of public service failure (or at least exacerbated by it) is manifestly the wrong way to go about it.

The thinking behind the enforcement mantra involves several distinct strands of behaviour control which have developed since Labour came to power in 1997. Defending defenceless neighbourhoods ravaged by a minority of aggressive families and individuals is one. A belief that with a bit of encouragement communities (however defined) will learn to re-establish informal social control is another. An expectation that formal, cooperative, arrangements at local government level, always under the watchful eye of central government, will solve the problems of crime and disorder that residents, voluntary organisations and businesses identify, is a third. Fourthly, reduction of visible signs of disorder (whether human or inanimate) by means of the third strand is expected to reduce fear of crime and assist the community solidarity intended in the second strand. Fifthly, the process is to be fostered through new styles of policing (or the reintroduction of old styles) that favour visibility, attention to petty crime and disorder, and direct engagement with the populace.

Other countries have their own versions of most of these ideas. The Dutch, as described above, have adopted authoritarian regulation of public space in the name of public safety but still pursue ideals of community enhancement and support. In most west European countries, socially excluded areas and the minority groups within them attract programmes of improvement at the same time as they arouse suspicion in majority populations – sometimes ratcheted up to fear and aggression through images of terror and evidences of crime. These are the populations most on the receiving end of tough community safety measures. Versions of community policing are widely adopted, as are 'zero-tolerance' techniques inspired from America. The United States has also provided numerous examples of civil enforcement against disorder which have penetrated British and Dutch practice. But, at least as shown in the Netherlands and Sweden, social interventions exist that act in a preventive capacity to reduce the likelihood of problematic individuals causing alarm and distress in their neighbourhoods.

Britain differs in its particular emphasis on individual control (as distinct from control of identified disorderly groups) that is expressed above all in the anti-social behaviour order. The use of the term 'anti-social' stresses the exclusionary approach to persons seen as social pariahs unworthy of membership of their communities. Thus enforcement, involving the curtailment of ordinary liberties, is promoted as the only effective policy. Attention to the causes of bad behaviour, whether individual or structural, rarely form a part of the policy. As argued earlier, support systems that might have prevented many people acting in a way that is highly distressing to their neighbours are largely lacking. The government has recognised the degree of distress that can be caused, but has failed to provide lasting solutions, despite many good initiatives intended to help parents and improve the prospects of the most deprived neighbourhoods. If it is correct to link anti-social behaviour with income polarisation, then the policies which aim to increase the disposable incomes of poor families should eventually play their part. Not only might behaviour improve, but greater economic security should in theory (Maruna and King, 2004) reduce punitiveness and favour more holistic solutions.

The most intractably disorderly and unpleasant families – the prototype 'nasty neighbours' – have to be taken in hand somehow, not just evicted from one neighbourhood to another. Recognising this, and adopting after a long delay a model successfully pioneered in Dundee (Dillane et al., 2001) and later in Rochdale, it is now official policy to provide the intensive support and resocialising that seems usually to work. As this scheme spreads, there are bound to be new concerns about the selection and degree of coercion applied in these cases. However dreadful they are, these people have rights too.

The shrill, simplistic message sent out by the Home Office's 'Together' campaign has not been to the taste of many local practitioners. They are made to jump through performance hoops which, as Stenson and Edwards (2004) point out, are inimical to the diversity of need and practice found in different places. On the ground a combination of prevention and enforcement is the usual approach (Millie et al., 2005), even though expressive local cultures vary in one direction or the other. The locally varied applications of central policy noted by Stenson and Edwards continue to make their mark, as shown by differences in Milton Keynes and Nottingham. It cannot be mere chance that, by October 2004, Greater Manchester had imposed 608 ASBOs to Thames Valley's 69. Figures like this are a reminder that not only local government but, perhaps even more importantly, the cultures of different police forces carry great weight in the interpretation of community safety.

The police seem to have been a major influence in transforming the ASBO from an occasional substitute for criminal prosecution to a useful adjunct to a criminal conviction. This is the way that most ASBOs are now imposed. All the arguments about whether the order is strictly civil or covertly criminal need revisiting in the light of this little-remarked transformation. The closer that the order is tied to a sentence, the more urgent the need to review issues of evidence and proportionality.

One odd aspect of the story told in this book is the way that the use of the term 'anti-social', originally used to describe aggressive or selfish individual behaviour affecting neighbours, has been adopted instead of the more neutral 'disorder' to describe a diverse mix of environmental and human incivilities that affect neighbourhoods in a more impersonal and generalised way. There are no 'victims' of litter, graffiti or passive gatherings of youths – just people who don't like these things or say they make them feel fearful. For years the British Crime Survey has included perceptions about a standard list of 'disorders', classified by type of neighbourhood – but only in 2002 did the same list suddenly appear rebranded as 'anti-social behaviour'. The focus of the 'Together' campaign against anti-social behaviour has been largely environmental in scope, as are most sections of the Anti-Social Behaviour Act 2003. It seems that only by invoking the enemy within will enough attention be paid to mundane municipal housekeeping duties – and the regulation of begging, public drinking and prostitution then be seen as just one of these street-cleansing functions. The Clean Neighbourhoods and Environment Act 2005 speaks for itself – it is all about the detail of enforcing rules against disorder, right down to the behaviour of dogs.

Almost unnoticed is the continued and growing burden of enforcing good behaviour carried by local authorities and social landlords in the regulation of tenants. Long past are the days when housing law was just about land and property rights. Now the possession of a social tenancy is treated as a privilege to be earned, conditional on the good behaviour of the tenant, his or her family and visitors. The threat of eviction or reduced status is ever present, with the future possibility of housing benefit removal not finally ruled out. Far more people are at the receiving end of tenancy controls than ever receive ASBOs (although the two often go together). The Housing Act 2004 conveys a power to local authorities to adopt licensing controls over private landlords in whole neighbourhoods (approved centrally), especially those destabilised by low demand where anti-social behaviour is said to be prevalent. Some of the worst disorder occurs in areas of mixed tenure and it is now expected that proxy responsibility imposed on private landlords will be sufficient to enforce codes of good behaviour on tenants otherwise beyond the reach of local authority discipline. Time will tell whether this is a fig leaf or a birch.

Whole geographical areas designated for special measures by reason of anti-social behaviour, widely defined, links this new housing policy with the powers, under s. 30 of the Anti-Social Behaviour Act, for police to operate zones within which groups of more than two people are forbidden to gather and curfews may be imposed on children aged under 16. These powers can be applied for six months at a time in any area where anti-social behaviour is 'serious and persistent'. In the way that legislation tends to proliferate by borrowings from previous statutes, so one can imagine that this format – bad behaviour = bad area = areal restrictions – may in future be adopted to justify other forms of local control.

In turn this fits with a policy preference for dealing with neighbourhoods, or 'communities', on an individual basis, if necessary by means of by-passing conventional authorities and appealing directly to residents. The Home Office declared its four-year strategic plan (2004–8) to include 'enabl[ing] the public to take their part in tackling anti-social behaviour by getting involved in their communities and by holding public services to account to ensure they do more to support the law-abiding majority'. It goes on to promise that '[s]pecialist anti-social behaviour prosecutors and anti-social behaviour courts will deliver justice more effectively and ensure a greater level of accountability to the public on the problems that can make people's lives a misery'.

Now it has to be acknowledged that the Home Office is not the department to deliver the better education, jobs, social services and health services that might help to deal with 'problems that can make people's lives a misery'. Because anti-social behaviour is a Home Office idea and its self-appointed responsibility, it has to be seen to be doing new things. If the consequence is yet more ASBOs – and individuals empowered to demand them, as David Blunkett wanted – there will indeed be issues of accountability. Yet it is hard to see what specialist anti-social behaviour courts can do that ordinary courts are not already doing. And how will these new courts relate to the promised 'community courts' (a pilot introduced in 2004) or will they take them over?

Community courts raise concerns about proportionality and equality of justice. But they may, as originally planned, provide a venue for genuine problem-solving, maybe substituting restorative justice mechanisms for conventional courtroom procedure in suitable cases. Alternatively they may simply serve up a parade of local youths, alcoholics and drug addicts to be labelled, shamed and expelled along the lines of so much that has already happened. The Home Office plan looks to be pointing in that direction. Community as the locus of crime prevention always carries the risk of selective, vengeful and discriminatory mindsets, as Nelken (1985) warned twenty years ago. But in the hands of local people things could work out differently – punitiveness is not a universal trait, especially when the facts are known (Maruna and King, 2004), and those held accountable could indeed be local agencies in the guise of the deliverers of public services rather than the enforcers. But, as the Local Government Association has made plain, central government cannot be left out of the loop when funding restrictions and centrally imposed targets have diverted resources from many things that directly address the causes of bad behaviour.

   The communitarian philosophy that provides the moral fervour behind the appeal to 'community' as the basis for improving the quality of life has the attraction of focusing on the middle, 'parochial', level of social control (Hunter, 1985). (Literally parochial, now that parish councils are to be empowered to issue fines for minor disorder.) There is a lot of agreement that the ability to maintain behavioural norms does depend in varying degrees on neighbourly support and willingness to intervene when necessary. But even between poor neighbourhoods this type of cohesiveness differs, and it may be absent from some affluent areas, whose residents get on well enough without it since wealth itself is a great protector. The government assumes that informal social control is the vital ingredient for reducing bad behaviour in deprived areas, and that it can be regained through a mixture of exhortation and banishment of people deemed to have proved themselves unworthy of belonging. The recipe does not address the matter raised so urgently by W. J. Wilson (1996): if the structures of civil society have vanished, how can poor people, excluded from mainstream society physically and economically, be expected to manage order on their own? Such communities suffer from uncontrolled crime and disorder through the very fact of their isolation and lack of support. The people (children and adults) whose behaviour needs controlling are equally part of the syndrome and part of the community. Policies that fail to recognise these connections cannot provide any long-term answers.

Appendix 1

Number of anti-social behaviour orders – by area and type of court

Number of anti-social behaviour orders reported to the Home Office as either issued or refused, at all courts, by area and type of court, from 1 April 1999 to 30 September 2004

CJS area	Total applications refused	Magistrates courts		Total ASBOS issued	The Crown Court Total ASBOS issued on conviction	County courts Total ASBOS issued	All courts	
		Total ASBOS issued on: application	conviction				Total ASBOS issued	Total applications[1] /on convictions
Avon & Somerset	–	43	49	92	14	1	107	107
Bedfordshire	–	14	12	26	5	–	31	31
Cambridgeshire	–	25	17	42	3	–	45	45
Cheshire	–	41	32	73	3	–	76	76
Cleveland	2	38	2	40	–	–	40	42
Cumbria	1	22	23	45	3	–	48	49
Derbyshire	–	22	17	39	8	–	47	47
Devon & Cornwall	–	17	23	40	30	–	70	70
Dorset	–	24	4	28	–	–	28	28
Durham	–	46	6	52	1	–	53	53
Essex	–	17	23	40	1	1	42	42
Gloucestershire	–	14	6	20	3	–	23	23
Greater London[1]	9	179	164	343	17	4	364	373

	Total applications refused	Magistrates courts Total ASBOS issued on: application	conviction	Total ASBOS issued	The Crown Court Total ASBOS issued on conviction	County courts Total ASBOS issued	All courts Total ASBOS issued	All courts Total applications[1]/on conviction
Greater Manchester	5	355	177	532	70	6	608	613
Hampshire	4	54	25	79	9	4	92	96
Hertfordshire	1	31	26	57	5	–	62	63
Humberside	–	37	25	62	1	–	63	63
Kent	4	52	25	77	3	–	80	84
Lancashire	2	77	54	131	15	1	146	148
Leicestershire	–	7	7	14	6	–	21	21
Lincolnshire	–	3	8	11	4	–	15	15
Merseyside	5	90	22	112	4	2	118	123
Norfolk	1	41	13	54	4	–	58	59
Northamptonshire	–	18	11	29	2	–	31	31
Northumbria	–	47	21	68	5	–	73	73
North Yorkshire	–	19	12	31	3	–	34	34
Nottinghamshire	–	37	30	67	9	–	76	76
South Yorkshire	–	63	36	99	1	3	103	103
Staffordshire	–	32	40	72	5	2	79	79
Suffolk	1	20	52	72	4	2	78	79
Surrey	–	25	5	30	–	–	30	30
Sussex	1	74	24	98	7	1	106	107
Thames Valley	1	37	28	65	2	2	69	70
Warwickshire	–	36	8	44	1	1	46	46

West Mercia	–	116	21	137	–	–	137	137
West Midlands	1	138	118	256	12	3	271	272
West Yorkshire	1	242	49	291	8	–	299	300
Wiltshire	4	5	7	12	1	–	13	17
England	**43**	**2,158**	**1,222**	**3,380**	**269**	**33**	**3,682**	**3,725**
Dyfed Powys	–	3	15	18	–	–	18	18
Gwent	–	17	5	22	–	2	24	24
North Wales	–	13	20	33	3	–	36	36
South Wales	–	31	32	63	2	1	66	66
Wales	**–**	**64**	**72**	**136**	**5**	**3**	**144**	**144**
Total all courts E & W	**43**	**2,222**	**1,294**	**3,516**	**274**	**36**	**3,826**	**3,869**
percentage of total applications[1] on conviction	*1*	*57*	*33*	*91*	*7*	*1*	*99*	*100*

[1]Includes ASBO applications refused.
[2]Including City of London.
Source: Home Office.

Appendix 2

ASBO breaches and custodial sentences given – 1 June 2000 to 31 December 2003[1] by area and age group

Number of anti-social behaviour orders (ASBOs) issued, breached and where breach resulted in a custodial sentence

CJS area	ASBOs issued				ASBOs breached				Custodial sentence given for breach of an ASBO[2]			
	Total	Age at date of issue of ASBO			Total	Age at date of breach of ASBO			Total	Age at date of breach of ASBO		
		10–17	18 & over	not known		10–17	18 & over[3]	not known		10–17	18 & over[3]	not known
Avon & Somerset	47	19	27	1	17	6	11	0	8	2	6	0
Bedfordshire	22	9	13	0	12	5	7	0	6	2	4	0
Cambridgeshire	19	13	6	0	8	8	0	0	3	3	0	0
Cheshire	43	20	23	0	15	5	10	0	10	4	6	0
Cleveland	26	21	5	0	17	13	4	0	4	2	2	0
Cumbria	30	11	18	1	17	3	14	0	12	2	10	0
Derbyshire	20	7	13	0	11	4	7	0	6	3	3	0
Devon & Cornwall	20	7	13	0	8	2	6	0	6	1	5	0
Dorset	8	7	1	0	2	2	0	0	1	1	0	0
Durham	34	18	16	0	26	9	17	0	16	4	12	0

Essex	15	5	10	0	2	1	1	0	2	1	1	0
Gloucestershire	10	7	3	0	5	4	1	0	3	2	1	0
Greater London	146	53	86	7	46	11	35	0	31	3	28	0
Greater Manchester	317	206	107	4	138	86	52	0	88	56	32	0
Hampshire	44	25	16	3	20	11	9	0	12	4	8	0
Hertfordshire	31	21	9	1	9	4	5	0	6	2	4	0
Humberside	23	9	13	1	10	5	5	0	6	3	3	0
Kent	51	27	24	0	7	5	2	0	1	0	1	0
Lancashire	68	49	19	0	37	25	12	0	17	7	10	0
Leicestershire	10	7	3	0	4	4	0	0	1	1	0	0
Lincolnshire	8	4	4	0	5	2	3	0	1	0	1	0
Merseyside	71	42	29	0	22	16	6	0	10	6	4	0
Norfolk	25	10	11	4	11	3	8	0	1	0	1	0
Northamptonshire	11	9	2	0	1	0	1	0	1	0	1	0
Northumbria	47	22	25	0	15	5	10	0	7	2	5	0
North Yorkshire	15	7	8	0	8	3	5	0	3	2	1	0
Nottinghamshire	32	15	17	0	13	5	8	0	7	3	4	0
South Yorkshire	52	24	28	0	24	11	13	0	15	6	9	0
Staffordshire	46	20	25	1	15	6	9	0	8	3	5	0
Suffolk	33	16	17	0	9	3	6	0	5	1	4	0
Surrey	10	6	4	0	4	0	4	0	2	0	2	0
Sussex	46	29	16	1	18	12	6	0	6	3	3	0
Thames Valley	26	7	15	4	8	3	5	0	3	1	2	0
Warwickshire	29	18	11	0	14	6	8	0	3	0	3	0
West Mercia	100	46	54	0	48	18	30	0	28	7	21	0

| | ASBOs issued | ASBOs issued | | | | ASBOs issued | | | | Custodial sentence gven for breach of the ASBO[2] | | | |
| | Total | Age at date of issue of ASBO | | | | Age at date of breach of ASBO | | | | Total | Age at date of breach of ASBO | | |
		10–17	18 & over	not known	Total	10–17	18 & over[3]	not known	Total		10–17	18 & over[3]	not known
West Midlands	163	58	93	12	81	35	46	0	53	20	33	0
West Yorkshire	110	76	34	0	49	31	18	0	23	14	9	0
Wiltshire	7	4	3	0	3	2	1	0	2	1	1	0
England	1,815	954	821	40	759	374	385	0	417	172	245	0
Dyfed Powys	11	0	11	0	5	0	5	0	4	0	4	0
Gwent	10	6	4	0	5	3	2	0	3	1	2	0
North Wales	20	13	7	0	11	7	4	0	4	2	2	0
South Wales	36	18	18	0	13	8	5	0	9	4	5	0
Wales	77	37	40	0	34	18	16	0	20	7	13	0
Total England and Wales	1,892	991	861	40	793	392	401	0	437	179	258	0
Percentage of total ASBOs issued	100	52	46	2	42	21	21	0	23	9	14	0

Percentage of total ASBOs breached by age group	100	100	100	100	100	42	40	47	0
Percentage of custodial sentences given for breach of an ASBO by age group			100	100	100	55	46	64	0

1. Breaches are counted in this table on a persons basis, i.e. multiple breaches (occurring at the same time), or where the order has been breached on more than one occasion, are all counted as one breach. The breach resulting in the severest penalty for a person is used.

2. Excluding 2 persons given a fully suspended sentence and 8 cases where a sentence of one day in police cells was given.

3. Includes breaches where the ASBO recipient was a juvenile when the order was given.

Source: Home Office.

References

Abbreviations:

CIH   – Chartered Institute of Housing
DTLR   – Department for Transport, Local Government and the Regions
JRF   – Joseph Rowntree Foundation
ODPM   – Office of the Deputy Prime Minister

Ahmed, E., Harris, N., Braithwaite, J. and Braithwaite, V. (2001) *Shame Management Through Reintegration.* Cambridge: Cambridge University Press.

Aitken, S. (2001) *Geographies of Young People. The Morally Contested Spaces of Identity.* London and New York: Routledge.

Albrecht, H.-J. (2002) 'Immigration, crime and unsafety', in A. Crawford (ed.), *Crime and Insecurity. The Government of Safety in Europe.* Cullompton: Willan.

Anderson, S., Kinsey, R., Loader, I. and Smith, C. (1994) *Cautionary Tales.* Aldershot: Avebury.

Ashford, B. and Morgan, R. (2004) 'Criminalising looked-after children', *Criminal Justice Matters*, 57, Autumn: 8–9, 38.

Ashworth, A. (2004) 'Social control and "anti-social behaviour": the subversion of human rights?', *Law Quarterly Review*, 120, April: 263–91.

Ashworth, A., Gardner, J., von Hirsch, A., Morgan, R. and Wasik, M. (1998) 'Neighbouring on the oppressive: the government's Community Safety Order proposals', *Criminal Justice*, 16(1): 7–14.

Aye Maung, N. (1995) *Young People, Victimisation and the Police. British Crime Survey Findings on the Experiences and Attitudes of 12–15 year olds,* Home Office Research Study No. 140. London: Home Office.

Baillergeau, E. and Schaut, C. (2001) 'The security issue in the Netherlands and Belgium', *European Journal of Criminal Policy and Research*, 9: 427–46.

Baumgartner, M. (1984) 'Social control in suburbia', in D. Black (ed.), *Towards a General Theory of Social Control*. Orlando, FL: Academic Press.

Beck, U. (1992) *Risk Society: Towards a New Modernity*. London: Sage.

Beckett, K. and Western, B. (2001) 'Governing social marginality', *Punishment and Society*, 3(1): 43–59.

Bellair, P. (1997) 'Social interaction and community crime: examining the importance of neighbor networks', *Criminology*, 35(4): 677–701.

Biderman, A., Johnson, L., Mcintyre, J. and Weir, A. (1967) *Report on a Pilot Study in the District of Columbia on Victimisation and Attitudes Towards Law Enforcement*, President's Commission on Law Enforcement and Administration of Justice, Field Surveys 1. Washington, DC: US Government Printing Office.

Bland, N. and Read, T. (2000) *Policing Anti-Social Behaviour*, Police Research Series 123. London: Home Office.

Blom, M., Oudhof, J., Bijl, R. and Bakker, B. (2005) '*Verdacht van criminaliteit* [Suspects of Crime]. The Hague: Ministerie van Justitie, WODC, Cahier 2005–2.

Body-Gendrot, S. (2000) *The Social Control of Cities? A Comparative Perspective*. Oxford: Blackwell.

Bottoms, A. and Wiles, P. (1986) 'Housing tenure and residential crime careers in Britain', in A. Reiss and M. Tonry, (eds), *Communities and Crime*. Chicago: University of Chicago Press.

Bottoms, A. and Wiles, P. (1995) 'Crime and insecurity in the city', in C. Fijnaut et al. (eds), *Changes in Society, Crime and Criminal Justice. Volume 1. Crime and Insecurity in the City*. Antwerp: Kluwer Law International.

Bottoms, A. and Wiles, P. (2002) 'Environmental criminology', in M. Maguire, R. Morgan and R. Reiner (eds), *The Oxford Handbook of Criminology*, 3rd edn. Oxford: Oxford University Press.

Bottoms, A. and Wilson, A. (2004) 'Attitudes to punishment in two high-crime communities' in A. Bottoms, S. Rex and G. Robinson (eds), *Alternatives to Prison: Options for an Insecure Society*. Cullompton: Willan.

Bottoms, A., Mawby, R. and Xanthos, P. (1989) 'A tale of two estates', in D. Downes (ed.), *Crime and the City*. London: Macmillan.

Boutellier, H. (2001) 'The convergence of social policy and criminal justice', *European Journal of Criminal Policy and Research*, 9(4): 361–80.

Boutellier, H. (2004) *The Safety Utopia: Contemporary Discontent and Desire as to Crime and Punishment*. Dordrecht: Kluwer Academic Publishers.

Bowling, B. (1998) 'The rise and fall of New York murder: zero tolerance or crack's decline?', *British Journal of Criminology*, 39(4): 531–54.

Bratton, W. (1997) 'Crime is down in New York City: blame the police', in N. Dennis (ed.), *Zero Tolerance: Policing a Free Society*. London: Institute for Economic Affairs.

Bright, S. and Bakalis, C. (2003) 'Anti-social behaviour: local authority responsibility and the voice of the victim', *Cambridge Law Journal*, 62(2): 305–34.

Brown, A. (2004) 'Anti-social behaviour, crime control and social control', *Howard Journal*, 43(2): 203–11.

Brown, A., Barclay, A., Simmons, R. and Eley, S. (2003) *The Role of Mediation in Tackling Neighbour Disputes and Anti–social Behaviour*. Edinburgh: Scottish Executive Social Research.

Bullock, K. and Jones, B. (2004) *Acceptable Behaviour Contracts: Addressing Antisocial Behaviour in the London Borough of Islington*, Home Office On-line Report 02/04. London: Home Office.

Burney, E. (1999) *Crime and Banishment: Nuisance and Exclusion in Social Housing.* Winchester: Waterside Press.

Burney, E. (2002) 'Talking tough, acting coy: what happened to the Anti-social Behaviour Order?', *Howard Journal*, 41(5): 341–56.

Burney, E. (2003) 'Punishment without crime: civil law and public protection'. Unpublished paper to Socio-Legal Studies Association annual conference.

Burney, E. (2004) 'Nuisance or crime? The changing use of anti-social behaviour control', *Criminal Justice Matters*, 57, Autumn: 4–5.

Burney, E. (forthcoming) 'No spitting: regulation of offensive behaviour in England and Wales', in A. von Hirsch and A. Simester (eds), *Incivilities: Regulating Offensive Behaviour.* Oxford: Hart Publishing.

Bursik, R. (1988) 'Social disorganisation and theories of crime and delinquency', *Criminology*, 26: 519–51.

Bursik, R. and Grasmick, H. (1993) *Neighborhoods and Crime. The Dimensions of Effective Community Control.* Lanham, MD: Lexington Books.

Campbell, B. (1993) *Goliath: Britain's Dangerous Places.* London: Methuen.

Campbell, S. (2002) *A Review of Anti–social Behaviour Orders*, Home Office Research Study 236. London: Home Office.

Cheh, M. (1998) 'Civil remedies to control crime: legal issues and constitutional challenges', in L.G. Mazerolle and J. Roehl (eds), *Civil Remedies and Crime Prevention*, Crime Prevention Studies Vol. 9. Monsey, NY: Criminal Justice Press.

CIH (1995) *Neighbour Nuisance: Ending the Nightmare*, Good Practice Briefing No. 3. Coventry: Chartered Institute of Housing.

Clapham, D. (1997) 'The social construction of housing management', *Urban Studies*, 34: 761–74.

Cockburn, J. (1977) 'The nature and incidence of crime in England 1559–1625: a preliminary survey', in J. Cockburn (ed.), *Crime in England 1550–1800.* London: Methuen.

Cohen, S. (1972) *Folk Devils and Moral Panics.* London: Paladin.

Cohen, S. (1985) *Visions of Social Control.* Cambridge: Polity Press.

Collishaw, S., Maughan, B., Goodman, R. and Pickles, A. (2004) 'Time trends in adolescent mental health', *Journal of Child Psychology and Psychiatry*, 45(8): 1350–62.

Commission of the European Communities (2000) *The Prevention of Crime in the European Union. Reflection on Common Guidelines and Proposals for Community Financial Support*, COM/2000/0786.

Council of Europe (2003) *Violence in Schools – A Challenge for the Local Community.* Strasbourg: Council of Europe Publishing.

Crawford, A. (1997) *The Local Governance of Crime: Appeals to Community and Partnerships.* Oxford: Clarendon Press.

Crawford, A. (2001) 'Joined–up but fragmented: contradiction, ambiguity and ambivalence at the heart of New Labour's "Third Way"', in R. Matthews, and J. Pitts (eds), *Crime, Disorder and Community Safety.* London: Routledge.

Crawford, A., Lister, S., Blackburn, S. and Burnett, J. (2005) *Plural Policing: The Mixed Economy of Visible Security Patrols.* Bristol: Policy Press.

Croll, A. (1999) 'Street disorder, surveillance and shame: regulating behaviour in the public spaces of the late Victorian British town', *Social History*, 24(3): 250-68.

Currie, E. (1997) 'Market, crime and community. Toward a mid-range theory of post-industrial violence', *Theoretical Criminology*, 1(2): 147–72.

Curtis, T. C. (1977) 'Quarter Sessions appearances and their background: a seventeenth–century regional study', in J. S. Cockburn (ed.), *Crime in England 1550–1800*. London: Methuen.

Davey, B. (1983) *Lawless and Immoral: Policing a Country Town 1838–1857*. Leicester: University of Leicester Press.

Deehan, A. and Saville, E. (2002) 'Alcohol related crime and disorder: the first audit and strategy documents from crime and disorder partnerships', *Crime Prevention and Community Safety: An International Journal*, 4(2): 33–7.

Dignan, J., Sorsby, A. and Hibbert, J. (1996) *Neighbour Disputes: Comparing the Cost Effectiveness of Mediation and Alternative Approaches*. Sheffield: University of Sheffield Centre for Criminological and Legal Research.

Dillane, J., Hill, M., Bannister, J. and Scott, S. (2001) *Evaluation of the Dundee Families Project*. Glasgow: University of Glasgow Centre for the Child and Society and Department of Urban Studies.

Ditton, J., Bannister, J., Gilchrist, E. and Farrall, S. (1999) 'Afraid or angry? Recalibrating the "fear" of crime', *International Review of Victimology*, 6(2): 83–99.

Dodd, T., Nicholas, S., Povey, D. and Walker, A. (2004) *Crime in England and Wales 2003/2004*. Home Office Statistical Bulletin 10/04. London: Home Office.

Downes, D. (1988) *Contrasts in Tolerance. Post-war Penal Policy in the Netherlands and England and Wales*. Oxford: Clarendon Press.

Downes, D. (1998) 'The buckling of the shields: Dutch penal policy 1985–1995,' in R. Weiss and N. South (eds), *Comparing Prison Systems*. Amsterdam: Gordon & Breach.

DTLR (2002) *Tackling Anti-Social Tenants: A Consultation Paper*. London: DTLR.

Edwards, A. (2002) 'Learning from diversity: the strategic dilemmas of community-based crime control', in G. Hughes and A. Edwards, (eds), *Crime Control and Community. The New Politics of Public Safety*. Cullompton: Willan.

Edwards, A. and Benyon, J. (2000) 'Community governance, crime control and local diversity'. *Crime Prevention and Community Safety: An International Journal*, 2(3): 35–54.

Eisner, M. (2003) 'Towards more effective youth violence prevention – an overview', in Council of Europe, *Violence in Schools – A Challenge to the Local Community*. Strasbourg: Council of Europe.

Elias, N. (1978) *The Civilising Process. Vol. 1: The History of Manners*, trans. E. Jephcott. Oxford: Blackwell.

Emmison, F. (1973) *Elizabethan Life: Morals and the Church Courts, mainly from Esssex Archidiaconal Records*. Chelmsford: Essex Record Office.

Emsley, C. (1983) *Policing and Its Context 1750–1870*. Basingstoke: Macmillan.

Emsley, C. (1996) *Crime and Society in England 1750–1900*, 2nd edn. Harlow: Pearson.

Estrada, F. (2001): 'Juvenile violence as a social problem. Trends, media attention and societal response', *British Journal of Criminology*, 41: 639–55.

Estrada, F. (2004) 'The transformation of the politics of crime in high crime societies', *European Journal of Criminology*, 1(4): 419–43.

Estrada, F. and Nilsson, A. (2004) 'Exposure to threatening and violent behaviour among single mothers – the significance of lifestyle, neighbourhood and welfare situation', *British Journal of Criminology*, 44(2): 168–87.

Etzioni, A. (1993) *The Spirit of Community. The Reinvention of American Society*. New York: Touchstone.

Evans, K., Fraser, P. and Walklate, S. (1996) 'Whom can you trust? The politics of grassing on an inner city housing estate', *Sociological Review*, 44: 361–80.

Farrell, G. (1992) 'Multiple victimisation: its extent and significance', *Internationational Review of Victimology*, 2(3): 85–102.

Farrington, D. (2002) 'Developmental criminology and risk-focused prevention', in M. Maguire, R. Morgan and R. Reiner (eds), *The Oxford Handbook of Criminology*, 3rd edn. Oxford: Oxford University Press.

Field, F. (2003) *Neighbours from Hell: The Politics of Behaviour*. London: Politico's.

Foreman, A. (2004) 'Sites of contention: young people, community and leisure space', in W. Mitchell, R. Burton and E. Green (eds), *Young People, Risk and Leisure. Constructing Identities in Everyday Life*. Basingstoke: Palgrave Macmillan.

Foster, J. (2002) '"People pieces": the neglected but essential elements of community crime prevention', in G. Hughes and A. Edwards (eds), *Crime Control and Community. The New Politics of Public Safety*. Cullompton: Willan.

Foster, J. and Hope, T. (1993) *Housing, Community and Crime: The Impact of the Priority Estates Project*, Home Office Research Study 131. London: Home Office.

Garland, D. (2001) *The Culture of Control*. Oxford: Oxford University Press.

Gemeente Rotterdam (2004) *Veiligheidsindex 2004*. Rotterdam: Programmabureau Veilig.

Giddens, A. (1990) *The Consequences of Modernity*. Cambridge: Polity Press.

Gilling, D. (2001) 'Community safety and social policy', *European Journal of Criminal Policy and Research*, 9: 381–400.

Gillis, J. (1975) 'The evolution of juvenile delinquency in England 1890–1914', *Past and Present*, 67: 96–126.

Girling, E., Loader, I. and Sparks, R. (2000) *Crime and Social Change in Middle England. Questions of Order in an English Town*. London: Routledge.

Gray, K. and Gray, S. (1999) 'Civil rights, civil wrongs and quasi-public space', *European Human Rights Law Review*, 1: 46–102.

Greene, J. (1999) 'Zero tolerance: a case study of police policies and practices in New York City', *Crime and Delinquency*, 45(2): 171–87.

Halligan-Davis, G. and Spicer, K. (2004) *Piloting 'On the Spot Penalties' for Disorder: Final Results of a One-Year Pilot*, Home Office Research Findings 257. London: Home Office.

Hallsworth, S. and Young, T. (2004) 'Getting real about gangs', *Criminal Justice Matters*, 55: 12–13.

Hanak, G. (2004) *Contexts of Insecurity: The Case of Vienna.* Paper presented to the European Society of Criminology Conference, Amsterdam.

Harcourt, B. (2001) *Illusion of Order: The False Promise of Broken Windows.* Cambridge, MA: Havard University Press.

Hauber, A., Hofstra, B., Toornvliet, L. and Zanbergen, A. (1996) 'Some new forms of functional social control in the Netherlands and their effects', *British Journal of Criminology*, 36(2): 199–219.

Hayward, R. and Sharp, C. (2005) *Young People, Crime and Antisocial Behaviour: Findings from the 2003 Crime and Justice Survey*, Findings 245. London: Home Office.

Hedge, J. (2002) *A Priority in Common. A Resource Book on Anti-Social Behaviour.* Chilton: Thames Valley Partnership.

von Hirsch, A. and Simester, A. (eds), (forthcoming) *Incivilities: Regulating Offensive Behaviour.* Oxford: Hart Publishing.

von Hofer, H. (2003) 'Prison populations as political constructs: the case of Finland, Holland and Sweden', *Journal of Scandinavian Studies in Criminology and Crime Prevention*, 4(1): 21–38.

von Hofer, H. (2004) 'Crime and reactions to crime in Scandinavia', *Journal of Scandinavian Studies in Criminology and Crime Prevention*, 5(2): 148–66.

Home Office (1991) *Safer Communities: The Local Delivery of Crime Prevention Through the Partnership Approach*, The Morgan Report. London: Home Office.

Home Office (1998) *Draft Guidance Document: Anti-Social Behaviour Orders*, London: Home Office.

Home Office (1999) *Crime and Disorder Act 1998. Anti-Social Behaviour Orders: Guidance.* London: Home Office.

Home Office (2000) *Crime and Disorder Act 1998. Anti-Social Behaviour Orders: Guidance on Drawing up Local ASBO Protocols.* London: Home Office.

Home Office (2001) *Antisocial Behaviour and Disorder: Findings from the 2000 British Crime Survey*, Research Findings 145. London: Home Office.

Home Office (2003a) *A Guide to Anti-Social Behaviour Orders and Acceptable Behaviour Contracts.* London: Home Office.

Home Office (2003b) *Together – Tackling Anti-Social Behaviour. Action Plan.* London: Home Office.

Home Office (2004) *Defining and Measuring Anti-Social Behaviour.* Home Office Development and Practice Report 26. London: Home Office.

Hood, R. and Joyce, K. (1999) 'Three generations: oral testimonies on crime and social change in London's East End', *British Journal of Criminology*, 39(1): 136–60.

Hope, T. (1996) 'Communities, crime and inequality in England and Wales', in T. Bennett (ed.), *Preventing Crime and Disorder: Targeting Strategies and Responsibilities.* Cambridge: University of Cambridge Institute of Criminology.

Hope, T. (2001) 'Crime victimisation and inequality in a risk society', in R. Matthews and J. Pitts (eds), *Crime, Disorder and Community Safety: A New Agenda?* London: Routledge.

Hope, T. and Hough, M. (1998) 'Area, crime and incivility: a profile from the British Crime Survey', in T. Hope and M. Shaw (eds), *Communities and Crime Reduction.* London: HMSO.

Hopkins Burke, R. (2000) 'The regulation of begging and vagrancy: a critical discussion', *Crime Prevention and Community Safety: An International Journal*, 2(2): 43–52.

Hopkins Burke, R. and Morrill, R. (2002) 'Anti-social Behaviour Orders: an infringement of the Human Rights Act 1998?', *Nottingham Law Journal*, 11(2): 1–16.

Hornqvist, M. (2004) 'Risk assessments and public order disturbances: new European guidelines for the use of force?', *Journal of Scandinavian Studies in Criminology and Crime Prevention*, 5(1): 4–26.

Hough, M. (1995) *Anxiety about Crime: Findings from the 1994 British Crime Survey*, Home Office Research Study 147. London: Home Office.

Hughes, D. (2000) 'The use of possessory and other powers of local authority landlords as a means of social control, its legitimacy and some other problems', *Anglo-American Law Review*, 29(2): 167–203.

Hughes, G. (1996) 'Communitarianism and law and order', *Critical Social Policy*, 49: 17–41.

Hughes, G. (2000) 'In the shadow of crime and disorder: the contested politics of community safety in Britain', *Crime Prevention and Community Safety: An International Journal*, 2(4): 47–59.

Hunter, A. (1985) 'Private, parochial and public order: the problem of crime and incivility in urban communities', in G. Suttles and M. Zald (eds), *The Challenge of Social Control*. Norwood, NJ: Ablex.

Hunter, C. and Nixon, J. (2001) 'Taking the blame and losing the home: women and anti-social behaviour', *Journal of Social Welfare and Family Law*, 23(4): 395–410.

Hunter, C., Nixon, J. and Shayer, S. (2000) *Neighbour Nuisance, Social Landlords and the Law*. Coventry: CIH and York: JRF.

Hunter, C., Nixon, J. and Shayer, S. (2003) *Initiatives by Social Landlords to Tackle Anti-social Behaviour*. Sheffield: Sheffield Hallam University.

Innes, M. (2004a) *Understanding Social Control. Deviance, Crime and Social Order*. Maidenhead: Open University Press.

Innes, M. (2004b) 'Reinventing tradition? Reassurance, neighbourhood security and policing', *Criminal Justice*, 4(2): 151–71.

Innes, M. and Fielding, N. (2002) 'From community to communicative policing: "signal crimes" and the problem of public reassurance', *Sociological Research Online*, 7(2): http://www.socresonline.org.uk/7/2/innes.html.

Jackson, J. (2004) 'Experience and expression: social and cultural significance in the fear of crime', *British Journal of Criminology*, 44(6): 946–66.

Jacobs, J. (1961) *The Death and Life of Great American Cities*. New York: Random House.

Jacobson, J. and Saville, E. (1999) *Neighbourhood Warden Schemes: An Overview*, Home Office Crime Reduction Series Paper 2. London: Home Office.

Janson, G. (2004) 'Youth justice in Sweden', in M. Tonry and A. Doob (eds), *Youth Crime and Youth Justice. Comparative and Cross National Perspectives*, Vol. 31 Crime and Justice: a Review of Research. Chicago: University of Chicago Press.

Johnston, M. and Jowell, R. (2001) 'How robust is English civil society?', in *British Social Attitudes 2001–2002*. London: Sage.

Jones, D. (1982) *Crime, Protest, Community and Police in Nineteenth-Century Britain*. London: Routledge.

Jones, T. and Newburn, T. (2002) 'The transformation of policing? Understanding current trends in policing systems', *British Journal of Criminology*, 42(1): 129–46.

Jones, T., MacLean, B. and Young, J. (1986) *The Islington Crime Survey*. Aldershot: Gower.

Junger-Tas, J. (2004) 'Youth Justice in the Netherlands', in M. Tonry and A. Doob (eds), *Youth Crime and Youth Justice: Comparative and Cross-National Perspectives*, Vol. 31 'Crime and Justice: A Review of Research. Chicago: University of Chicago Press.

Karn, V., Lickiss, R., Hughes, D. and Crawley, J. (1993) *Neighbour Disputes: Responses by Social Landlords*. Coventry: Institute of Housing.

Keenan, P. (1998) 'Residential mobility and low demand: a case history in Newcastle', in S. Lowe, S. Spencer and P. Keenan (eds), *Housing Abandonment in Britain. Studies in the Causes and Effects of Low Demand Housing*. York: Centre for Housing Policy, University of York.

Kelling, G. and Coles, C. (1996) *Fixing Broken Windows*. New York: Free Press.

van Kesteran, J., Mayhew, P. and Nieuwbeera, P. (2000) *Criminal Victimisation in 17 Industrialised Countries: Key Findings from the International Crime and Victims Survey*. The Hague: NSCR/WODL.

Krudy, M. and Stewart, G. (2004) 'Real life ASBOs: trouble-makers or merely troubled?', *Criminal Justice Matters*, 57, Autumn: 10–11.

Labour Party (1995) *A Quiet Life: Tough Action on Criminal Neighbours*. London: Labour Party.

Lacey, N. and Zedner, L. (1998) 'Community in German criminal justice: a significant absence?', *Social and Legal Studies*, 7(1): 7–25.

Lagrange, R., Ferraro, K. and Supancic, M. (1992) 'Perceived risk and fear of crime: role of social and physical incivilities'. *Journal of Research in Crime and Delinquency*, 29(3): 34.

Lenke, L. and Olsson, B. (1995) 'Sweden: zero-tolerance wins the argument?' in N. Dorn et al. (eds), *European Drug policy and Enforcement: Local, National and Pan-European International Realities*. London: Macmillan.

Lenke, L. and Olsson, B. (2002) 'Swedish drug policy in the twenty-first century: a policy model going astray'. *Annals of the American Academy of Political and Social Science*, 582: 64–79.

Lewis, D. and Maxfield, M. (1980) 'Fear in the neighbourhood: an investigation on the impact of crime', *Journal of Research in Crime and Delinquency*, 17: 160–89.

Liddle, M., Warburton, F. and Feloy, M. (1997) *Nuisance Problems in Brixton: Describing Local Experiences, Designing Effective Solutions*. London: NACRO.

Lindstrom, P. (1996) 'Family interaction, neighborhood context, and deviant behavior'. *Studies in Crime and Crime Prevention* 5: 113–9.

Local Government Association (2004) *Sustainable Solutions to Anti-Social Behaviour*. London: LGA.

Loeber, R., Farrington, D., Stouthamer–Loeber, M. and van Kammen, W. (1998) *Anti-Social Behaviour and Mental Health Problems. Explanatory Factors in Childhood and Adolescence*. London: Lawrence Erlbaum Associates.

Lupton, R., Wilson, A., May, T. et al. (2002) *A Rock and a Hard Place: Drug Markets in Deprived Neighbourhoods*, Home Office Research Study 240. London: Home Office.

MacDonald, R. (1997) 'Youth, social exclusion and the millenium', in R. Macdonald (ed.), *Youth, the Underclass and Social Exclusion*. London and New York: Routledge.

Macdonald, S. (2003) 'The nature of the Anti-Social Behaviour Order – *R (McCann and Others)* v *Crown Court at Manchester*', *Modern Law Review*, 66(4): 630–9.

Macmurray, J. (1961; new edition 1991) *The Form of the Personal Vol. 2: Persons in Relation*. London: Humanities Press International.

Madge, N. (2004) 'Anti-social behaviour orders: case law reviewed', *Legal Action*, December: 20–2.

Maruna, S. and King, A. (2004) 'Public opinion and community penalties', in A. Bottoms, S. Rex and G. Robinson (eds), *Alternatives to Prison: Options for an Insecure Society*. Cullompton: Willan.

Mason, D. (2005) 'ASBOs – use and abuse', *New Law Journal*, January: 129.

Matthews, H., Limb, M. and Taylor, M. (2000) 'The "street as thirdspace"', in S. Holloway, and G. Valentine (eds), *Children's Geographies: Playing, Living and Learning*. London and New York: Routledge.

Matthews, R. and Pitts, J. (2001) 'Introduction: beyond criminology?', in R. Matthews and J. Pitts (eds), *Crime, Disorder and Community Safety*. London: Routledge.

Matthews, R. (1992) 'Replacing "broken windows": crime, incivilities and urban change', in R. Matthews and J. Young (eds), *Issues in Realist Criminology*. London: Sage.

Mayhew, H. (1862/1950) *London's Underworld*, selections from vol. 4 of *London Labour and the London Poor*, ed. P. Quennell. London: Spring Books.

Mazerolle, L. G. and Roehl, J. (eds), (1998) *Civil Remedies and Crime Prevention*. Crime Prevention Studies 9. Monsey, NY: Criminal Justice Press.

Meek, R. (2005) *Once upon a Time in the West. Stories of the Social Deprivation of Young People in Rural South-West England*. London: Howard League for Penal Reform.

Merton, R. (1938) 'Social structure and anomie', *American Sociological Review*, 3: 672–82.

Millie, A., Jacobson, J., McDonald, E. and Hough, M. (2005) *Anti-Social Behaviour Strategies: Finding a Balance*, a report for the Joseph Rowntree Foundation. Bristol: Policy Press.

Mitchell, E. (2005) 'Tackling anti-social behaviour', *New Law Journal*, 18, February: 250–1.

Morgan, R. (2005) 'Anti-social behaviour: getting to the root of the problem', *Howard League Magazine*, 1: 13–14.

Muncie, J. (1999) *Youth and Crime: A Critical Introduction*. London: Sage.

Murray, C. (1990) *The Emerging British Underclass*. London: Institute of Economic Affairs.

Murray, C. (1994) *Underclass: The Crisis Deepens*. London: Institute of Economic Affairs.

National Association of Probation Officers (2004) *Antisocial Behaviour Orders – Analysis of the First Six Years*, Briefing Paper 14–04. Available at: www. napo.org.uk.

National Council for Crime Prevention (BRÅ) (2000) *The Criminalisation of Narcotic Drug Misuse – An Evaluation of Criminal Justice System Measures*, Brå-report 2000: 21. Stockholm: BRÅ.

Nelken, D. (1985) 'Community involvement in crime control' *Current Legal Problems*, 38: 259–67.

Nelken, D. (2002) 'Comparing criminal justice', in M. Maguire, R. Morgan and R. Reiner (eds), *The Oxford Handbook of Criminology*, 3rd edn. Oxford: Oxford University Press.

Newburn, T. and Sparks, R. (2004) *Criminal Justice and Political Cultures*. Cullompton: Willan.

Nicholas, S. and Walker, A. (eds) (2004) *Crime in England and Wales 2002/2003: Supplementary Volume 2: Crime, Disorder and the Criminal Justice System – Public Attitudes and Perceptions*, Home Office Statistical Bulletin 02/04. London: Home Office.

Nilsson, A. and Estrada, F. (2003) 'Victimisation, inequality and welfare during an economic recession. A study of self reported victimisation in Sweden 1988–1999', *British Journal of Criminology*, 43: 655–72.

Nixon, J., Blandy, S., Hunter, C. and Reeve, K. (2003) *Tackling Anti-Social Behaviour in Mixed Tenure Areas*. London: ODPM.

Oberwittler, D. (2004) 'A multi-level analysis of neighbourhood contextual effects on serious juvenile offending. The role of sub-cultural values and social disorganisation', *European Journal of Criminology*, 1(2): 201–35.

O'Donnell, M. and Sharpe, S. (2000) *Uncertain Masculinities: Youth, Ethnicity and Class in Comtemporary Britain*. London: Routledge.

ODPM (2004) *Survey of English Housing Provisional Results*. Available at: www.odpm.gov.uk.

Ogbourn, M. (1993) 'Ordering the city: surveillance, public space and the reform of urban policing in England', *Political Geography*, 12: 505–21.

Padfield, N. (2004a) 'Anti-Social Behaviour Act 2003', *Current Law Statutes*, 2003: 38.

Padfield, N. (2004b) 'The Anti-Social Behaviour Act 2003: the ultimate nanny state?', *Criminal Law Review*: 712–27.

Pakes, F. (2004) 'The politics of discontent: the emergence of a new criminal justice discourse in the Netherlands', *Howard Journal*, 43(3): 284–98.

Palme, J., Bergmark, Å., Bäckman, O., Estrada, F., Fritzell, J., Lundberg, O. and Szebehely, M. (2002) 'Welfare trends in Sweden. Balancing the books for the 1990's', *Journal of European Social Policy*, 12: 329–46.

Pantazis, C. (2000) '"Fear of crime", vulnerability and poverty: evidence form the British Crime Survey', *British Journal of Criminology*, 40(3): 414–36.

Paradine, K. (2000) 'Using civil law to tackle crime and disorder', *New Law Journal*, November: 1614.

Pearson, G. (1983) *Hooligan. A History of Respectable Fears*. London: Macmillan.

Pearson, G. (1987) 'Deprivation, unemployment and heroin use', in N. Dorn and N. South (eds), *A Land Fit for Heroin? Drug Policies, Prevention and Practice*. Basingstoke: Macmillan Education.

Pearson, G., Blagg, H., Smith, D., Sampson, A. and Stubbs, P. (1992) 'Crime, community and conflict: the multi-agency approach', in D. Downes (ed.), *Unravelling Criminal Justice*. London: Macmillan.

Pettersson, T. (2003) 'Ethnicity and violent crime: the ethnic structure of networks of youths suspected of violent offences in Stockholm', *Journal of Scandinavian Studies in Criminology and Crime Prevention*, 4: 2.

Pettersson, T. and Tiby, E. (2002) 'The production and reproduction of prostitution'. *Journal of Scandinavian Studies in Criminology and Crime Prevention*, 3: 2.

Phillips, T. and Smith, P. (2003) 'Everyday incivility: towards a benchmark', *Sociological Review*, 51(1): 85–108.

Pitts, J. and Hope, T. (1997) 'The local politics of inclusion: the state and community safety', *Social Policy and Administration*, 31(5): 37–38.

Pratt, J. (2000) 'Emotive and ostentatious punishment: its decline and resurgence in modern society', *Punishment and Society*, 2(4): 417–39.

Prime Minister's Strategy Unit (2004) *Alcohol Harm Reduction Strategy for England.* London: Cabinet Office.

Putnam, R. (2000) *Bowling Alone.* New York: Simon & Schuster.

Radzinowicz, L. (1956) *A History of English Criminal Law, Vol 2: Enforcement of the Law.* London: Stevens & Sons.

Rentoul, J. (1995) *Tony Blair.* London: Little, Brown.

Richardson, A. and Budd, T. (2003) *Alcohol, Crime and Disorder: A Study of Young Adults.* Home Office Research Study 263. London: Home Office.

Roberts, E. (1984) *A Woman's Place. An Oral History of Working-Class Women 1890–1940.* Oxford: Blackwell.

Roberts, R. (1971) *The Classic Slum.* Manchester: Manchester University Press.

Rosen, B. (1991) *Witchcraft in England 1558–1618.* Amherst, MA: University of Massachussets Press.

Ross, C., Mirowsky, J. and Pribesh, S. (2001) 'Powerlessness and the amplification of threat: neighbourhood disadvantage, disorder and mistrust', *American Sociological Review*, 66 August: 568–91.

Rutherford, A. (2000) 'An elephant on the doorstep: criminal policy without crime in New Labour's Britain', in P. Green and A. Rutherford (eds), *Criminal Policy in Transition.* Oxford: Hart Publishing.

Samaha, J. (1974) *Law and Order in an Historical Perspective. The Case of Elizabethan Essex.* New York: Academic Press.

Sampson, R. and Groves, W. B. (1989) 'Community structure and crime: testing social disorganisation theory', *American Journal of Sociology*, 94: 774–802.

Sampson, R. and Raudenbush, S. (2001) *Disorder in Urban Neighbourhoods – Does It Lead to Crime?* Washington, DC: National Institute of Justice.

Sampson, R., Raudenbush, R. and Earls, E. (1997) 'Neighborhoods and violent crime: a multi-level study of collective efficacy', *Science*, 277: 918–24.

Scott, S. and Parkey, H. (1998) 'Myths and reality: neighbour nuisance problems in Scotland', *Housing Studies*, 13(3): 325–45.

Scottish Affairs Committee (1996) *Housing and Anti-Social Behaviour*, Parliamentary Papers, HC 160 1996/7. London: Stationery Office.

Sessar, K., Herrmann, H., Keller, W., Weinrich, M. and Breckner, I. (2004), Insecurities in European Cities. Crime-Related Fear Within the Context of New Anxieties and Community-Based Crime Prevention. Unpublished report to the European Commission.

Sharpe, J. (1984) *Crime in Early Modern England 1550–1750.* London: Longman.

Shaw, C. and McKay, H. (1942) *Juvenile Delinquency and Urban Areas.* Chicago: University of Chicago Press.

Simester, A. and von Hirsch, A. (2002) 'Rethinking the Offense Principle', *Legal Theory*, 8: 269.

Singer, L. (2004) *Reassurance Policing: An Evaluation of the Local Management of Community Safety*, Home Office Research Study 288. London: Home Office.

Skogan, W. (1990) *Disorder and Decline: Crime and the Spiral of Decay in American Neighbourhoods*. New York: Free Press.

Smith, S. (1986) *Crime, Space and Society*. Cambridge: Cambridge University Press.

Social Exclusion Unit (2000a) *Report of Policy Action Team 8: Anti-Social Behaviour*. London: Cabinet Office.

Social Exclusion Unit (2000b) *National Strategy for Neighbourhood Renewal. Policy Action Team Report Summaries: A Compendium*. London: Cabinet Office.

Social Exclusion Unit (2002) *Report of Policy Action Team 12: Young People*. London: Cabinet Office.

Sparks, R. (1992) *Television and the Drama of Crime*. Buckingham: Open University.

Stanley, K. and Asta Lohde, L. (2004) *Sanctions and Sweeteners. Rights and Responsibilities in the Benefits System*. London: Institute of Public Policy Research.

Stenson, K. (2002) 'Community safety in middle England – the local politics of crime control', in G. Hughes and A. Edwards (eds), *Crime Control and Community: The New Politics of Public Safety*. Cullompton: Willan.

Stenson, K. and Edwards, A. (2004) 'Policy transfer in local crime control: beyond naïve emulation', in T. Newburn and R. Sparks (eds), *Criminal Justice and Political Cultures*. Cullompton: Willan.

Stenson, K. and Watt, P. (1999) 'Crime, risk and governance in a southern English village', in G. Dingwall and S. Moody (eds), *Crime and Conflict in the Countryside*. Cardiff: University of Wales Press.

Stephen, D. and Squires, P. (2003) *Community Safety, Enforcement, and Acceptable Behaviour Contracts*. Brighton: Health and Social Policy Research Centre, University of Brighton.

Storch, R. (1977) 'The problem of working-class leisure. Some roots of middle-class moral reform in the industrial north: 1825–1850', in A. Donajgrodsky (ed.), *Social Control in Nineteenth Century Britain*. London: Croom Helm.

Sumner, C. (1990) 'Rethinking deviance', in C. Sumner (ed.), *Censure, Politics and Criminal Justice*. Milton Keynes: Open University Press.

van Swaaningen, R. (1997) *Critical Criminology. Visions from Europe*. London: Sage.

van Swaaningen, R. (2004) 'Sweeping the street clean: Rotterdam's idea of "community safety" in 2004'. Unpublished paper, GERN Justice and Community Seminar, Dublin.

van Swaaningen, R. (2005) 'Public safety and the management of fear', *Theoretical Criminology*, 39(3): 289–305.

Taylor, D. (2002) *Policing the Victorian Town. The Development of the Police in Middlesbrough c.1840–1914*. Basingstoke: Palgrave Macmillan.

Taylor, I. (1999) *Crime in Context: A Critical Criminology of Market Societies*. Oxford: Polity Press.

Taylor, R. (2001) *Breaking Away from Broken Windows*. Boulder, CO: Westview Press.

Terpstra, J. and Bakker, I. (2004) 'Justice in the community in the Netherlands. Evaluation and discussion' *Criminal Justice* 4(4): 375–93.

Tham, H. (1995) 'From treatment to just deserts in a changing welfare state', *Scandinavian Studies in Criminology*, 14: 89–122.

Tham, H. (1998): 'Swedish drug policy: a successful model?', *European Journal of Criminal Policy and Research*, 6: 3.

Tham, H. (2001) 'Law and order as a leftist project? The case of Sweden', *Punishment and Society*, 3(3): 409–26.

Thames Valley Partnership (2004) Report on the first year of activity from November 2002 to November 2003, unpublished report on the Mending Fences Project. Chilton: Thames Valley Partnership.

Thorpe, K. and Wood, M. (2004) 'Anti-social Behaviour', in S. Nicholas and A. Walker (eds), *Crime in England and Wales 2002/2003: Supplementary Volume 2: Crime, Disorder and the Criminal Justice System – Public Attitudes and Perceptions*, Home Office Statistical Bulletin 02/04. London: Home Office.

Tonry, M. (2004) *Punishment and Politics*. Cullompton: Willan.

Trickett, A., Ellingworth, D., Hope, T. and Pease, K. (1995) 'Crime Victimisation in the Eighties', *British Journal of Criminology*, 35 (3): 343–359.

Wakefield, A. (2003) *Selling Security. The Private Policing of Public Space*. Cullompton: Willan.

Walklate, S. and Evans, K. (1999) *Zero Tolerance or Community Tolerance?* Aldershot: Ashgate.

Whitehead, C., Stockdale, J. and Razzu, G. (2003) *The Economic and Social Costs of Anti-Social Behaviour*. London: London School of Economics.

Wikstrom, P.-O. (1991) *Urban Crime, Criminals and Victims: The Swedish Experience in an Anglo-American Perspective*. New York: Springer Verlag.

Wilkstrom, P.-O. (2002) *Adolescent Crime in Context. The Peterborough Youth Study: Report to the Home Office*. Cambridge: University of Cambridge Institute of Criminology.

Wikstrom, P.-O. and Dolmen, L. (2001) 'Urbanisation, neighbourhood social integration, informal social control, minor social disorder, victimisation and fear of crime', *International Review of Victimology* 8: 121–40.

Wikstrom, P.-O. and Loeber, R. (2000) 'Do disadvantaged neighborhoods cause well-adjusted children to become adolescent delinquents?: A study of male serious juvenile offending, individual risk and protective factors, and neighborhood context', *Criminology*, 38: 1109–42.

Wiles, P. (1999) 'Troubled neighbourhoods', in *Public Safety in Europe*. Twente: International Police Institute.

Willmott, S. and Griffin, C. (1996) 'Men, masculinity and the challenge of long-term unemployment', in M. Mac an Ghaill (ed.), *Understanding Masculinities*. Buckingham: Open University.

Willow, C. (2005) 'ASBOs: not meeting children's needs', *Howard League Magazine*, 1: 7–8.

Wilson, J. and Kelling, G. (1982) 'Broken windows: the police and neighbourhood safety', *The Atlantic Monthly*, March: 29–37.

Wilson, S. (1978) 'Vandalism and 'defensible space' on London housing estates', in R. Clarke (ed.), *Tackling Vandalism*, Home Office Research Report 47. London: Home Office.

Wilson, W. J. (1996) *When Work Disappears: The World of the New Urban Poor*. New York: Alfred A. Knopf.

Wood, M. (2004) *Perceptions and Experience of Anti-Social Behaviour: Findings from the 2003/2004 British Crime Survey*, Home Office Online Report 49/04. London: Home Office.

Wood, M. (2005) *The Victimisation of Young People: Findings from the Crime and Justice Survey 2003*, Findings 246. London: Home Office Research Development and Statistics Directorate, available from http://www.homeoffice.gov.uk/rds/pubintro1.html.

Young, J. (1999) *The Exclusive Society*. London: Sage.

Young, M. and Willmott, P. (1957) *Family and Kinship in East London*. London: Routledge & Kegan Paul.

Zedner, L. (2002) 'Dangers of dystopia in penal theory', *Oxford Journal of Legal Studies*, 22: 339–65.

Index